GERMAN
HUMANISM
AND
REFORMATION

The German Library: Volume 6

Volkmar Sander, General Editor

GERMAN
HUMANISM
AND
REFORMATION

Edited by Reinhard P. Becker

Foreword by Roland H. Bainton

CONTINUUM · NEW YORK

ACKNOWLEDGMENTS

Every reasonable effort has been made to locate the holders of rights to the selections included here. We gratefully acknowledge permission to reprint from the following publication:

Martin Luther, "To the Christian Nobility of the German Nation," from *Three Treatises,* copyright © 1970 by Fortress Press. Used by permission.

1982

The Continuum Publishing Company
575 Lexington Avenue, New York, NY 10022

Copyright © 1982 by The Continuum Publishing Company

Introduction© 1982 by Reinhard P. Becker
Foreword© 1982 by Roland H. Bainton

Printed in the United States of America

Library of Congress Cataloging in Publication Data

Main entry under title:

German humanism and reformation.

(The German library)
1. Humanism—Addresses, essays, lectures.
2. Germany—Intellectual life—Addresses,
essays, lectures.   I. Becker, Reinhard P.
II. Series.
B821.G44   1982   001.3'0943   82-7278
ISBN 0-8264-0251-8   AACR2
ISBN 0-8264-0261-5 pbk

Contents

Foreword

This volume supplies some of the important documents of the Renaissance and Reformation. The Renaissance is commonly described as the period in western history from 1300 to 1600, beginning with Dante and ending with Shakespeare. With this definition the Reformation is a phase of the Renaissance. There was a close affinity. The Renaissance was a reformation, the Reformation was a renaissance. Both were primitivist, that is, looking to the remote past for a model after which to reform their own society.

The term "humanist" is applied to those who delved in the literature of the classical age and this literature itself was reformatory, though the age of Augustus was actually one of corruption. The sway of Rome had been extended from the wall of Hadrian in Scotland to the Euphrates and the conquered peoples enslaved. The roads and the seas were open, making possible an extensive influx of orientals into Italy often importing along with themselves orgiastic religions. Expanding cities introduced urban vices. The writings of the moralists of this period, Greek and Roman, were the sources on which the humanists drew for their picture of the golden age. The Reformation leaders drew from the early Christian writings—some of which by the year 400 had been formed into the canon of the New Testament—composed primarily of the interpretations of the early Fathers.

The most intense decades of reformatory activity were the early years of the sixteenth century. Certain external factors here were influential. There was of course the discovery of America to the west. The impact on ideas was not immediate. Schdel in his history of the world published in 1493 never mentioned Columbus. But before too long the new world was contributing not simply gold but ideas. Ever since the formulation of Augustine the view had been held that a war could never be just on both sides. This view was challenged by Vittoria when his fellow Spaniards were invading the lands of the Indians. The invasion was theoretically just because the prevailing interpretation of law placed the whole earth at the service at all. But the natives, ignorant of such law, were equally just in defending their territories against the interlopers. If then war could be just on both sides, international law needed to be codified and a court established to evaluate claims. Here was the germ of an idea that would come to fruition centuries later.

The rounding of the cape of Africa commenced a trend toward equality for blacks. In the mystery plays of the Middle Ages one of the Wise Men, Casper by name, was a black buffoon. But when his land proved to be a continent, to the Magi were allocated Europe, Asia, and Africa. The seed of the idea of racial equality was planted.

The advance of the Turks on the eastern side had equally significant effects. The first edict of complete religious liberty in Europe was promulgated in 1525 in Transylvania because the Turks had obtained suzerainty over this area and would not suffer their Christian vassals to decimate each other. When in 1453 Constantinople fell into the hands of the Turks, an exodus to Italy ensued on the part of a number of Greeks, who brought with them classical manuscripts later to be printed by Aldus Manutius of Venice.

The period of the Renaissance and Reformation is commonly regarded as one of universal efflorescence. In a measure this is the case but in varying degrees. Thorndike in his history of science thought this period less productive than the preceding. But some advance certainly there was. The discoveries of Galileo, though rejected by Rome, received ultimate vindication. The views of Copernicus were published by the Lutheran Osiander, and Luther, though not persuaded, did not impede publication.

Astronomy and astrology were allied. The astrologer was a court figure. Melanchthon dabbled in astrology. Luther scoffed. That astrology which predicted the deaths of individuals was subject to legal penalty. Servetus, having correctly foretold an eclipse of Mars, went on to predict disasters in which many princes would be killed. Brought to trial, he saved himself by pointing out that his forecast was concluded with the words "which may God avert." Not the stars but God controlled.

In the field of physiology notable advances were made, especially in the great anatomical work of Vesalius. Servetus, along with him, tested the implication of the scriptural text which said that the soul is in the blood. To govern the whole body the soul must be able to get around. Circulation is imperative. He discovered that the blood does not, as previously held, seep through the wall of the heart, but the entire bloodstream passes through the pulmonary artery to the lungs and there is aerated and changes color. Now since God *breathed* into man the breath of life, there is a close relationship between respiration and inspiration. Lacking a microscope to discover the capillaries, Servetus could not demonstrate the complete circulation. Paracelsus also contributed to medical advance by invoking the air of chemistry and psychology. Carl Jung observed, "We see in Paracelsus not only a pioneer in the domains of chemical medicine, but also in those of empirical psychological healing science."

As for economic advance the current view is that the Renaissance was a period of affluence. Lopez has demonstrated that it was actually a time of economic decline, but the inequity of distribution was such that some were affluent enough to be lavish patrons of the arts. One need not here recount the roster of great painters, sculptors, and architects in Italy, the Netherlands, France and Spain, and in Germany as well with Dürer, Schongauer, and the Cranachs. At the same time some religious bodies were iconoclastic in obedience to the command "You shall not make. . . . any likeness of anything that is in the heaven above or that is in the earth beneath" (Ex. 20:4). The Zwinglians would not allow the crucifix in the church. Calvinists, though banning the crucifix, would allow the cross. Erasmus had misgivings about the cross on the banners of those who went out to slaughter the Turks.

As for literary art Erasmus wrote a treatise on the proper style for letter writing. Before him Conrad Celtis had dealt with the art of versification and of setting Latin verse to music. For one syllable there should be only one note. No slurring. The Council of Trent undertook a revision of the liturgy, including the musical portions. Luther regarded music after theology as the greatest gift of God. He loved the polyphonic music of the Netherlands, which he described as a square-dance in heaven with the notes bowing to their partners. At the time when Catholic-Protestant estrangement was bitter, Luther wrote to Senfl, the composer and organist of the rabid Catholic dukes of Bavaria, saying, "I hope a letter from me will not endanger you." Music was above the confessions. Luther revived congregational singing in unison. Zwingli, who sharply distinguished flesh and spirit, not only, as we noted, rejected images to delight the eye, but music to titillate the ear, and in the sacrament he would not admit that bread and wine feed the spirit. He retained the Lord's Supper simply because commanded as a memorial. Calvin allowed hymns and metrical versions of the Psalms.

In the field of jurisprudence Roman law was superseding the Germanic, which allowed communal ownership by the peasants of some waters for fishing and some lands for hunting. Roman law recognized only private ownership. In consequence the nobles took possession of the common areas for themselves. This was one of the grievances leading to the great Peasants' War.

The greatest factor favoring the flourishing of Renaissance and Reformation was a lull in the vigilance of the Inquisition in the pivotal decade around 1500. The Holy Office had been at its peak in the thirteenth century in the effort to suppress the pululation of sects after the collapse of the great Gregorian reform of the late eleventh and early twelfth centuries.

The attrition of inquisitorial power begot a liberal Catholic reformatory movement that had its adherents in all countries of Europe. In England one thinks of More and Colet, in Spain of Vives and Ximines, in Italy of a large concourse: Contarini, Sadoleto, Bembo, Carnesechi, Giberti, Vergerio, and a number of women; Vittoria Colonna, Catarina Cibo, Julia Gonzaga, and still others. In Germany there come to mind Reuchlin, Wimpheling, Sebastian Brant, Hans Sachs, Pirckheimer, Ulrich von Hutten. In France there was Lefevre and in what was to be Holland the peer of them all, Erasmus of Rotterdam.

The main instrument for the propagation of their program was, as noted above, literary. They undertook to make available the major works of classical and Christian antiquity, Greek and Latin.

Erasmus edited alike Suetonius and Jerome. His most significant work was the issue in print for the first time of the New Testament in Greek in 1516. A few years later Ximines in Spain brought out the entire Bible in Hebrew, Aramaic and Greek. This endeavor prompted Erasmus to formulate principles for the determination of the authenticity of variant readings in the manuscript texts. The shorter version should be preferred because a scribe would not omit any of the holy word but might amplify. Again, the more difficult reading had greater claim since the copyist would not make the clear obscure but might make the obscure clear. Lorenzo Valla showed that language itself could date documents. The Donation of Constantine, which conferred upon the pope jurisdiction over the West, was manifestly a forgery because it employed terminology not in use in the days of Constantine.

To the texts of the ancients were added modern manuals of devotion such as Erasmus' *Handbook of the Christian Soldier,* a collection of prayers and paraphrases of the gospels. These of course were not controversial. Another genre was critique of abuses in the Church with irony and ridicule. A precedent for this style was at hand in Lucian of the classical age and Boccaccio in the contemporary. Examples in this volume are *The Ship of Fools* and the *Praise of Folly,* though the latter is actually not as stinging as Erasmus' anonymous skit "Pope Julius Excluded from Heaven."

Into this atmosphere of comparatively innocuous mockery burst Luther with passionate outrage. In many respects he was a medieval figure. In his day tremors occasioned by the fear of death slackened. After the Black Death the most popular publication was the *Ars Moriendi,* [The Art of Dying]. If a tremor remained, the reason had altered. The motto of Erasmus was *Concedi Nullo* [I yield to no one]. Accused of arrogance, he replied that not he was the speaker, but instead Death. He feared that he might be cut off without completing his earthly mission rather than that Christ the judge would consign him to the place where the fire is not quenched. Luther, struck to earth by lightning, screamed, "St. Anne help me, I will become a monk" on the assumption that monasticism would save him from the wrath of God. He himself said that what distinguished him from earlier reformers was that they attacked the life, he the doctrine.

He did indeed revive the doctrine of original sin, which meant that man could never be good enough to bargain with God over meritorious deserts. This undercut the doctrine of indulgences which implied that the saints were an almost-necessary aid to salvation. Their superfluous virtues could by the pope be transferred to those in arrears. The time in purgatory could then be reduced. Luther's blast in the Ninety-Five Theses in 1517 swiftly moved from indulgences to papal infallibility. Rome, not wishing to offend Luther's prince and supporter, Frederick the Wise, dallied with the insurgent for three years. In the meantime many of the humanists rallied to his side. Erasmus wrote to Frederick saying, "Luther is a good man and a good man cannot have a very bad theology. Luther if wrong should be convinced, not coerced. And you are the one to see that he be given a fair hearing." Among other supporters were Hutten, Pirkheimer, Dürer, Hans Sachs, Sebastian Brant, the Reuchlinists in general, and most emphatically Melanchthon.

Luther's reform differed from others not simply because it was doctrinal but because it was directed to the common man. He not only debated ideas, he changed practices. The Mass was turned into German. The cup was given to the laity (long since a demand of the Hussites). Dietary stipulations, pilgrimages, penances were dropped. For the common man this meant an emancipation. The role of the Church in politics was undercut. The argument had been that since priests alone could save souls by administering the sacraments, which civil rulers could never do, therefore the pope might dictate civil appointments. Luther's doctrine of the priesthood of all believers undercut this reasoning and gave the magistrate a different status.

Among the media employed by Luther was, as we have seen, the revival of congregation hymn-singing. A Jesuit later said that Luther damned more souls with his songs than with his sermons. A further device was the substitution of the popular tract for the massive tome. The pamphlets (*Flugschriften*) in the vernacular were small, cheap, and illustrated with woodcuts. The *Ship of Fools* was printed in this fashion. The Reformation may be said to have invented the cartoon. A pamphlet contrasting Christ and Antichrist had, among other woodcuts, on one page Christ washing the disciples' feet, on the other the Pope having his toes kissed.

The Roman Church responded with the Counterreformation.

Burckhardt rightly said that Luther saved the papacy. In place of the secularized popes of the Renaissance came the puritan popes who turned savagely not only against the Protestant reformation but also that of the liberal Catholics. Pope Paul IV put all the works of Erasmus on the index even though they had little to do with religion. The Inquisition was reinstated.

While Catholic reform assumed two forms, Protestantism broke into many more. Some have been called magisterial because supported by the magistrates. This was true in the case of the churches of Luther, Zwingli, Calvin, and Cranmer. Other forms were disowned by the major groups and persecuted by the magistrates: Anabaptists, Schwenkfelders, individualists including mystics, rationalists, and sometimes revolutionaries.

An important factor was the view of the future. Some like Thomas Müntzer thought that Christ was already at the door and all his opponents should be slaughtered. Luther hoped to complete his commentary on Daniel before Christ should come. Calvin allowed an indefinite span of years. Hope for the future fluctuated. Erasmus and More thought the succession to the throne of the learned Henry VIII marked the revival of the golden age. But when Henry became engaged in wars on the continent, Erasmus said, "This is the worst century since Jesus Christ." Whether it was, is of course questionable. But the texts in this present volume do make clear that it was certainly an age of political and religious chaos as well as of intellectual ferment.

ROLAND H. BAINTON

Introduction

The German nineteenth century in its rediscovery of the past and its quest for national heroes saw German Humanism and its leading figures in a romantic and rather dramatic light. The fifteenth and sixteenth centuries were portrayed as a period in which youthful and enlightened generations of intellectuals who embraced the new ideas of the Renaissance and postulated drastic reforms of academic studies radically confronted the Scholastics who desperately clung to the rigid academic traditions of the "dark" Middle Ages. One assumed that there ran a clear front line between these two camps, on one side of which were the Scholastics, firmly entrenched in the universities, stubbornly resisting any suggestion of change, and on the other side of which were the young revolutionary and idealistic Humanists, fighting passionately to bring light into their darkness. During the last hundred years the understanding of German Humanism has sobered and clarified considerably. It has become evident that the "darkness" and adherence to tradition were not so rigid on the one side, and the desire for change and the enlightenment were not so brilliant on the other. If there was a front line at all, it frequently ran through the minds of the individual personalities. This means, of course, that the pains of change, since they were felt in the consciousness of the individual, were often much more traumatic and dramatic than nineteenth-century scholars imagined. These were truly generations born on a threshold, shaken and often confused by the violence of the change that took place within them.

The fifteenth and sixteenth centuries saw the birth of a new social class, the merchants and patricians, who, after establishing lucrative trade routes to the Orient, within a few generations amassed giant fortunes, created a new life-style in the cities, and presented an ever-growing political and economic challenge to the nobility. The political power of the emperors continued to be weakened by the endless struggle with Rome for secular authority, which seriously affected security and law and order in the country. Luther's Reformation dealt a terrifying blow to people's confidence in the teachings of the Church, and the bloody Peasant Wars of 1525 added the passionate demands of farmers and workers for social justice and human dignity to the general turmoil. In this context of universal restiveness and brewing upheavals the German Humanists remodeled in the course of about a hundred years the educational programs and intellectual values of their society.

In defining the goals and activities of this movement one must not overlook the essential differences between Italian and German Humanism. They reacted against entirely different cultural backgrounds, and they grew and built upon different historical traditions. Humanism in Germany developed a specific literary and academic character combined with deep religious concerns. Paul Oskar Kristeller offers a concise definition of German Humanism in his book *Renaissance Thought,* where he describes it as a cultural and educational program that concentrated on an important but limited area of studies that involved primarily neither classics nor philosophy but what might be roughly characterized as literature.

Recent scholarship tends to divide German Humanism into three phases. The earliest awakening of Humanist interests in terms of Kristeller's definition can be observed in Prague under Emperor Charles IV. There, in 1348, he founded a university, the first one in Central Europe, and his reform of the imperial chancellery initiated a new awareness of good style in official Latin documents. His chancellor, Johann von Neumarkt, published a book of forms for government documents that had a decisive influence on the style of public writings both in German and in Latin. The second phase is characterized by contacts with the Italian Renaissance. Traveling scholars and poets like Rudolf Agricola (1444–1485), Rudolf von Langen (1438–1519), and Peter Luder studied in Italy and came back to Germany filled with admiration for Renaissance letters, and brought this inspiration into the German universities. This new interest was further stimulated by the Reform councils of Basel and Constance and through visits to Germany by such illustrious Italian scholars as Aeneas Silvius, Vergerio, and Poggio. In the final and very decisive phase of German Humanism three successive generations of Humanists shook off their dependence on the Italian Renaissance, distanced themselves from the academic methods of Scholasticism, and led Humanist studies to widespread popular success in Germany.

After their return from Italy, many Humanist scholars wandered from one German university to another, offering lectures on Cicero, Seneca, Terence, and Horace and encouraging their students to study Greek literature and philosophy. They formed circles in many German cities and at universities where scholars shared their interest in these new educational programs, and pooled their findings and their insights. One of the earlier centers of such activities was Heidelberg where Johann von Dahlberg (1455–1503), who had studied at Ferrara, gathered at the court of the Elector Philip (1448–1508) a group of scholars interested in the new learning. This group at times included such fascinating men as Rudolf Agricola, Peter Luder, and Johann Reuchlin (1455–1522). Similar centers sprang up for a while in cities like Strasbourg (around Sebastian Brant [1458–1521]), Basel, Nuremberg, Augsburg, Ingolstadt, Leipzig, Erfurt, and Vienna. One of the most dynamic forces in the proliferation of Humanist activities was Conrad Celtis (1459–1508), who traveled extensively throughout the country and established a number of learned sodalities to gather materials on German history (a new concern in this generation) for a voluminous standard work that Celtis planned to edit but which never materialized.

Of outstanding significance in the first third of the sixteenth century was the group of scholars who gathered in Nuremberg around Willibald Pirckheimer (1470–1530), whose grandfather and father had sought a Humanist education in Italy and whose patrician family combined cultural sophistication with considerable wealth. Willibald, whose own Humanist interests had been kindled in Italy, compiled in his magnificent house in Nuremberg one of the two finest private libraries north of the Alps. His house, his collection of books (which had been started by his grandfather), and his extraordinary learning attracted many visiting scholars and made him a focal figure in the Humanist activities in that region.

Another prestigious center of Humanist learning was Erfurt.

Here, too, from the beginning of the sixteenth century into the 1530s, there was a steady coming and going of the leading Humanist scholars and poets. Mutianus Rufus (b. 1471), a clergyman in the nearby town of Gotha, and Crotus Rubianus (c. 1480–1539) were the magnetic figures that held this circle together for many years. Mutianus was a theologian and a fascinating philosopher whose hospitable house in Gotha harbored the other remarkable private library of that era. He corresponded on intimate terms with most Humanists throughout his life and his correspondence is a treasure of information about their personalities, interests, and goals. When Johann Reuchlin rather late in his life became engrossed in an ugly controversy with the Dominicans in Cologne over the alleged anti-Christian ideas in Jewish religious books, it was Crotus who wrote the scathing satire, *Letters of Obscure Men*, that ended this embarrassing quarrel by making a laughing stock of Reuchlin's adversaries. Crotus' close friend Ulrich von Hutten (1488–1523) later added a sequel to the original satire.

Nothing gave the Humanists of this generation so great a sense of solidarity as their united stand against the vicious attacks made on the venerated Reuchlin, for they all looked up to him as one of the earliest pioneers of the new learning. Reuchlin was a lawyer and an adviser to Emperor Maximilian (reigned 1493–1519) who had devoted himself to the study of Greek and Hebrew. He was a shining example of the new scholar who strove for expertise in the philological crafts and found new and sophisticated approaches to literature and philosophy.

The only personality in this period whose prestige was comparable to Reuchlin's (and even exceeded it abroad) was Erasmus of Rotterdam (1466–1536). Aloof from the various groups and factions, he personified all the virtues and interests of a Humanist. He challenged the traditional values in academic learning, he had high standards of scholarship, he recognized the importance of literature, he published editions of Greek authors and translated some of their works into Latin, he took an interest in pedagogy, he held Humanistic views on theological questions and took an unyielding critical stand against the abuses of the clergy.

German Humanism reflected a changing attitude toward learning and the values and principles of education in general, just as the Reformation reflected the individual's changing position vis-à-vis the Church and religion in general. The activities and interests of the German Humanists included the study of the classical languages, the translating, reading, editing of, and commenting on classical literatures, the close collaboration with publishers and printers who were highly dependent on their scholarly skills, a rethinking of the role religion played in their society and in their personal lives, and a growing uneasiness about social justice and political choices on the threshold of a new age.

R.P.B.

JOHANN VON TEPL

Johann von Tepl (c.1351–1415) is a very early and quite astonishing figure in German Humanism. After serving for a time as headmaster of the Latin School in his native Saaz in Bohemia, he spent the rest of his life as a lawyer in Prague. The following text is a landmark in early Humanist literature. Bold and unprecedented in the choice of German as its language, it reflects in the challenge of Death and his authority over Life more than any other work of the fifteenth century the awakening of a new mentality. Johann, whose wife had died in childbed in 1400, wrote this dialogue with a grief that still retains much of its passion. His sense of literary form, his command of the leading philosophical and theological arguments of the late Middle Ages, and his poetic insistence on the dignity of a personal pain that defies the consolations of religion and philosophy make this work a supreme example of the shifting attitudes in early German Humanism. It was written around 1401.

Death and the Ploughman

THE PLOUGHMAN: Grisly destroyer of men, baleful scourge of the world, vile slayer of mankind, my curse upon you, O Death! May God who created you hate you, may calamities heap themselves on you; may misfortune cleave to you in all its might: may you be dishonored forever!

May fear, and distress, and misery not depart from you wherever you go; suffering and sorrow go with you on all your ways; bitter doubts, fear of shame to come, and ignominious hurt weigh heavily upon you at all times; may heaven, earth, sun, moon and stars, seas and waters, mountains and fields, valleys and meadows, the pit of hell, and all that has life and being foully offend you and bring you nought but loss and be a curse to you for all eternity!

May you be sunk in wickedness, may you be wasted with pitiful miseries and languish forever under the grievous, imperishable contempt of God and men and all created things!

Shameless wretch, may your evil memory live on and endure without end; may glooms and terrors dog your footsteps, wander where they will: let me and all men cry Murder on you and wring their hands!

DEATH: Hark! Hark! Hark! New marvels! Terrible and unheard-of tidings assail Our ears. But We know naught of him who brings them. Threats, curses, wringing of hands, lamentations and cries of murder and all manner of uproar have left us unscathed hitherto. Nevertheless declare yourself, son, and make known what woe has befallen you through Us and whence this unseemliness, to which We have been unused, although We have trespassed on

3

the pastures of many sagacious and high-born, fair, lordly, and vainglorious persons, so that sorrow enough has fallen to the lot of widows and orphans in all lands.

You behave as if you were in earnest with your accusation and were hard pressed by lawful necessity. But your accusation is without rhyme or reason, and We take note from your lamentations and outcries that you will not be moved from your complaint. Yet if you are mad, or raging, or deluded, or otherwise out of your mind, pause, contain yourself, and be not too quick with your grievous curses; have a care lest you be troubled with after-rue! Do not imagine that you could ever weaken Our sublime and mighty power.

But now declare yourself and do not conceal in what ways We have done you so heavy a wrong. We shall be justified in your eyes, for all Our ways are just. We know not why you charge Us so presumptuously!

THE PLOUGHMAN: I call myself a ploughman; my pen is my plough, and I live in the land of the Bohemians. Always you will be loathsome and repugnant and hateful to me, for you have plundered the twelfth letter of my alphabet with terrible hand, the essence of my joys; you have pitilessly plucked the sweet summer flower of my delight from my heart's garden; with evil cunning you have stolen my fortune's stay from me, my chosen dove! You have worked irretrievable loss upon me. Consider for yourself whether I am not right to remonstrate, to rave, to accuse: through you I am robbed of joy-bringing life, cheated of my happy days and despoiled of all gladsome possessions. Cheerful and contented I was at all times before this, short and joyous was each hour of day and night, both in like measure rich in joys and delights, every year was a year of grace.

Now they call out to me: Be off! Over the turbid potion, on the dry branch, embittered, benighted, withered, I live and weep without cease! The wind drives me along, I swim through the flood of the wild sea, the waves overpower me and my anchor finds no hold. Therefore I will cry without cease: Death, be you accursed!

DEATH: We marvel and are astonished at this unheard-of onslaught which We have never experienced before. If you are a ploughman living in the land of the Bohemians, We hold that you do Us a mighty injury, since of late We have accomplished nothing of note in Bohemia save in one snug and comely little town perched bravely on a mountain; four letters—the eighteenth, the first, and the twenty-third—wove the wreath of its name. There on an honest, happy daughter of men We ended Our work of grace; her letter was the twelfth. She was upright and steadfast; We can well speak in this way for We were present when she was born. Honor sent her a cloak for her lap and a garland; the cloak and her garland she bore with her untorn and unsullied to the grave. Our witness and hers is the knower of all hearts. Clear of conscience, sweet-natured, loyal, truthful, and above all kindly she was to all men. In truth a woman so constant and so homely has seldom been committed to Us. She it must be whom you mean, for We know of none other.

THE PLOUGHMAN: Yes, my lord Death, I was her husband, she was my beloved. You have taken her away, the gracious delight of my eyes; she is gone, my shield against adversity; gone is my wishing wand. Gone, gone! Now I, poor ploughman, stand here alone. Vanished is my bright star from heaven, the sun of my salvation is gone to rest; it will never rise again. Never will my day-star rise again; the gleam has faded, I have none to drive away my sorrow anymore; dark night is everywhere before my eyes. I do not think that aught can bring me joy again, for the proud banner of my joys is, alas, brought low.

From the bottom of my heart at all times let the cry of Murder go forth in the year, on the day, of my misfortune and the piteous hour when my steadfast diamond was broken, when the staff that was my true guide was pitilessly snatched from my hand and the way closed to my young fountain of delight!

Woe without end, sorrow without cease, miserable decay, violent and eternal fall be your portion forever! May you perish befouled with iniquity, sunk in shame, dishonored, amid weeping, wailing, and gnashing of teeth; may you rot in the depths of hell! God take your strength from you and scatter it like dust! And may the Devil plague you for all eternity!

DEATH: A fox smote a sleeping lion on the cheek: his belly was torn open; a hare tweaked a wolf: to this day he wears no tail; a cat clawed a dog that wanted to sleep: she must bear the dog's enmity forever. In like manner you seek to vex Us. Yet We believe that slave remains slave, and master is master still. We want to give proof that We weigh rightly, judge rightly, and do rightly in the world; spare none because he is noble, heed not knowledge, nay, not even the greatest, consider not beauty, and take no account of either gifts of love, or sorrow, or age, or youth, or anything else. We do as the sun, which shines upon good and evil alike: We draw both good and evil under Our dominion.

Every master who can command the spirits must at the last deliver up his own spirit to Us. The witches and warlocks cannot endure before Us; it avails them nothing that they ride upon broomsticks, that they ride upon goats. The physicians who are cunning to prolong the lives of men must also be our prey; not wholesome roots and herbs, not ointments or apothecary's powders can help them. Even if We reckoned only the generations of butterflies and grasshoppers that have perished, the reckoning would not be enough. Wherefore, then, moved by ill-will or love or sorrow, should We let men live? All the kingdoms of the world would be Ours today, all the kings would have placed their crowns on Our head, their scepters in Our hand; the pope's throne and his miter with the triple crown would now be in Our power.

Therefore let your curses be, tell no more tales with your chattering tongue, cease to beat air, and the chips will not fall into your eyes.

THE PLOUGHMAN: Could I curse, revile, and contemn so that worse and yet worse might befall you, it would be no more than you deserve of me for your scurviness! After great grief there is to be in all justice great wailing: I were not human did I not bewail the wondrous gift which none may give but God. I shall mourn always: my glorious falcon is flown, my virtuous wife. Rightly I lament, for she was nobly born, rich in honor, fair of face, and in person shapely above all her companions, true and modest in word, chaste of body, kind and merry in all she did: I fall silent, I lack strength to count up the many honors and virtues that were her portion from God—you yourself know them, Death.

With full justice I call you to account for this great heart's sorrow. And truly, were any goodness in you, you would have pity! I will turn from you, say nothing good of you, set my face against you with all my strength forever and ever: may all creation help me to do you battle, may all things that are in heaven, in earth, in hell, hate and abhor you!

DEATH: God has apportioned the throne of heaven to the good, the pit of hell to the wicked, and the fields of earth he has apportioned to Us. Peace and reward await the virtuous in heaven, pain and punishment the sinners in hell: the globe of the earth and the sea's flood with all that in them is, these the mighty prince of the world has committed to Us with the commandment that We root and weed out all things superfluous. Consider, fool, prove and engrave it on your mind with the needle of wit: Had We not, from the time the first man rose from the clay, weeded out men from upon the earth, beasts and reptiles from the wildernesses and wastes, the multitude of slippery scaled fishes from the deep—no man could live for little gnats, no man could stir out of doors for wolves, one man would devour another, one beast another, every living thing another, for nourishment would be wanting and earth too narrow. He is a fool who bewails what is mortal. Let be! the living to the living, the dead to the dead, as always. Consider rather, foolish man, of what you lament and of what you should lament.

THE PLOUGHMAN: I have lost my highest treasure beyond recall. Wherefore should I not be sad and sorrowful, when I must live to the day of my death bereft of all joys? God in His charity, the Lord in His mightiness, avenge me on you, sorrow-maker!

You have cut me off from delight, bereft me of dear days, stripped me of great honors. For great honors I enjoyed when that good, that pure daughter fondled the children fallen into her chaste nest! Dead is the mother hen that reared such chicks. O God, O mighty Lord, how brave was my countenance when she walked in honor with modest step so that all people looked at her lovingly and said, "Thanks, praise, and honor be to this dear woman, God grant her and her nestlings all good things!" Had I but known to give thanks to God then, I had reasons enough! What poor man had He so richly favored?

Say what you will, he whom God has blessed with a pure, chaste, and beautiful wife knows the gift for a gift, a blessing above all earthly blessings. O almighty Lord of heaven, how favored is he whom You have joined to a spotless wife! Rejoice in your honest wife, good husband, rejoice in your good husband, honest wife! God give you both joy. What does the fool know who has never drunk of this young fountain? And even though grievous injury and heart's sorrow have befallen me, yet I thank God with fervent heart that I have known a blameless wife. But you, wicked Death, adversary of all men, may you be hateful to God forever!

DEATH: You have not drunk from the fountain of wisdom; your words betray you. You have not looked into the workings of nature, nor glimpsed the connections between the things of this world, nor gazed upon the changes of the earth; you are a cub of no understanding. Look how the lusty roses and the strong-smelling lilies of the garden, the strength-giving herbs and the joy-bringing flowers of the fields, the firm-standing rocks and the high-sprouting trees of the wild plains, the powerful bears and the mighty lions of the sinister deserts, the tall-statured heroes and fleet-footed, venturesome mortals, skilled masters of all knowledge, how all earthly things, be they ever so cunning and artful and strong, and no matter how long they guard themselves and go their ways—all, all are brought to nothing and everywhere decay. And if all the generations of men that have been, are, and will be must so pass from being to not-being, why should the beloved whom you mourn not rejoice that it happens to her as to all others and to all others as to her? You yourself shall not escape Us, little as you think of it now. One after another! everyone among you must exclaim. Your lament is as nothing; it cannot help you, it comes from a dumb mind.

THE PLOUGHMAN: I put my trust in God, who is my Lord and yours. He will shield me from you and severely avenge me of the wrong you have wrought against me. You juggle with your words, you mix false with true and would snatch the immeasurable sorrows of my mind, heart, and reason from my sight, head, and understanding. In vain, for the pain of my loss is bitter, past all retrieval.

My healing physic in all trouble and adversity, God's servant, supporter of my will, attendant of my body, guardian of her honor and mine—in these things she was untiring day and night. Whatever was entrusted to her she rendered back again whole, pure, and untarnished, often multiplied. Honor, discipline, the virtues of charity and loyalty, moderation, care, and modesty dwelt continually in her court; shame held the mirror of honor before her eyes always; God was her benevolent supporter. Toward me also He was gracious and well disposed for her sake; the honor of my house had won the favor of God. Great her reward and recompense, Bountiful Requiter of all true laborers, Lord of all wealth! Be more gracious to her than ever I could wish! Oh, oh, oh, infamous murderer, Death, vile maw of iniquities, may the hangman be your judge and bind you on his block before me as you cry for pardon!

DEATH: Could you but measure, weigh, calculate, or consider things aright, you would not let such words fall from your empty head. You curse and call for vengeance unmerited and without reason. Wherefore such foolishness? We have told it before, how everything cunning and rich in skill, noble and honorable, fruitful and earthly, and all that lives must perish at Our hand, and still you clamor and declare all your happiness is in your spotless wife. If happiness lies in women, as you say, We might counsel you to continue happy in them. But beware lest it turn to unhappiness!

Tell Us: When you took your much belauded wife did you find her dutiful or make her so? If you found her dutiful, then seek with understanding and you will find many other dutiful and honest women in the world, of whom one may be meet for your espousal. But if you made her dutiful, be glad: you are a living master who understands how to rear and fashion a dutiful wife.

But I will tell you something else: The more you have of love, the more of sorrow will befall you. Had you abstained from love, you would be free of sorrow; the greater the happiness in knowing love, the greater the sorrow of its lack. Wife, child, riches, and all earthly goods bring but a little joy at the beginning and more sorrow at the end; all love upon earth must turn to sorrow: sorrow is the end of love, joy's end is mourning, after desire comes disgust, liking is turned to loathing, good will to ill. All living things run to this end. Learn this better if you wish to talk cleverly!

THE PLOUGHMAN: After injury comes mockery, as the smitten well know. Even thus is it with me, hapless wretch that I am! You have made me a stranger to joy and the companion of sorrow, and long as God wills it I must suffer you. Dull-witted as I am, little as I can do and little as I have gleaned from the learned masters, yet I know that you are the destroyer, robber of my honor, thief of my joys, despoiler of my good days, wrecker of my delights and of all that made life winsome to me. Wherein shall I now rejoice? Where shall I find comfort? Whither fly for refuge? Where shall I seek salvation? Where shall I turn for true counsel? All is gone! My joy is fled before its time; too early it has vanished; all too soon you snatched her from me, my faithful darling, when so ruthlessly you robbed me of my wife and my children of their mother.

Helpless, alone, and full of sorrow I am left unrecompensed by you; never could you requite me for the great wrong you have done. What say you, Death, breaker of all men's marriages? No man can earn or obtain anything good from you; after your evil-doing you make reparation to none; again I remark, mercy is not in you. Curses are your custom, grace you nowhere know. The benefits you show to men, such kindness as men receive from you, the reward you give people, the end you prepare for them—may He send you this who has life and death in His hand!

Lord of the heavenly hosts, requite me for this mighty loss, the great wrong, the bitter woe and the grievous crime! Avenge me on the arch-fiend, Death, O God, avenger of all evildoing!

DEATH: Better silence than foolish speech. After foolish speech strife, after strife enmity, after enmity disquiet, after disquiet pain, after pain days of woe, after days of woe consuming remorse—such is the lot of a mind deranged.

You declare war upon Us. You accuse Us of having worked you an injury in respect of the wife loved so well. It was done to her kindly and graciously: in the merriness of her youth, in the pride of her body, in the prime of her life, at the height of her regard and with honor untarnished, We received her into Our favor. All wise men have praised and wanted that, when they said, Best to die when best to live! He who longs for death has no good death; he who cries out to die has lived too long; pain and trouble are the lot of him who is weighed down with age; for all his wealth he is poor!

On the festival of the keeper of the heavenly gate, six thousand five hundred and ninety-nine years from the beginning of the world, We bade the blessed sufferer in childbed depart from the brief misery of this life, thinking that she should come into God's heritage of eternal joy, everlasting life, and perpetual peace. Hateful as you are to Us, We would wish you and grant you this: that your soul may come together with hers in the house of heaven, your body be united with hers, bone for bone, in the grave of earth. We warrant that you will profit by her good deeds. Therefore silence; hold your peace! As little as you can take away the light from the sun, the chill from the moon, the heat from the fire, or the wet from the water, so little can you rob Us of Our power!

THE PLOUGHMAN: For excuse the guilty needs, in truth, fair words! Even so you. Sweet and sour, soft and hard, amiable and sharp is your way with those whom you think to deceive. I see it with my own eyes. Gloss as you may, I do know that I must still lack my sweet wife thanks to your ruthless violence. And I know too that such power belongs to none save to God and yourself. But by God I have not been thus visited: Had I sinned against God—as has happened often enough—He would have been avenged on me, or she, who was without blemish, would have made amends. You are the evildoer. Therefore I would know who you are, what you are, and where you are, whence you are and what good you are that you have so much power and provoke me so cruelly without warning, that you lay waste my garden of blessings, undermine my strong tower and cause it to fall?

God, comforter of all sad hearts, comfort and requite me, poor, distressed sorrowing man that I am, sitting all alone! Ordain Thy punishment, O Lord, make Thy reckoning, hold in check and wipe out this abominable Death, who is Thy enemy and ours! O Lord, in truth in all Your creation nothing is more abominable, nothing more hideous, nothing more infamous, more bitter, or more unjust than Death! He troubles, brings confusion upon all Your earthly dominion; he takes the dutiful rather than the undutiful; the bad, the old, the infirm, and the useless he often leaves behind, but the good and the useful he snatches all away! Judgment, O Lord, on the false judge!

DEATH: They that have no understanding call evil good and good evil; likewise you. You accuse Us of false judgment and are therefore unjust: of this We shall convince you.

You ask who We are. We are God's hand, the Lord Death, an honest reaper. Our scythe swings of itself: white, black, red, brown, yellow, green, blue, gray, and all manner of bright flowers and grasses We cut down one after another, regardless of their brilliance, their virtue, and their strength. Its lovely hue, its rich scent, avail the violet nothing. Behold, that is justice. The Romans and the poets accorded Us justice as Our due portion, for they knew Us better than you.

You ask what We are. We are nothing and are yet something. Nothing, because We possess neither life nor being nor form and are not spirit, nor visible, nor tangible. Something, because We are the end of life and being, and the beginning of not-being, a mean between the two. We are a fate that brings all men to their fall. The mighty giants must fall before Us, all beings that have life must by Us suffer change. Our guilt is clear for all to see!

You ask where We are. We are invisible; yet Our likeness was found painted on the wall of a temple in Rome in the form of a man, with eyes bound, riding upon an ox. This man wielded a hoe in his right hand and in his left a spade, with which he smote the ox. A great crowd of people assailed him, striking at him and beating him; all conditions of men, each with his own implement, and among them there was even a nun with her psalter. They struck and hurled themselves upon the man on the ox and their blows were meant for Us; yet Death triumphed and buried them all. Pythagoras likens Us to the effigy of a man with the eyes of a basilisk which roam to the very ends of the earth, and at the sight of which every living creature must perish.

You ask whence We are. We come from the earthly paradise. There God created Us and called Us by our right name, when he said: In the day that you eat of the fruit you will surely die. Therefore We write Ourselves thus: Death, Lord and Master upon earth, in the air and on the waters of the deep.

You ask what good We are. You have now heard that We bring the world more of good than of harm. Cease, therefore, let that suffice and be thankful to Us that We have done so graciously by you!

THE PLOUGHMAN: Old men tell strange tales, learned men unknown tales, much-traveled men and men against whom none may speak lying tales, because they cannot be brought to book for outlandish things. And because you also are such an old man you may well be puffed up with conceits.

But even though you were fallen into paradise as a reaper and have the semblance of justice, your scythe still cuts unevenly. Right sturdy flowers it weeds out and leaves the thistles standing; tares remain, the good herbs must all perish. You declare that your scythe swings of itself. How comes it, then, that it leaves more thistles than good flowers unhurt, more plumbago than camomile, more unworthy people than worthy?

Count them up and show me the sum with your fingers: where are the good, the notable men of old? I think that you have them all. Among them is my love; only dust and ashes remain for me. Where are they who dwelt on earth and spoke with God, and won grace and favor with Him, and compassion? Where are they who sat on the earth, yet went among the stars and divided the planets? Where are they, the wise, the masterful, the just, the valiant men of whom the chronicles tell us so much? You have murdered them all and my tender darling; the vile still live.

Whose is the guilt? If you dared to confess the truth, Lord Death, you would name yourself. You firmly declare how justly you judge, sparing no one, how your scythe fells them one by one. I stood and saw with my eyes two mighty armies, each more than three thousand strong, fighting on a green heath; they waded in blood up to the calves. In their midst you were busily hewing and hacking them down on all sides. In each army you slew many; many you left. More lords than serfs lay dead. You cast them out one from another like sleepy pears. Was that mown justly? Is that justly judged? Does your scythe swing of itself?

Hither, my children, gather round! Let us ride out to meet him, let our tongues offer praise and honor to Death, who holds such just court! God's justice is scarce so just!

DEATH: He who has no understanding of things cannot speak of them. Even so with Us. We did not know that you were such a proper man. We have long known you, but forgotten you.

We were there when the Sibyl left you her cunning, when the Lord Solomon on his deathbed bequeathed you his wisdom, when God apportioned to you all the power he had lent to Moses in Egypt, when you took the lion by his leg and smote him against a wall; We saw you number the stars, count up the sands of the sea and its fishes, and measure the raindrops; We saw with enjoyment the race you undertook with the hare; at Babylon before the sultan We saw you taste meat and drink in high honor, and when you bore aloft the banner before King Alexander, conqueror of the world, We looked and gave you the honor gladly. And when you disputed in the Academy at Athens with the high, knowledgeable masters who held wise discourses on the Divine and understood all great things, and when you vanquished them with your knowledge, then We had especial joy; and when you instructed Nero that he act righteously and show patience, We harkened delighted. We were amazed when you brought the Emperor Julius Caesar over the wild sea in a coracle in the teeth of the tempest. In your workshop We saw you fashion a fine garment of rainbows; in it were worked angels, birds, four-footed beasts, and all manner of fishes; the owl and the ape were also borne among them in the weft. But especially We laughed and were loud in your praises when at Paris you sat on Fortune's Wheel and performed your dance on the hides, when you worked Black Magic and caught the Devil in a curious glass. And when God summoned you to his council to discuss the fall of Eve, then We perceived very clearly the depths of your wisdom.

Had We known you so well before, We would have given way to you; We would have let your wife and all men live forever. Yes, We would have done that in your sole honor, for truly you are a wondrous clever donkey!

THE PLOUGHMAN: Mockery and ill-treatment men must often endure for the sake of truth. Even so with me. You praise me for impossible things, you devise preposterous achievements for me, you turn your wrath on my head. You have treated me sorely, and that hurts me all too much. Yet when I speak of it you are hateful toward me and are full of wrath. For he who does evil and will not bow himself nor accept and suffer correction, but presumptuously opposes all things, let him take care lest he encounter enmity.

Take example from me: however evilly, however unjustly, however spitefully you have used me these many days, still I suffer it and do not avenge it as I should. Even now I will prove myself the better of us two: if I have done anything unfair or unhandsome toward you, inform me of it and I will gladly make amends. But if such be not so, then repair my loss or tell me how I may recover from my heart's great sorrow. Never was such wrong done to any man. But that you may have proof of my understanding, either make good the ill you have done her for whom I mourn, I and my children, or else come with me and lay this matter before God, who is the sole true judge of you and me and all the world. You could easily have prevailed upon me; I wanted to leave it to you. I trusted that you would come to see the injustice of your ways and recompense me for so great a wrong. Act with understanding, otherwise the hammer must meet the anvil, and violence violence, come what may!

DEATH: Fair speeches soften men's hearts, understanding leads to comfort, patience brings honor, an angry man is no man at all. Had you addressed Us so kindly before, We would in kindness have told you that you were wrong to weep and bewail the death of your wife.

Have you not heard of the philosopher who resolved to take his life in the bath, or have you not read in his books that no man should bewail mortality? If you did not know it, know it now: as soon as man is born, he has received an earnest that he must die. The beginning is sister to the end. He who is sent out has a duty to return. No man should fight against what must come in its season; what all men must suffer no man should resist. What a man borrows he should repay. All men dwell in misery upon earth; they must pass from being to nothingness. Man's life goes by on swift feet: now living, now in a hand's turn dead. To conclude with one brief sentence: each and every man owes Us a death and has death for his inheritance.

But if you bewail your wife's youth, you do wrong, for as soon as a man comes into life he is straightway old enough to die. Think you, perhaps, that old age is a noble possession? Not so, it is full of sickness and of toil, unshapely, cold, and an offense to all. It is good for nothing and unprofitable in all things: ripe apples fall often into the mud, dropping pears often splash into the puddle.

Or if you bewail her beauty, you do childishly: either age or death must destroy the beauty of each one. All rosy mouths must pale, all ruddy cheeks must blench, all bright eyes grow dim. Have you not read, as Hermes the philosopher teaches, that a man should guard against fair women, when he says, "Hard it is, despite daily care, to keep what is beautiful, because all men desire it; but it is easy to keep what is ugly, because it is displeasing to all men." So cease to lament! Do not mourn a loss that you cannot retrieve!

THE PLOUGHMAN: "Receive gentle correction with all gentleness, a wise man acts accordingly," I hear the wiseacres saying. Your correction is not unbearable. But if a good chastener is to be a good counselor, advise and instruct me how I may root out and drive away from my heart such unutterable sorrow, such lamentable woe, such affliction beyond all bounds from my head and from my understanding! God knows that grief past all telling has fallen upon me since my modest, true, and steadfast spouse was snatched from my house, for she is dead, I am a widower, and my children become orphans.

O Lord Death, the whole world cries out against you, and I cry with them. Yet never was man so evil that he was not in something good. Therefore counsel me, help me, and show me how I may cast out this great grief from my bosom, and my children be recompensed for the loss of so blameless a mother; else I must remain heartsick and they mirthless forever. And you should not take this ill of me, for I perceive that even among the unreasoning brutes one will grieve for his mate out of inborn instinct.

Help, counsel, and restitution you owe me, for you have done me hurt. Should that not be forthcoming, then, even though God in His omnipotence could find nowhere an instrument of vengeance, I would still be avenged upon you, and pick and shovel would be needed once more!

DEATH: Quack, quack, quack! goes the goose—one preaches what one wants. You mete by the same measure. We have already proved that it is foolish to bewail mortality. Since We are the excise officer to whom all men must pay duty for their lives, why do you resist? For truly he who would deceive Us, deceives only himself.

Desist therefore and hearken: life is made for death's sake; were there no life, We would not be, Our office would have no meaning, neither would there be any order in the world. Either you are too full of sorrow, or else you lack reason. If you are unreasonable, pray God that he may lead reason to you; but if you are sorrowful, cease, let be, learn that man's life on earth is but a breath.

You ask for counsel how you may drive sorrow from your heart. Aristotle taught of old time that joy, sorrow, fear, and hope, these four, bring trouble upon all the world and especially upon those who know not how to guard against them. Joy and fear make time short, sorrow and hope make time long. He who has not wholly cast out these four from his heart must have cares always. After joy comes tribulation, after love comes sorrow here upon earth. Love and sorrow dwell one with another: one's end is the other's beginning. Love and sorrow are the same as if a man should clutch a thing to his heart and not let it go, even as no man can be poor who is contented and no man rich who is discontented;

for contentment and discontentment do not dwell with possessions or with any earthly things, but in the heart. He who does not drive away all love from his heart must bear abiding sorrow to the end of his days. Cast out remembrance of love from the heart, from the head, and from the understanding, and straightway you will be quit of sorrow. So soon as you have lost a thing which you cannot regain, act as though it had never been yours: away flies your mourning on the instant.

But if you do not act so, much sorrow is still before you; for heartsickness will befall you after the death of any of your children, and heartsickness also to them, to them and to you, when you have to depart from them. You ask that they may be recompensed for the loss of their mother: can you bring back the years that are gone, the words that are spoken, the maidenhood that is despoiled? If so, you can bring back the mother of your children. I have counseled you enough. Have you understanding, blockhead?

THE PLOUGHMAN: In the long run we perceive the truth; soonest learnt, soonest done. Your words of wisdom are sweet and full of cheer, but I have had enough. Yet should joy, love, delight, and sportiveness be cast out from the world, it would fare ill with us. In this matter I will draw upon the Romans. They themselves were wont and taught their children to hold love in high esteem, to practice tilting, fencing, dancing, racing and jumping, and all manner of virtuous entertainments in time of idleness, thinking that they would be exempt from evildoing the while. For the heart of man cannot remain idle: either good or evil must be in his thoughts always. Even in sleep the heart is not idle. If, therefore, good thoughts be taken from the heart, evil thoughts will enter in. Good out, evil in; evil out, good in: such alternation must continue to the end of time. Since joy, modesty, shame, and other good manners were driven from the world, the world has become full of evil, malice, infamy, perfidy, mockery, and treachery, as you see daily.

Should I, therefore, root out the remembrance of my most beloved wife from my heart, evil thoughts would enter in again: so much the more, then, will I keep remembrance of my dear wife forever. If great love be changed into great sorrow, who may forget it so soon? Only evil folk can do that. Good friends think continually on one another; far journeys, long years, cannot divide dear friends. If my wife be dead in the body, in my thoughts she lives always.

Lord Death, you must counsel more truly if your counsel is to bring help; else you, like a bat, must endure the enmity of birds!

DEATH: Joy but not too much joy, sorrow but not too much sorrow, a wise man harbors in gain or in loss: you do not likewise. He who asks counsel and does not follow the counsel is not to be counseled at all. Our friendly encouragement falls on stony ground.

Yet be you joyful or be you sorrowful We would bring out the truth into the light of the sun; let him see it and hear it who will. Your limited understanding, your stunted thoughts, your hollow heart, lead you to make of men more than they can be. You make of a man what you desire. Yet man cannot be anything more than that which, with the permission of all good women, I shall now set forth: man is conceived in sin, nourished on foul and unnamable corruptions in the womb; he comes naked into the world and smeared like a beehive—a thing of disgust, a noisome mass, a vessel of filth, food for worms, an abode of stinks, a loathly slop tub, a packet of carrion, a barrel of scum, a bottomless sack, a dripping sieve, a bladder of wind, a gobbling mouth, an insatiable orifice, an open cesspool, a stinking pisspot, a reeking bucket, a foul-smelling swill, a den of thieves, a pit of abominations, a dissembling dummy, a bag full of holes, and a painted deception. Let him hear who will: Every man born of woman has nine holes in his body, and out of them all there flows so loathly and so pestilent a nastiness that nothing is more noisome on this earth. Never did you see a person so beautiful but you would shudder, had you the eyes of a lynx and could see through him within. Strip the fairest woman of the clothier's colors, and you will see an outrageous doll, a swift-fading flower, a short-lived phantom, and a soon-sagging mound of earth. Show me a handful of beauty among all the beautiful women who lived a hundred years ago—unless it be those painted on the wall—and take the emperor's crown for your own!

Therefore let go joy, let go sorrow! Let the Rhine run his course like other waters, you clever man from Donkeytown!

THE PLOUGHMAN: For shame! you bag of infamies! See how

you destroy and dishonor and make a nothing of a man, God's most excellent and dearest creation, thereby reviling the Godhead itself! Now I know that you are full of lies and were not made in paradise, as you say. Had you come into the world in paradise, you would know that God created man and all things and saw that they were good; that He placed man above them all, gave him power over all to set his foot upon them, so that man should have dominion over the beasts of the earth, the fowls of the air, the fishes of the deep, and all the fruits of the earth, as indeed he has. Were man so vile, evil, and corrupt as indeed you say, God had wrought corruptly and unprofitably. Had God's almighty and excellent hand fashioned the impure and loathly thing you describe, He had been a culpable creator. Neither would the word stand that God created all things and placed man over them and saw that it was good.

Death, cease your vain clamor! You bring shame upon God's fairest creation. Angels, devils, goblins, and flibbertigibbets, they be all spirits in God's power: but man is the most estimable, the most dextrous, the freest work of God. God fashioned him in His own image, as He Himself has spoken at the beginning of creation.

Where did any craftsman ever make so cunning and rich a work, so masterly a little ball as the head of a man? In it is hidden a wondrous art unknown to all the gods. There in the eyeball is the sight, the surest witness of all, ingeniously worked in the semblance of a mirror: it reaches to the clear horizon of heaven. There in the ear is the hearing, which works afar, latticed most excellently by a fine membrane for the receiving and distinguishing of many sweet sounds. There in the nose is the smell, going in and going out through two holes artfully contrived for the agreeable enjoyment of glad and delightful scents: herein lies the nourishment of the soul. There in the mouth are the teeth, grinding the daily food of the body; also the thin leaf of the tongue, which brings all men intelligence of one another; and there, too, is the delicious tasting and testing of every kind of food. In the head, furthermore, are the thoughts that come from the depths of the heart; with them a man can swiftly reach out, however far he will: with his thoughts a man climbs to the Godhead, and beyond. And man alone is endowed with reason, the divine treasure. He alone possesses the fair body which none but God can fashion, and in which all excellence, all art, and all knowledge are worked with wisdom. Let be, Death! You are man's enemy: therefore you speak no good of him.

DEATH: Sneers, curses, wishes, however many, can fill no sack, however small. Moreover chatterers are not to be combated with words. Your opinion that man is the summit of all art, beauty, and perfection rests on itself alone; he will nevertheless fall into Our net, be caught in Our snare.

Grammar, foundation of all good speech, avails nothing with her sharp and well-set words. Rhetoric, blossoming ground of fair language, avails nothing with her flowery sentences and fine phrases. Logic, careful divider of truth and untruth, avails nothing with her veiled explanations and crooked paths to truth. Geometry, weigher and measurer of the earth, avails nothing with her unerring degrees, her exact measurements. Arithmetic, rapid balancer of numbers, avails nothing with her calculations and reckonings, her nimble figures. Astronomy, mistress of the firmament, avails nothing with her power of the stars, her influence of the planets. Music, orderly helpmeet of the song and the voice, avails nothing with her sweet sounds, her delicate harmonies. Philosophy, field of wisdom, tilled and sown across and across by the science of nature and for the attainment of good manners, avails nothing with all her perfections. Medicine, distiller of sustaining potions; geomancy, cunning answerer of questions on earth by determination of planets and by the signs of the heavenly girdle; pyromancy, winged and truthful presager by fire; hydromancy, diviner of the future by the workings of water; astrology, interpreter of the ways of earth by heavenly marvels; cheiromancy, foreteller of things to come by the lines of the hand; necromancy, mighty conjurer of spirits by sacrifices to the dead, by fingers, and by seals; arithmomancy, art of secret numbers, with her strong prayers and potent spells; alchemy, with her wondrous transmutation of metals; augury, which understands the cries of birds and prophesies the future from them; haruspicy, which sees visions in the smoke from the altar of sacrifice; pedomancy, which works sorceries with the entrails of children, and ornithomancy, with the entrails of fowls; even the lawyer, that unscrupulous Christian, avails nothing with his advocacy of right and wrong and his crooked judgments—these and other arts related to those herein named, all will avail nothing. Every man must be overthrown by Us, is grist to Our mill, and will be pounded beneath Our rollers. Mark Us well, you saucy bumpkin?

THE PLOUGHMAN: Requite not evil with evil; be patient—so the teachers of virtue admonish. This path I too will tread, that I may see whether, perchance, you will turn patient after impatience.

I perceive from your words that you think to advise me truly. Since truth is in you, give me true counsel as upon oath: In what manner shall I now live my life? Hitherto I have been dearly and delightfully wedded; where shall I turn now? To worldly or to unworldly condition? Both are open to me. I have proved the ways of all manner of men in my thoughts, I have appraised and weighed them diligently: I found them all imperfect, brittle, and full of sin. And now I am in doubt where to turn, for the life of all men is troubled with infirmities. Counsel me, Death, for counsel is needed.

I have looked into my heart and I hold firmly that a pure and godly household cannot be save in marriage. By my soul I say that if I knew I would prosper in marriage as before, I would live all my days in that state. Blest, contented, merry, and well-liking is a man who has an upright wife, wherever he may be. To such a man it is a joy to seek nourishment and to strive after honor. To him it is a joy also to repay honor with honor, truth with truth, good with good. He need not guard his wife, for an upright wife is her own best guardian. But he who may not believe and trust his wife must have continual care.

Lord of heaven above, Prince of all joys, happy is he whom Thou hast blest with a pure partner of his bed. Let him look to heaven and give thanks to Thee daily with upraised hands. Death, do your worst, Lord of so much power!

DEATH: Praise without end, profanation without purpose, such is the habit of many men in all their undertakings. Yet there should be reason and moderation to praise and profanity so that one may use it aright when one has need of it.

You praise marriage immoderately. Yet We would say this of marriage without giving offense to chaste women: As soon as a man takes a wife, straightway the two of them are in Our prison. Straightway he has a duty, an appendage, a tailpiece, a yoke, a handsleigh, a horse collar, a burden, a heavy load, a besom, and a daily blight which he cannot be rid of unless We grant him of Our grace. A man with a wife has thunders, showers of hail, foxes, and serpents in his house all the days of the year. A woman strives always to be the man: If he blows hot, she blows cold; if he wants this, she wants that; if he goes here, she goes there—of such play he becomes sick and defeated. Deceits and trickeries, flatteries, caressings and purrings, carpings, hissings, laughings and weepings, she has them all in a moment—to them she is born. Slothful to work, brisk to lewdness, tame and wild she is as soon as she feels the need! No counsel but she will always gainsay it; not to do what is commanded, and to do what is forbidden—in this she is very zealous. This is too sweet for her, that too bitter; this is too much, that too little; now it is too early, now too late—in this manner everything becomes the victim of her carpings. Yet if anything is praised by her, it is fit only to be displayed in the pillory and made mock of: so their life passes with jests and derision. There is no mean for a married man—be he too pleasant or be he too sharp, in either case he will be the loser; yet be he not half so pleasant or sharp, there is still no mean for him: all turns to loss or reproach in the end. Every day new entreaties or chidings; every week unexpected demands of murmurings; every month new nastiness or abomination; every year new clothes or daily bickerings—all this must a married man suffer, do what he will. As for the vexations of the night, let me pass over them in silence; at Our age we are ashamed.

If We would not spare the upright women, of the undutiful We could sing and say much. Therefore have a care what you praise, you who know not gold from lead!

THE PLOUGHMAN: Revilers of women must be reviled, say the masters of truth. How now, Death? Your senseless slandering of women, although you did it with their permission, turns to your disgrace and their shame.

In the writings of many wise masters we read that no one can prosper without the guidance of a wife. For the possession of wife and children is not the least part of earthly happiness. With such a truth did the wise Mistress Philosophy comfort that consoler, Roman Boethius. Every sensible and wise man can be my witness: No man can be schooled save in the school of women. Say what you will, a well-bred, fair, chaste, and virtuous woman is above all earthly treasures. Never did I see a right true man and brave but he was guided by a woman's persuasion. And wherever good men gather together you see it every day: in all public places, in all courts, in all tournaments, in all adventures women acquit themselves the best. He who has committed himself to a woman's service refrains from all evildoing. Good breeding and honor women teach in their school. And women have power over earthly pleasures also; they bring it about that all prettiness and pleasant dalliance be done to their honor. The threat of a chaste woman's finger chastens a good man more than the prick of weapons.

But to speak shortly and with no nonsense: Worthy women are the sustenance, the mainstay, and multiplication of the world. Nevertheless, with gold there must be lead, with corn thistles, with all coins clippings, and with women viragoes; but the good should not suffer for the bad. Mark that, captain of the heights!

DEATH: A knob of base metal for a nugget of gold, a turd for a topaz, a flint for a ruby—thus mistakes the fool; the haystack is a mountain, the Danube is the sea, the buzzard is a noble falcon—thus says the simpleton. You likewise praise the delight of the eyes; the why and the wherefore of things you see not at all. You do not know that everything on this earth is either lust of the flesh or lust of the eyes or worldly pride. Lust of the flesh seeks after pleasure, lust of the eyes covets wealth and possessions, worldly pride strives after honors. Wealth brings miserliness, pleasure makes unchaste, honors breed pomps and boasting; hazards and fear must always come from possessions, evil thoughts and sin from pleasure, vanity from honors. If only you could rightly understand that you would find vanity everywhere; then be it joy or be it sorrow that fell to your lot, you would suffer in patience and not plague Us with your complaints.

But as little as the ass understands how to play the harp, so little can you perceive the truth. Therefore We are in such distress on your account. When We parted young Pyramus from Thisbe the maid, who were one soul and one flesh, and divided them one from another, and when We caused Trojan Paris and Grecian Helen to die, We were not so sorely plagued as by you. Neither were We so mightily vexed on account of the Emperor Charles, nor the Margrave William, nor Dietrich von Bern, nor Boppe the Strong, nor Siegfried the leather-skinned. Many men still mourn Aristotle and Avicenna, and yet We remain undisturbed. When David the patient king and Solomon the shrine of wisdom died, We were accorded more thanks than curses. They who lived once are all departed; you, and all who now are or will be, must follow them. Yet We, Death, remain master here!

The Ploughman: Out of his own mouth shall a man be judged, especially when he says now this, now that.

You said before that you were something and yet nothing; that you are no spirit and are the end of life, and that all men upon earth are committed to your charge. But now you say that we must all depart and that you, Death, will remain master here! Two contradictory words cannot together be true. For if we all must depart this life and if all life on earth is to have an end, and if you are, as you say, life's end, I must ask: When there is no more life and when, therefore, there is no dying and no death anymore, where will you be, Death? You cannot dwell in heaven, for heaven is granted only to good spirits, and you are not a spirit, as your words have said. If, then, you have nothing more to do upon earth and the earth itself no longer endures, you must straightway go down to hell; there you must groan for all eternity. Then, too, the living and the dead will be avenged upon you.

No man can be guided by your contrary words. Are all earthly things made and fashioned so evilly, contemptibly, and unprofitably? Never since the beginning of the world has God been so charged! He has esteemed virtue, abhorred evil, forgiven and punished the sinner until now; and I hold that He will continue in this wise. From youth up I have read, marked, and learned in the books that God is the creator of all things. You say that all earthly life must have an end. But Plato and other philosophers hold, as against this, that in all matters the confounding of one thing is but the bringing forth of another, and that all rests on rebirth. They say, further, that in heaven, as upon earth, all is but a whirl of everlasting change.

With your fickle discourse, whereon no man may build, you would frighten me from my accusation. Therefore, you despoiler, I call upon God, my savior! And may He shower evil upon you, Amen!

Death: Often a man who begins to speak knows not how to cease until he be interrupted. You are hewn from the same block.

We have said it once and say it again and will make an end of it: The earth and all that it contains are founded on inconstancy. In this time the earth has become truly changeable, for all things have changed about: the great multitude of the people has but the back to the front, the front to the back, the undermost to the top, the top to the undermost, and the wrong they have made the right. But we have brought all the generations of men into the steadiness of the flaming fire. To snatch at the rainbow, and to find a good, true, and constant friend, are alike possible upon earth. All men are more disposed to evil than to virtue. And if any do what is good, he does it for fear of Us. All men and all their works are full of vanity. Their body, their wife, their children, their honor, their possessions, and all their strength flee away, in a moment they vanish, on the wind they are scattered; neither shape nor shadow remains.

Mark, note, look, and behold what the children of men now do upon earth: how they probe and explore mountain and valley, hill and dell, fields, pastures, and wildernesses, and fathom the depths of the sea and the womb of earth for the sake of worldly possessions; how they dig deep mines and sink shafts into the earth and ransack her rich veins, looking for shining ores which they prize above all things because they are scarce; how they hew wood in the forests, make walls and fences, and stick houses together like the swallows; plant orchards and set graftings; till the soil, build vineyards, erect mills, accumulate tithes, hunt fishes and game, and pursue the chase; raise great herds of cattle, have menservants and maidservants, ride upon high horses, fill their houses and coffers with gold, silver, and precious stones, and rich garments and all manner of goods and possessions; relish luxury and pleasure, which they pursue day and night—what, then, is this? All is vanity and a pollution of the soul, passing as the day of yesterday, which is past. With war and with robbery they win it; the more they possess, the more they have robbed. And to new strife and discord they leave it for an heritage.

Oh, mortal man lives in fear perpetually, in misery, in weariness, in care, in terror and trembling, in days of sickness and sorrow, in grief and toil and woe and affliction and all manner of adversity. And the more a man possesses of earthly goods, the more adversity will befall him. Yet this is the most grievous of all, that no man can know when, where, and how We will come upon him of a sudden and force him to go the way of all flesh. This burden is the lot of master and man, husband and wife, rich and poor, good and bad, young and old. O painful certainty, how little the fool heeds it! When it is too late, they all wish to be pious! Vanity of vanities, all is vanity and vexation of the spirit.

Therefore let be your lament and enter into what condition you will; everywhere you will find frailty—vanity is everywhere. But turn yourself from evil and do good; seek peace and pursue it continually; above all earthly things set a clear, unalloyed conscience. And for that we have done right by you, We will come with you before God, the everlasting, the great, and the strong.

THE JUDGMENT OF GOD: The Spring, the Summer, the Autumn, and the Winter, the four helpers and quickeners of the year, fell out in a great dispute. Each of them praised himself for his good will in rain, wind, thunder, hail, snow, and all weathers, and each one claimed that his work was best.

The Spring said that he quickened and rounded all fruit; the Summer said that he made the fruit timely and ripe; the Autumn said that he brought into barn, cellar, and house all fruit; the Winter said that he consumed and used up all fruit and drove away the venomous worm. So they praised themselves and disputed zealously, but they had forgotten that the power was from God.

Both you do likewise: The accuser bewails his loss as though it were his rightful inheritance; he does not consider that it was bestowed by Us. Death praises himself for his just dominion, which he has received in fee from Us alone. The one bewails what is not his; the other boasts a power that is not of himself. Yet the battle is not without sense. You have both fought well. Sorrow drives the one to accuse, and the accusation drives the other to speak truth. Therefore, Ploughman, yours be the honor; yours, Death, the victory. Each man owes his life to Death, his body to earth, his soul to Us.

THE PLOUGHMAN'S PRAYER TO GOD: Just and eternal Keeper of the world; God of all gods; awful and wonderful Lord of lords; Almightiest of spirits; Prince of all princes; Source from which all goodness flows; Holiest of the holy; Crown-giver and the Crown; Rewarder and the Reward; Elector in whose hand is all election;

Blesser of those to whom Thou givest life; Joy and Delight of the Angels; Molder of forms most high; Patriarch and Child; hear me!

O Light that needs no other light; Light that outshines and darkens all external light; Radiance from before which all other radiance flees; Radiance like to which all light is as darkness; Light beside which all is shadow; Light that in the beginning said, "Let there be light!"; Fire that burns unquenched, everlastingly, without beginning or end: Hear me!

Holiness above all things holy; Way without false turnings to life everlasting; Best than which there is no better; Life from which all things live; Truth of Very Truth; Wisdom embracing all wisdom; Issue of all strength; Perceiver of all right and wrongdoing; Succor in all errors and transgressions; Quencher of all thirsts; Comforter of the sick; Seal of highest majesty; Keystone of heaven's harmony; Knower of all hearts; Shaper of all countenances; Planet holding in sway all planets; Sovereign Influence of the stars; Mighty Master of the heavenly court; Law before which the orbits of heaven can never more bend from their fixtures; Bright Sun: Hear me!

Assuagement of all fevers; Master of all masters; Only Father of all creation; Ever-present Watcher of all ways and at all arrivals; Almighty escort from womb to tomb; Artificer of all forms; Foundation of all good works; Lover of all truth; Hater of all corruption; Only Just Judge; Arbiter from whose decree no single thing may depart evermore: Hear me!

Balm of our weariness: Fast Knot which none may unloose; Perfect Being having power over all perfection; Very Knower of all secrets and of things known to none; Giver of eternal joys; Bestower of earthly blessedness; Host, Ministrant, and Friend to all good men; Hunter to whom no track is hid; Mold of all thought; Judge and Unifier; Measurer and Container of all circles; Gracious Harkener to all them that call upon Thee: Hear me!

Never-failing support of the needy; Comforter of them that hope in Thee; Feeder of the hungry; All-powerful Creator of Being from Nothing and of Nothing from Being; Quickener of all beings, momentary, temporal, or eternal. Preserver and Destroyer of life; Thou who imaginest, conceivest, givest form to, and takest away all things: Hear me!

Everlasting Light; Eternal Luminary; True-faring Mariner whose vessel never founders; Ensign beneath whose banner victory is sure; Author of Brightness; Architect of the foundations of the earth; Tamer of the seas; Mingler of the inconstant air; Kindler of fire; Creator of all elements; of the thunder, of the lightning, of the mist, of the hail, of the snow, of the rain, of the rainbow, of the dew and the mildew, of the wind, of the frost, and of all their workings, Sole Craftsman; Monarch of the heavenly host; Emperor in whose service none may fail; All-gentlest, All-Strongest, and All-merciful Creator: Pity me and hear me!

Store from which all treasures spring; Fountain from which all pure streams flow; Shepherd from whom none goes astray; Lodestar to which all good things strain and cleave as the bees to their queen; Cause of all causes: Hear me!

Good above all goods, most august Lord Jesus, receive graciously the soul of my dear and best-beloved wife, grant her eternal peace, refresh her with the dew of Thy grace, keep her under the shadow of Thy wing, accept her, Lord, into Thy perfect satisfaction, where the least and the greatest alike have their contentment! Let her, O Lord, from whom she is come, dwell in Thy kingdom with the blessed, the everlasting spirits!

I grieve for Margaretha, my chosen wife. Grant her, gracious Lord, in the mirror of Thine almighty and eternal Godhead, wherein the choirs of angels have their light, to see and contemplate herself everlastingly, and everlastingly rejoice.

May all things that live under the blazon of the eternal standard-bearer, all creatures whatsoever, help me to say with heart tranquil and serene. Amen.

Translated by K. W. Maurer

SEBASTIAN BRANT

Sebastian Brant (1458–1521) was born in Strasbourg and became one of the leading exponents of Humanism. He began his studies in 1475 at the University of Basel, where he earned his baccalaureate in 1477. He received his law degree at Basel in 1484 and his doctorate in law in 1489. He taught law at Basel (and was for a time dean of the faculty) until 1499. His publications in those years reflect his interest in the sources of and commentaries on Roman and canon law, as well as in religious and political topics. Like many Humanists, he took a strong interest in printing and had a decisive influence on the magnificent Basel book industry as an anonymous adviser and editor in Bergmann von Olpe's important printshop. His *Ship of Fools* (1494) vividly documents how in his generation the borderline between tradition and the changing concepts and values of the new epoch could run through the consciousness of one individual. This book became an enormous success in Europe because it anthologized much of the traditional wisdom and morality (which Brant gleaned from classical, biblical, and medieval sources), but at the same time gave early glimpses of the new trends beginning to take shape in academic, spiritual, and social life.

From
The Ship of Fools

A Prologue to
the Ship of Fools

*For profit and salutary instruction, admonition and pursuit of wis-
dom, reason, and good manners: also for contempt and punishment of folly, blindness, error, and stupidity of all stations and
kinds of men: with special zeal, earnestness, and labor compiled
at Basel by Sebastian Brant, doctor in both laws.*

All lands in Holy Writ abound
And works to save the soul are found,
The Bible, Holy Fathers' lore
And other such in goodly store,
So many that I feel surprise
To find men growing not more wise
But holding writ and lore in spite.
The whole world lives in darksome night,
In blinded sinfulness persisting,
While every street sees fools existing
Who know but folly, to their shame,
Yet will not own to folly's name.
Hence I have pondered how a ship
Of fools I'd suitably equip—
A galley, brig, bark, skiff, or float,
A carack, scow, dredge, racing boat,

31

A sled, cart, barrow, carryall—
One vessel would be far too small
To carry all the fools I know.
Some persons have no way to go
And like the bees they come a-skimming,
While many to the ship are swimming,
And each one wants to be the first,
A mighty throng with folly curst,
Whose pictures I have given here.
They who at writings like to sneer
Or are with reading not afflicted
May see themselves herewith depicted
And thus discover who they are,
Their faults, to whom they're similar.
For fools a mirror shall it be,
Where each his counterfeit may see.
His proper value each would know,
The glass of fools the truth may show.
Who sees his image on the page
May learn to deem himself no sage,
Nor shrink his nothingness to see,
Since none who lives from fault is free;
And who would honestly have sworn
That cap and bells he's never worn?
Whoe'er his foolishness decries
Alone deserves to rank as wise,
Whoever wisdom's airs rehearses
May stand godfather to my verses!
He'd injure me and have no gain
If he would not this book retain.
Here you will find of fools no dearth
And everything you wish on earth,
The reasons why you're here are listed,
Why many fools have ay existed,
What joy and honor wisdom bears
And why a fool in danger fares,
The world's whole course in one brief look—
Are reasons why to buy this book.
In jest and earnest evermore
You will encounter fools galore.

The wise man's pleasure I will win,
While fools speak oft of kith and kin,
Fools poor and rich, high-bred and tyke,
Yes, everyman will find his like,
I cut a cap for every chap,
But none of them will care a rap,
And if I'd named and then apprized him,
He'd say I had not recognized him.
I hope, though, men who're really wise
Will find a deal to praise and prize,
And out of knowledge say forsooth
That I have spoken but the truth.
If I were sure that they'd approve
I'd care not what the fools reprove.
Naught else but truth the fool must hear,
Although it pleases not his ear.
Terence asserts that truth can breed
Deep hate, and he is right, indeed,
And he who blows his nose too long
Will have a nosebleed hard and strong,
And he whom evil tempers pall
Will often agitate his gall,
And so not deeply am I riled
When I by rabble am reviled,
Because my teachings seem too good.
Fools ever have misunderstood
And spurned and laughed at wisdom's touch,
Of simpletons this book tells much.
But pay more heed, I beg you do,
To common sense and honor's due
Than e'er to this poor verse or me,
In truth I've slaved laboriously
That 'mongst these leaves these idiots might
Foregather; I have worked at night
While snug in bed they slumbered tight
Or gambled, freely drinking wine,
And never thought of me and mine.
Some rode about in sleds on snow
With frozen ear or frostbit toe,
Some pranced like lovesick calves elated,

And others losses estimated
That they had undergone that day,
And how themselves they would repay,
Or how tomorrow they would ply
Their falsehoods, sell, deceive, and buy.
In pondering these many pranks,
The pranks of countless stupid cranks,
'Tis wonder not that anxious fear
Lest rhyming bring me hate and jeer
Has robbed of sleep my nights so drear.
Both men and women, all mankind
Their image in this glass will find,
That both I mean will follow soon,
For man is not the only loon,
'Mongst women fools are hardly fewer,
I'll deck their heads and veils demure
With fool's cap, though I'm sure it hurts,
For girls, too, have on idiot's skirts.
Some clothes they wear would put to shame
Full many a man's unblemished name,
Shoes pointed, bodice cut too low,
So that their breasts might almost show,
And rags they wrap into their braids,
And build huge horns upon their heads,
The giant oxen mocking they
Parade about as beasts of prey.
But honorable women should
Forgive me what I say, I would
Not wish to injure their good name,
I'd stress the bad ones' evil fame,
Full scores of whom deserve a trip
Aboard our crowded idiot's ship.
With caution everyone should look
To see if he's in this my book,
And who thinks not will say that he
Of wand and fool's cap may be free.
Who thinks that he is not affected
To wise men's doors be he directed,
There let him wait until mayhap
From Frankfurt I can fetch a cap.

Who everywhere would innovate
Arouses scandal, wrath, and hate,
A dunce's stupid traveling mate.

4. Of Innovations

An erstwhile quite disgraceful thing
Now has a plain, familiar ring:
An honor 'twas a beard to grow,
Effeminate dandies now say no!
Smear apish grease on face and hair
And leave the neck entirely bare,
With rings and many a heavy chain,
As though they were in Lienhart's train;

Vile sulphur, resin curl their hair,
An egg white's added too with care,
That curls may form in basket-pan,
The curls amid the breeze they fan,
Or bleach them white in sun and heat,
For lice no ordinary treat;
Their number now would wax untold,
Since modern clothes have many a fold,
Coat, bodice, slipper, also skirts,
Boots, pants, and shoes and even shirts,
Fur hoods, cloaks, trimmings not a few,
The Jewish style seems smart and new.
The styles change oft, are various,
It proves that we are frivolous.
Shameless and fickle I do brand
Style slaves who live in every land;
Their coats are short and shorter grow,
So that their navels almost show.
Shame, German nation, be decried!
What nature would conceal and hide,
You bare it, make a public show,
'Twill lead to evil, lead to woe,
And then grow worse and harm your name;
Woe's every man who rouses shame,
Woe's him too who condones such sin,
His wages will be paid to him.

My rope pulls many fools about,
Ape, cuckold, ass, and silly lout,
Whom I seduce, deceive, and flout.

13. Of Amours

Dame Venus I, with rump of straw,
Fools do regard me oft with awe,
I draw them toward me with a thrill
And make a fool of whom I will,
My clients, who could name them all?

Whoever's heard of Circe's stall,
Calypso, famous sirens' bower,
He knows my skill and knows my power.
Whoever thinks he's very shrewd
In idiot's broth will soon be stewed,
Whom I decide to wound by stealth
Through herbs will not regain his health.
My little son stark blind is he
Since lovesick swains can never see;
My son's a child, he never grew,
For lovers act like children too.
They seldom speak a serious word,
Their speech like children's is absurd.
My son goes naked every day,
Love can't be hid and tucked away;

Since evil loves are flighty things
My offspring wears a pair of wings;
Amours are changeful, fickle e'er,
There's naught more fitful anywhere;
And Cupid brings along his bow,
While round his waist two quivers show.
In one, barbed arrows he doth bear,
To shoot the fools who have no care.
Whom once these sharp gilt barbs do hit,
Deprived are they of sense and wit,
They dance about like fools insane.
The other pouch doth bolts contain,
They're dull and leaded, hardly light,
One causes wounds, the other flight.
Whom Cupid strikes, Amor ignites,
So that the fire his vitals bites
And he cannot put out the flame
That killed Dido of ancient fame
And caused Medea, cruel mother,
To burn one child and slay another.
Tereus would not have been a bird,
Pasiphaë the steer'd avoid,
Phaedra would Theseus not pursue
And passion for her stepson shew,
For Nessus death would not have loomed
And Troy would never have been doomed,
Scylla would leave her father's hair,
Hyacinth be a flower fair,
Leander would not swim the sea,
Messalina pure and chaste would be,
And Mars in chains would never lie,
Procris from thickets green would shy,
Sappho would not fall off the cliff,
Sirens would not upset a skiff,
Circe no vessel would impede,
Pan, Cyclops play no plaintive reed,
Leucothoë would incense spare,
Myrrha would no Adonis bear,
And Byblis would her brother leave,

Through gold would Danaë not conceive,
In night Nyctimine not rejoice,
And Echo would not mock our voice,
Thisbe would dye no berries red,
Atalanta be no lion dread,
The Levite's wife none would disgrace,
Causing the death of one whole race;
David would not take Bersabë,
Samson would not trust Dalitë,
Solomon would not to idols pray,
Amnon his sister not betray,
And Joseph would not be undone
Nor Hippolytus, Bellerophon;
As horse the wise man would not fare,
And Vergil would not hang in air,
Ovid the emperor's friend would be,
Had he not learned love's artistry,
And more to wisdom's fount would go
If smitten not with lover's woe.
Who sees too much of woman's charms
His morals and his conscience harms;
He cannot worship God aright
Who finds in women great delight.
Clandestine love in every race
Is foolish, sinful, black disgrace;
Such love is still more foolish when
It seizes older wives and men.
Fool who from love takes inspiration
And means to practice moderation,
For wisdom's treasure rich and pure
Cannot be mingled with amour;
A lover's oft so blind indeed,
He thinks no one his loves will heed.
Such folly I can but deride,
This dunce cap's pasted to his hide.

Who never learns the proper things,
Upon his cap the dunce bell rings,
He's led by idiot's leading strings.

27. Of Useless Studying

Students should likewise not be skipped,
With fool's caps they are well equipped,
When these are pulled about the ear
The tassel flaps and laps the rear,
For when of books they should be thinking
They go carousing, roistering, drinking.
A youth puts learning on the shelf,
He'd rather study for himself
What's useless, vain—an empty bubble;
And teachers too endure this trouble,
Sensible learning they'll not heed,
Their talk is empty, vain indeed.

Could this be night or is it day?
Did mankind fashion monkeys, pray?
Was't Plato, Socrates who ran?
Such is our modern teaching plan.
Are they not bred to folly true
Who night and day with great ado
Thus plague themselves and other men?
No other teaching do they ken.
Of such men, writes Origines,
That froglike creatures quite like these
And gadflies who, unbidden, flew in,
Brought over Egypt rack and ruin.
In Leipzig students act this way,
In Erfurt, Mainz, Vienna, ay,
Heidelberg, Basel, anyplace,
Returning home in sheer disgrace.
The money's spent in idleness,
They're glad to tend a printing press
And, learning how to handle wine,
They're lowly waiters many a time.
Thus money spent to train and school
Has often gone to rear a fool.

He guards grasshoppers 'neath the sun,
Pours water into wells for fun,
Who guards his wife as 'twere a nun.

32. Of Guarding Wives

They harvest folly, sheer despair,
Who always watch their wives with care,
For she who's good will do the right,
And she who's bad will sin for spite
And manage well to perpetrate
Her evil plans against her mate.
For e'en a padlock placed before
The entrance, be it gate or door,
And many guards about the house

Can't keep her honest toward her spouse.
Danaë, held in tower, grieved,
And nonetheless a child conceived.
Penelope was loose and free,
And many suitors did she see.
Yet twenty years her husband strayed,
Still chaste and pure she always stayed.
Let only that one claim that he
Of his wife's base deceit is free
Who loves her so as to believe
That she would not her spouse deceive.
A pretty wife on folly's course
Is like unto an earless horse.
The man who plows with such a nag,

His furrows oft diverge and sag.
A wife who would be modest found
Should cast her eyes upon the ground
And not coquet whene'er she can
And not make eyes at every man,
Nor heed whate'er one says and does.
Panders will often wear sheep's clothes.
If Helen had not sent a note
In answering what Paris wrote,
And Dido through her sister Ann,
They'd not have wed a lecherous man.

The stupid oft by lust are felled
And by their wings are firmly held:
For many, this their end hath spelled.

50. Of Sensual Pleasure

A temporal pleasure's like unto
A brazen, sensual woman who
Infests the street and plies her trade,
Inviting every amorous blade
To come and practice fornication
At bargain rates—a great temptation—
She begs all men in shameless fashion
To join and quench her evil passion.
Fools seek her out, indifferent, low,
As oxen would to slaughter go,
Or like a harmless, frisky wether
That does not know about the tether
Until it feels the deadly dart
That's shot to penetrate its heart.
Remember, fool, your soul's at stake
And soon in deepest hell you'll bake
If such lewd women you frequent.
Shun lust, then blessings will be sent,
Seek not for lust, licentiousness
Like heathen king Sardanapalus,
Who thought that men should live on earth
In lust and joy and sensuous mirth,
Because they're over when one dies.
Such nonsense silly fools advise,
To trust in pleasures ever fleeing.
Yet this old king was quite far-seeing.
The man of lust and pleasures vain
Buys moderate joy with ample pain;
If temporal lust be sweet, my friend,
It's wormwood, mark its bitter end,
The whole world's base licentiousness
Turns finally to bitterness,
Though Epicurus placed his trust
In worldly joys and wanton lust.

For priesthood some declare desire,
They don a priest's or monk's attire,
But later their regret is dire.

73. Of Becoming a Priest

Another type I'd have you mark
That on the fool's ship should embark
Has recently been much increased,
For every peasant wants a priest
Among his clan, to dodge and shirk
And play the lord, but never work;
It's not done out of veneration
Or for the sake of soul's salvation,
They want a high-placed relative
On whom the other kin may live.
"Training," they say, "we need not give
Him much, he'll learn it easily,

No need for scholarship I see
So long as benefices be."
Priesthood to them is something slight,
As though it were a trifling mite;
Ofttimes young priests are now so crude,
They seem just like a monkey's brood,
Shepherds who flocks should tend and keep
But could be trusted with no sheep.
In church affairs they're as astute
As Miller's ass upon the lute.
But if to orders they're admitted
For this the bishops should be twitted,
Soul shepherds they should never be
Unless they're friends of decency.
Unwise the shepherd who'd abuse
His flock and all his sheep confuse,
But now these young and foolish beasts
Have one ambition—being priests,
This is the hope that they unfold,
But everything is not of gold
That on the saddle brightly gleams,
It's merely dung that costly seems.
A youth that enters priesthood's state
May later execrate his fate
Because he took the step in haste,
By begging later to be faced.
If he had had a living good
Before he donned the gown and hood,
It never would have gone so far.
Full many priestlings summoned are
And have to bless the fish and meat
At lordly feasts where others eat.
A patent's rented out and hired,
So that a title be acquired:
To cheat their bishop they believe,
But only their own selves deceive.
No poorer creature lives on earth
Than priests who suffer want and dearth.
They must pay fees to one and all,

To bishop, vicar, and fiscal,
Collator and to many a friend,
Housekeeper, children without end,
These lash him with a cruel whip
And land him on the dunce's ship.
Thus joy is killed and pleasures pass,
O God, so many priests say mass,
'Twere better far did they refrain
And graced the altar ne'er again.
Your sacrifices will not win
The Lord when done with sin in sin.
To Moses God the Lord did say
That every beast should stay away
And should not touch the holy mound,
Else black misfortunes would abound.
Uzzah, who saw the ark and dared
To touch it, was by death not spared;
Korah, Abiram, and Dathan
The censer touched and perished then.
The sacred meat seems good to eat,
With monkish coal some warm their feet,
Who'll later roast and stew in hell.
I'm preaching to the sensible.
Full many a youth ordained we see
Who has not reached maturity,
And ere he knows what it will do
Of good or bad, he's in the stew.
Habituation oft will do it,
But sadly some men have to rue it
And curse their friends with loud complaining
Who bear the blame for this ordaining.
Most enter monasteries blind,
Not old enough to know their mind,
They enter not by heaven's will
And only hope to eat their fill;
They pay no heed to priestly vow,
They never make a reverent bow,
Especially in orders where
Observing rules is very rare.

Such cloister-cats are insolent
Because they are not tied and pent.
Far better close the orders all
Than monks that into sinning fall.

Translated by Edwin H. Zeydel

DESIDERIUS ERASMUS

Erasmus of Rotterdam's (1466–1536) *Praise of Folly* is one of the most amazing books of its time. It deals in great detail with the whole scale of critical attitudes that the Humanists developed toward the state, the Church, the universities—in fact, toward every value and taboo that had been revered in the past. Under the veneer of scholarly witticism and cumbersome mythological lore smolders a fuse that would never again be completely extinguished.

In its radical indictment of all authority, this text has no parallel before or during Erasmus' lifetime—and, for that matter, rarely if ever afterward. In its relegation of all moral, political, and religious decisions to the discretion of the individual's free human will, it was a challenging document of the desire for change at the height of German Humanism.

The Praise of Folly

Preface

Desiderius Erasmus of Rotterdam to his Friend, Thomas More, Greetings!

As I left Italy for England a short time ago, I decided I would not waste all the time I would have to spend on horseback in idle chitchat or popular tales but rather would concern myself with questions related to those subjects in which we both have common interest, as well as in recalling the pleasant memories of friends, some of whom—very learned and very charming people—I had previously left here (in England). And the first one to come to mind was you, Morus. So, while far away from you, I took almost as much pleasure in recalling you as I used to experience in your company when we were constantly together. I'll be hanged if I've ever enjoyed anything more in my life. Since I felt impelled to do something, but since the time and circumstances did not seem to permit more serious scholarly activity, I toyed with the notion of producing a praise of Folly.

You may wonder what goddess Pallas put that idea into my head. Well, in the first place, it was your surname More that prompted me. It comes as close to the word *mōría* ("folly") as you yourself are remote from that concept. The general consensus of all is that you are as far from folly as it is possible to be. Next, I imagined that you would quite approve of this exercise in ironic wit, because you ordinarily immensely enjoy humorous efforts of this sort yourself, efforts that are on the learned side, if I am not mistaken, but are by no means ponderously insipid. Furthermore, in your own view of this mortal existence you play the part of a Democritus. Yet, endowed as you are with your own unique perspicacity, you are given to disagreeing drastically with the common herd, while being able, because of your incredibly amiable, easygoing nature, to get along with all sorts of people and to enjoy doing so.

May you, then, accept in good part this little exposition as a memento from a friend, and may you defend it against attack. Since it is dedicated to you, it is now yours and is no longer mine. There are bound to be disputatious people who will object to it. They will probably claim, on the one hand, that such trifles are too frivolous to befit a theologian and, on the other, too caustic to be appropriate for a humble Christian. And they will no doubt object that we are reviving ancient comedy, or Lucian, as we mordantly assail everything in sight. But I would like to remind any who take offense at the frivolity and playfulness of my argument that this is not an innovation on my part, but that there is ample precedent in the great authors of the past. Homer, those many ages ago, had fun with a battle between frogs and mice, Vergil with a gnat and a salad, Ovid with a nut. Polycrates eulogized Busiris, and Isocrates did likewise, though he had no use at all for Polycrates. Glaucon made a case for praising injustice; Favorinus did so for Thersites and the quartan fever; Synesius praised baldness; Lucian lauded the fly and the parasite. Seneca played with the pumpkinaceous apotheosis of Emperor Claudius; Plutarch had fun with a dialogue between Gryllus and Ulysses; Lucian and Apuleius with an ass; and somebody or other joked about the last will and testament of one Grunnius Corotta—a hog, as St. Jerome mentions.[1]

Well, if it makes them happy, let them think that I've been playing with figures on a chessboard all this time—or riding a hobbyhorse—to raise my morale. Is it not, though, an outrageous injustice, at a time when every station in life is allowed to enjoy its own special recreation, that scholarship and learning alone should be permitted none? Especially when we remember that literary trivia may lead to serious matters, and playfulness may be employed in such a way that any reader who is not a complete idiot may derive more profit from it than from the solemn pomposities of some people we could mention. For example, one man praises rhetoric or philosophy in a patchwork of oratory lifted from the works of others. Another portrays the glories of some prince. Another urges war against the Turks. Another predicts the future. And still another cooks up a series of petty essays on such a substantial topic as a lock of goat's wool. Nothing is more frivolous, granted, than treating serious topics frivolously. But nothing is more entertaining than treating light topics in such a way as to appear anything but frivolous. Others will judge me as they will. But unless self-love deceives me badly, I have praised Folly in a manner that is not altogether foolish.

To answer the other objection, that we mordantly assail everything, I can reply that men of wit have always been granted this liberty and may ridicule the foibles and manners of people with impunity, provided their liberty does not become license or their license viciousness. That's why I am surprised at the sensitivity of ears in these times which can apparently stand almost nothing but pompous and solemn forms of address. In fact, you will note that some are "religious" in such a distorted way that they can endure the most reviling insults against Christ Himself rather than hear a pope or prince indirectly assailed with the most harmless kind of humor, especially if something involving cash is concerned. But, I ask, if one censures the lives of men without mentioning anybody by name, does that not seem to be teaching and admonishing rather than biting? Otherwise, I pray, under how many headings am I taking myself to task? Also, one who spares no class of persons should be envisaged as angered at no individual but at the vices of all. Thus, if someone comes with the complaint that he has been libeled, he betrays either a guilty conscience or the fear that he may be guilty. St. Jerome resorted to that kind of writing and, indeed, with far greater freedom and acerbity (than I), and at times he did not fail to name names.

I not only name no names throughout this work but I also adopt such a temperate style that any sensible reader will soon realize that my aim has been to give pleasure, not biting satire. I never resort, à la Juvenal, to muckraking to turn up foul vices; my aim is to point out ridiculous situations rather than filthy ones. If, despite this, there is any reader whom this work is unable to please, let him remember that to be slandered by Folly is only a plus!

Since I have pretended that she herself is speaking, I naturally have had to preserve the verisimilitude of the part and not fall out of character.

I don't know why I am telling you these things, for you are such a skilled advocate that you can ably defend even undeserving causes. Farewell, learned More; defend your *Mōría* valiantly. From my rural retreat, June 9, 1508.[2]

Declamation

Folly speaks:

Regardless of how ordinary mortals may speak of me—for I am perfectly aware of how bad the name of Folly sounds, even to the biggest fools—I say I am the only one whose divine power can cheer up both gods and men. Ample proof of this is the fact that the moment I stepped forward to address this huge audience all faces lit up with a fresh and unusual cheerfulness, as you all relaxed your brows and applauded me with delighted smiles. Thus, as I look at those present, you seem flushed with nectar, like the Homeric gods, but not without a mitigating admixture of nepenthe. Yet a moment ago you were sitting there sad and worried, as if you had just emerged from the cave of Trophonius. Just as it occurs when the sun first shows his radiant visage to the earth, or the infant spring breathes forth the gentle west breezes after a harsh winter, so that a new aspect is imparted to everything, as a bright new coloring and a certain youthfulness return to the earth, so too do you assume a new look at the very sight of me. That which eminent orators in other circumstances can hardly achieve in lengthy and carefully wrought speeches, I have managed to attain in a moment through my appearance alone.

You shall now hear why I appear today in this unusual garb, provided you are willing to lend your ears to what I have to say— not the ears with which you listen to preachers, but the ones you prick up to hear peddlers, clowns, and jesters, those ears which our friend Midas once turned toward the god Pan. I choose to act the part of the rhetorician before you for a little while, but not one of the crowd of those who fill the heads of schoolboys with worrisome pedantries or who advocate a more than womanish obstinacy in argumentation. Rather I take as my model those ancient ones who shunned the questionable name of philosophers, preferring to be called Sophists. Their concern was to celebrate in eulogies the excellencies of gods and men of heroic stature. Therefore you shall have a eulogy, but not of Hercules or Solon, but of me, Folly.

I have no use for those wise people who maintain that it is most foolish and ill-mannered for a person to praise himself. Let it be foolish as they claim, as long as it is conceded that it suits me. And what is more suitable than for Folly to toot her own horn? For who can better portray me than myself—unless it should turn out that there is someone to whom I'm better known than to me? All in all, though, I regard what I'm doing as much more proper than what hordes of our leaders and scholars do all the time. With false modesty they are in the habit of hiring some sycophantic orator or babbling poetaster to praise them, and then they listen to their own praise from such creatures—sheer fiction, of course. Meanwhile the listener, blushing with feigned modesty, spreads his feathers like a peacock and perks up his crest, as the adulating speaker seeks to find a parallel among the gods themselves for this worthless nobody, exalting him as a paragon of all virtue, whereas the wretch himself knows he is farther removed from that state than infinity times two. The flattering speaker decorates a crow with the feathers of other birds, whitewashes an Ethiopian, and makes an elephant of a gnat. Finally, I act according to the well-known proverb which says he has a perfect right to praise himself who never encounters anyone else to do him that favor. In this connection, I must say that I am amazed at the ingratitude or, perhaps, the neglect of men. For, although all of them eagerly cultivate me and willingly acknowledge my benefits to them, no one has as yet come forth in all the ages to show gratitude for this in a testimonial oration. Meanwhile there has been no shortage of those who burn the midnight oil turning out elegant eulogies extolling Busiruses, Phalarises, quartan fevers, flies, baldness, and similar pests.

You will now hear from me an extemporaneous speech, quite uncontrived and therefore all the more truthful. I would not have you think that it is being delivered to display my wit, as is the practice of the general run of orators. As you well know, they are capable of giving a speech they have been working on for thirty years—sometimes it is the work of somebody else—while swearing that they have dashed it off in three days, for the fun of it, or that they have just dictated it. As for myself, I have always found it more satisfactory simply to speak whatever comes to my mind. I hope nobody will expect me to follow the practice of those ordinary speakers and classify myself by definition, still less to divide myself. For it would be just as unfortunate to limit one whose nature is of such universal extent as it would be to dissect her in whose worship all the world joins as one. And what sense would it make for me to give you a sketch or silhouette of myself, when you can see me face to face? I am, as you see, that true bestower of all good things, the one the Romans call *Stultitia* and the Greeks *Mōría*.

But what need was there for me to tell you this, as if my face and appearance did not proclaim clearly enough who I am? Anyone claiming me to be Minerva or the Spirit of Wisdom could be refuted by one good look at me, even if I did not speak a word, although speech is the least deceptive mirror of the mind. I have no need for disguise. I do not pretend one thing with my facial expression while nurturing another in my heart. In all ways I am so consistent within myself that even those claiming for themselves the role and name of wise men cannot conceal me, even though they strut about like apes in royal scarlet or asses in lion skins. No matter how cleverly they play their parts, their Midas-ears are bound to stick out at some point. An ungrateful bunch that, by Hercules, for although they are undeniably members of my sect, they are publicly so ashamed of my name that they hurl it at others as a term of special reproach. Therefore, since they are actually *Mōrótatoi* ("most foolish ones"), yet are anxious to look like wise men and regular Thaleses,[3] would it not be most proper for us to call them *Mōrosóphoi* ("sophomores")? This is by way of imitating our present-day rhetoricians, who imagine themselves to be positively divine if they can show themselves bilingual—like the horse leech—and regard it as a brilliant accomplishment to be able to weave occasional Greek words into their Latin speeches, even when they don't particularly fit. Then, if they are looking for especially esoteric effects, they dig up four or five obsolete words from moldy manuscripts in order to befog the poor reader, the idea being, obviously, that those who understand the words will be enormously pleased with themselves, and those who do not will be tremendously impressed; in fact, the less they understand, the more respect they will have for the author. For there is among our followers a not inelegant kind of delight which looks up to imported things, and the more exotic the better. Some, with slightly more gumption than others, laugh and applaud and asslike wag their big ears, so that the others present will think they understand and are saying, "Quite right, quite right!"

Now I return to my topic. You have the name of Men. What epithet should I add to it? What else but "most foolish," for how else should the goddess Folly address her initiates? Since, however, not many know the lineage from which I am sprung, I shall now attempt, with the favoring help of the Muses, to expound it. It was not Chaos or Orcus or Saturn or Iapetus or any other of that obsolete and crumbling group of gods who was my father. Rather it was Plutus/Riches who, notwithstanding Hesiod, Homer, and even Jove himself, is the father of gods and men. In days of old as at the present time, a mere nod from Plutus could turn everything sacred or profane upside down. By his will are governed all wars, peace, empires, constitutions, legal decisions, elections, marriages, treaties, pacts, laws, arts, sports, serious things—I'm running out of breath—in short, all public and private affairs of mortal men. Without his help the entire number of gods made up by the poets— I shall speak quite boldly and say even the supreme gods—would either simply not exist or would run a very meager household and be forced to "eat in." Pallas herself is unable to help one who arouses the wrath of Plutus; but one who enjoys his favor can tell mighty Jupiter and his thunderbolts to go to blazes. I boast of having him as my father. He did not create me out of his head, as did Jupiter the grim and dismal Pallas, but begot me of Neotes (Youth), the loveliest nymph of all, and the merriest. Nor did he do this within the cramped and straitening bonds of the marriage tie (the way the lame blacksmith[4] was born), but in a much more pleasant way by far, "mingled in love," as our Father Homer has it. But don't get me wrong; it was not the Plutus of Aristophanes, a broken-down old man with failing eyesight, who sired me. It was that same god while still hale and hearty and still fired by the passions of youth, and not by them alone, but also by nectar, which he happened to have imbibed at a feast of the gods—neat and in profusion.

If you are eager to know the place of my nativity—since these days much importance is attached to determining where a person emitted his first cries—let me say that I was not born in floating Delos, nor on the foaming sea, nor in deep caverns, but in the Blessed Isles, where all things grow without sowing or ploughing. In those islands there is neither toil nor old age nor any sickness. In the fields you never see an asphodel, mallow, leek, bean, or any other such trash, but your eyes and nose are enchanted by moly, panacea, nepenthe, sweet marjoram, ambrosia, lotus, rose, violet, hyacinth, and the gardens of Adonis. Since I was born among those delightful things, I did not begin life with an infant's cry but immediately laughed softly to my mother. I don't envy mighty Jupiter his nurse, a she-goat, because two most enchanting nymphs nursed me at their breasts, Methe (Drunkenness), daughter of Bacchus, and Apaedia (Ignorance), daughter of Pan. You see those two here today in the company of my other attendants and handmaidens. If you want to hear the names of all of them, by Hercules, you'll get only their Greek names from me. The one you see here with her haughtily raised eyebrows is, of course, Philautia (Self-Love). The one with the laughing eyes who is clapping her hands is called Kolakia (Flattery). The drowsy one half asleep over there is Lethe (Forgetfulness). The one leaning on her elbows with her hands folded is Misoponia (Laziness). The one wearing the wreath of roses and smelling of perfume is Hedone (Pleasure). The one with the deceitful eyes which she rolls this way and that is Anoia (Madness). She of the smooth skin and the well-rounded body is called Tryphe (Voluptuousness). You also see two male gods among these girls, one called Comus (Intemperance), and the other Negretos Hypnos (Deepest Slumber). With the faithful assistance of these servants in my retinue, I subject every sort of thing to my reign, even overruling rulers.

You've heard about my ancestry, my upbringing, and my companions. Now, so that no one will get the false impression that I have wrongly arrogated the name of goddess to myself, prick up your ears and hear what great advantages I bestow on gods and men, and learn how wide-ranging my divine power is. If, as someone has astutely written, being a god means, in the last analysis, helping men, and if those are deservedly admitted into the company of the gods who have shown mortals the use of wine, or grain, or other such conveniences, why should I not by rights be designated and regarded as the Number One of all gods, since I alone lavish all things on all men?

To start with, what can be dearer or more precious than life? But to whom, pray, can the origin of that life be more fittingly ascribed than to me? It is not the spear of mighty-sired Pallas nor the shield of cloud-herding Jupiter that begets and propagates the race of men. For even he who is father of gods and king of men, and who with a nod can make all Olympus tremble, has to put aside his three-pronged thunder and that grim countenance of his— with which, when he pleases, he terrifies all the gods—and assume another role, poor chap, when he wants to do what he is always doing, namely procreate offspring. Now the Stoics assert that they are the closest thing to gods. But show me one who is a Stoic three or four times over, or, if you will, six hundred times a Stoic, and if he doesn't exactly take off his beard, that symbol of wisdom, though held in common with billy goats, he will certainly have to set aside his supercilious arrogance, smooth the wrinkles from his brow, and temporarily jettison his ironclad principles and for a short while act the amorous fool. In short, a wise man has to summon me if he wants to become a father. Why should I not speak even more candidly with you, in keeping with my character? I ask you, is it the head, or the face, or the breast, the hand, the ear—all regarded as decent parts of the body—that generates gods or men? I think not; it is, rather, that part that is so foolish and even ridiculous that it cannot be mentioned without a laugh that is the propagator of the human race. That is the sacred fount from which all things derive their existence more truly than the famous four numbers of Pythagoras.[5] Tell me now, I beseech you, what man would be willing to stick his head into the halter of marriage if, following the practice of the wise, he were first to consider all the disadvantages of that life? Or what woman would let her husband come near her if she were aware of the perilous pangs of childbirth or the trouble of raising a child? Furthermore, if you all owe your existence to the marriage bed, and if marriage itself is due to my handmaiden Anoia (Madness), you must certainly realize what you owe to me. Moreover, what woman, having once experienced these things, would be willing to do so a second time unless attended by my powerful attendant Lethe (Forgetfulness)? And Venus herself would not deny, whatever Lucretius[6] may claim, that her own force would be defective and futile were it not for the addition of my divine power. Thus, from that crazy and ridiculous little game of mine are born both the supercilious philosophers (their place taken nowadays by those generally called monks) and the kings in their royal purple, as well as pious priests and thrice-holy popes, and, finally, the whole company of gods invented by poets, so numerous that Olympus, spacious as it is, can hardly accommodate the crowd.

Still, it is a small matter that the origin and source of life are due to me if I cannot prove that everything beneficial and agreeable in life is also the result of my kindness. For what would this life be, or would it even deserve to be called life at all, if you took pleasure away? You applaud. I knew that none of you would be so wise, or foolish—no, wise—as to fail to share that view. Even the Stoics themselves do not disdain pleasure, although they take great pains to pretend they do and publicly denounce it with a thousand condemnations, this, of course, so that when others have been scared away they can enjoy it more freely themselves. But let them explain to me, by Jove, what in life would not be sad, joyless, unattractive, tasteless, and bothersome without the added ingredient of pleasure, the spice of Folly. This is amply attested by Sophocles, who has never been sufficiently praised for his marvelous tribute to me, "Ignorance is Bliss." Be that as it may, let us examine the subject in detail. First, who does not know that the first period of a person's life is the happiest for him and the most agreeable to everybody else? What is it in children that makes us kiss, and hug, and fondle them, so that even an enemy would come to their aid, unless it is the seductive attractiveness of folly which Mother Nature wisely confers on newborn babes, so that by means of a sort of advance payment they are able to ease the toil of their nurses and gain the favor of those rearing them?

Then comes adolescence, to which all people are kindly disposed and are willing to lend a hand or to applaud. But, I ask, where does this charm of youth come from? Where, if not from me? From me, because of whose favor our youths know so little and are so little troubled. But when, having grown up, they begin to take on some of the aspects of manhood, as a result of training and experience, I'll be hanged if the luster of their charm does not gradually grow dim, their liveliness decline, their attractiveness cool, their vigor fade. The farther a person becomes removed from me, the less he really lives, until finally troublesome old age arrives, hateful to others, but even more so to itself. It would be unbearable for all humans if I did not, out of pity, once more come to the rescue. And just as the gods of the poets usually come to the aid of the dying through some metamorphosis, so too do I. I bring people back from the very jaws of death, back to their infancy. Hence those who say "they are in their second childhood" are not wide of the mark. If anyone wants to know how the metamorphosis is accomplished, I shall not conceal it. I lead them to the source of the River Lethe, for it rises in the Blessed Isles (only a narrow rivulet of it reaches the Underworld) so that, by drinking long draughts of oblivion there, they wash their minds clean of cares and become young again. But some will object that this only means they are made senile and foolish. True enough. But that's what becoming young is all about. What else does being young mean but to be foolish and lack understanding? Is it not the supreme joy of that age to know nothing? Who does not hate a child prodigy or despise a boy with the knowledge of a grown man? I agree with the saying currently making the rounds, "Hateful the boy who knows too much for his age." Then too, who could bear to have to associate with or transact business with an old man who, in addition to his wide experience in life, possessed a vigor of mind and a keenness of judgment to match? That's why, thanks to me, an old man dotes.

Yet this man of doting mind is free of all the cares that torment a wise man. Meanwhile, he is quite acceptable as a drinking companion. He does not feel that ennui that is often intolerable for a younger, more robust age. Once in a while, like the old man in Plautus, he resorts to reciting the three letters he has learned and to spell out in Latin, "I love (AMO)." If he were in his right mind he would be most wretched indeed. As it is he is, thanks to my efforts, happy, amusing to his friends, and there is never a dull moment in his company. In Homer, words sweeter than honey flow from the lips of Nestor, whereas Achilles' words are bitter and acrimonious. In the same author, the old men sitting on the wall[7] discourse eloquently and elegantly. In this respect old people, in fact, have an advantage over children, who, while sweet enough, are not great talkers, thus lacking one of life's chief joys. Apart from that, old people are extremely fond of children, and children, in turn, are delighted with the elderly. God brings like and like together. For how do the two groups differ, after all, except for the fact that old age is wrinkled and looks back on more birthdays? Otherwise, the white hair, toothless mouths, stunted bodies, their taste for milk, their babbling and chattering, their foolishness, their forgetfulness, their heedlessness—in short, all their other characteristics match completely. The farther along in age they get, the more the old resemble children until, in the manner of children, with no weariness of life or any awareness of death, they depart this world.

Let him who will compare this kindness of mine with the metamorphosis induced by other deities. It is best not to go into what they do when enraged but to look at what they do for the ones to whom they are well disposed. They turn such a person into a tree, or a bird, or a locust—even a snake—as if this meant not dying but being transformed. But I take the same person and lead him back to the happiest and best time of his life. If humans would completely avoid contact with wisdom and spend their lifetime in my company alone, there would be no old age, for they would enjoy perpetual youth. Don't you see that those seriously solemn chaps who bury themselves in the study of philosophy, or the ones who are condemned to the laborious and torturous activities of business, grow old before ever being young, all because through worrying and knocking their brains out they exhaust their spirits and dry up their vital juices? On the other hand, my Mor(e)ons are as sleek and plump as the proverbial Acarnanian hogs, have marvelous complexions, and are untouched by the burdens of age except, as sometimes happens, when they are contaminated by contact with wise men. Indeed the life of man is not destined to be happy in every respect. There is powerful support of these arguments in the proverb "Folly is the one thing that makes fleeting youth tarry and keeps ugly old age away." And it is asserted, not rashly, regarding the people of Brabant that whereas age makes others sensible, the Brabanters become more and more foolish the older they get. Yet there are no people more good-natured in everyday relationships than they, and none less cognizant of the miseries of old age. Close neighbors of them, both geographically and temperamentally, are my Hollanders[8] (why shouldn't I call them mine, since they are such ardent cultivators of Folly that they have earned themselves a name for it; and they are not only unashamed of that name but actually flaunt it).

Let foolish mortals go and seek their Medeas, Circes, Venuses, and Auroras and whatever fountain of youth they will. For all the time it is I that have that power and exercise it. In my possession is that magic elixir with which the daughter of Memnon prolonged the life of her grandfather Tithonus. I am that Venus through whose favor Phaeon was rejuvenated and was so deeply loved by Sappho. And those magic herbs, insofar as they exist, are mine, and those spells and that fountain which not only restores lost youth but, better yet, preserves it forever. If, then, you all accept the premise that nothing is better than youth and nothing more abominable than old age, you must realize how much you are indebted to me for preserving such a great good and averting such a great evil.

But why do I keep talking about mortals? Look at the boundless heavens; anyone may call me whatever name he wants to if he can find one single god who would not be disagreeable and contemptible were he not rendered acceptable by my divine power. Why is Bacchus always portrayed as a curly-haired youth? Simply because, being foolish and tipsy, he spends his life in feasts, dancing, and games and never has the slightest thing to do with Minerva. So far is he from wanting to be considered wise that he rejoices at being worshipped in frolic and sport. And he is by no means offended at the saying that gave him the nickname of fool: "More foolish than Morychius." For they changed his name to Morychius, since the boisterous and unrestrained country yokels used to smear him with new wine and fresh figs as he sat at the gates of his temple. What jeers ancient comedy hurled at him, for example, "O foolish god, you deserved to be born from your father's thigh!" But who would not rather be a stupid and foolish Bacchus, always ready for a good time, always having the exuberance of youth, and bringing joy and gladness to everybody, than to be a double-dealing Jupiter who terrifies everyone, or a grouchy Pan, who infects all things with his grumpiness, or Vulcan, who is covered with cinders and is always filthy from the sordid activity of his workshop, or even Pallas herself, always looking grim, with her Gorgon's head and her frightful spear? Why is Cupid always a young boy? Because he fools around and is incapable of doing anything sensible, or even of thinking of it. Why is golden Venus ever lovely and ever springlike? It is certainly because she is related to me. That's why her face has my father's coloring, and that's why she is always "Golden Aphrodite" in Homer. Finally, she is perpetually laughing, if we can believe the poets, or their emulators, the sculptors. And what deity did the Romans ever worship more devoutly than Flora, that inventor of all pleasures? Indeed, if anybody takes the pains to look up the life story even of the serious gods in Homer and other authors, he will find it replete with folly. But why is it necessary to recall the doings of other gods when you know perfectly well about the amours and dalliances of Jove the Thunderer himself, or of chaste Diana who, disregarding her sex, does nothing but hunt, meanwhile being hopelessly in love with Endymion?

Still, I'd rather let them hear their exploits told by Momus,[9] from whom they used to hear them frequently. But of late they became angry and cast him down to earth, together with Ate, merely because he annoyingly disrupted the happiness of the gods with his insistent wisdom. Yet no mortals think the poor exile deserves hospitality here on earth. There is particularly no room for him at the courts of princes, where Kolakia enjoys the top spot, and she could no more get along with Momus than a lamb with a wolf. Now they've gotten rid of this fellow, the gods carry on more licentiously than before, and more relaxedly, finding it easier to do whatever they want now that the critic has left.

What mad pranks will fig-wood god Priapus not provide? What games will Mercury, with his thefts and sleight-of-hand, not play? And does not Vulcan usually act the part of jester at the feasts of the gods, as he steps up the pace of the revelry, partly with his limping, partly with his sneers and jeers, and partly with his silly remarks? Then there is Silenus, that ancient lover, dancing his wild peasant dance, along with the Cyclops' hop and the barefoot dance of the nymphs. The half-goat Satyrs put on their ribald Atellan acts.[10] Pan makes them all laugh with some stupid song, and they'd rather hear him than the Muses themselves, especially when they are beginning to be saturated with nectar. But why should I recount the things that well-soused gods do after a feast? By Hercules, they are so silly that I sometimes can hardly refrain from laughing myself. Yet it is better in these circumstances to be mindful of Harpocrates (god of silence), in case some spy of the gods may overhear us telling the things of which not even Momus spoke with impunity.

But now it is time, following Homer's scheme, to leave heaven and come back to earth again and to perceive that nothing happy or joyous exists there except through my auspices. In the first place, you will note with what foresight Mother Nature, the source and creator of the human race, has seen to it that the spice of folly is never lacking. Now, according to the definitions of the Stoics, wisdom is nothing else but being governed by reason; folly, on the other hand, means being ruled by the power of the emotions. Therefore, how much more emotion did Jupiter provide than reason, in order that the life of mankind should not be completely sad and dreary? The proportion is about half an ounce to a pound. Besides that, he restricted reason to one small corner of the head and left all the rest of the body to the emotions. Then he set up two exceedingly violent tyrants, as it were, in opposition to reason: one, anger, occupying the citadel of the breast, thus including the heart, and the other, lust, which holds sway over a domain extending farther down to the area of the genitals. How effective reason is against these two is clearly seen in the life of the average man; for, whereas reason screams itself hoarse telling him what is right and decreeing codes of conduct, the other two (anger and lust) tell their king (reason) to go hang, and rudely shout him down until he is exhausted and ready to throw in the towel.

Now, to a man, who is born to transact important matters, a tiny bit more reason had to be dispensed, so that, in time of need, he could call on it as well as he could. But in other things he turned to me for advice, and I gave him advice worthy of myself. I told him to take a wife, a foolish creature, to be sure, and a silly one, but amusing and delightful too. With her foolishness she would, in the cozy familiarity of the marriage relationship, season and sweeten the sternness of the male disposition. If Plato hesitated as to where he should place woman—whether among the

rational beings or the animals—that merely indicated the conspicuous folly of the sex. If a woman wants to be considered wise, all
she does is to turn out to be a fool twice over—it's like taking a
bull to the gymnasium for a rubdown—it's against the will of Minerva, as they say, or "against the grain." Anyone who acts contrary to nature and puts on the semblance of a character not his
own merely compounds the offense. As the Greek proverb says,
an ape is always an ape, even if clad in royal purple. Similarly, a
woman is always a woman, that is, a fool, no matter what disguise she may adopt. Yet I do not believe that women are so foolish as to be incensed at me—who am both a woman and Folly—
for attributing folly to them. For if they consider the matter in the
proper light, they will have to admit that, because of folly, they
are in many respects better off than men. In the first place, they
have the gift of beauty, which they rightly prize above all else.
With the aid of beauty they can exercise tyranny over tyrants
themselves. Where else does a man's horrendous face come from,
with its rough skin, undergrowth of beard, and hint of senility,
but from the defect of being sensible? But women's cheeks are nice
and smooth, their voice gentle, their skin soft, almost conveying
the impression of perpetual youth. Furthermore, what else do they
want in life but to be as pleasing as possible to men? Is that not
the purpose of all their adornments and cosmetics, all their baths,
hairdos, creams, perfumes, and face, eye, and skin makeup? Of
course it is. And are they recommended to men by any auspice but
folly? What will men not let women get away with? And what is
the reward of that, other than pleasure? The only thing through
which women are pleasing is their folly. Nobody will ever deny
the truth of this who has thought about what nonsense a man
speaks to a woman and what silly little tricks he plays when he
has the desire to enjoy the pleasure afforded by a woman.

Now you have heard about the source from which the chief
charm in life derives. But there are some men, mostly old ones,
who prefer drinking to women, and who maintain that the greatest pleasure is to be found in drinking sprees. Whether there can
be any genuine entertainment without the presence of women I
leave to others to decide. This much is sure: without some added
spice of folly no banquet is any fun. Hence, if there is no one
present who can provoke laughter by real or make-believe folly,

the carousers send out for a paid comedian or bring in a silly parasite who drives away dullness and solemnity from the company with his foolish remarks. What's the use of filling the belly with all those fine delicacies, tasty viands, and marvelous foods if our eyes and ears—our whole mind—are not also fed with laughter, jokes, and humor? The only one to provide these desserts is myself. And all the other diversions of a feast—choosing a king by lot, drinking toasts, singing rounds and roundelays, dance, pantomime—were devised, for the consolation of mankind, not by the Seven Sages of Greece, but by me. It is the nature of such activities that the more folly there is in them, the more agreeable do they make the life of men; and that life can scarcely be called life at all if it is not happy. Yet it cannot be happy unless pastimes of this sort help us to dispel boredom, the close kin of unhappiness.

But there will no doubt be those who shun this kind of amusement and find contentment in the amicable association with friends and who say that, for them, friendship ranks higher than anything else. It is so necessary that neither air, fire, nor water are more so. It is, at the same time, so delightful that taking it away would be like taking the sun out of the sky. And it is, finally, so highly esteemed that even philosophers have no objection to naming it among the "greatest goods." But what if I claim that I am stem and stern of this great good? And I shall prove it, not by ambiguous syllogisms, dialectic subtleties, or any other sophistries of that sort, but I shall simply point straight at it. Come now! Closing one eye at your friends' vices, letting them pass, being blind to them and taken in by them, indeed even going so far as to admire certain conspicuous defects of your friends as if they were virtues—is that not closely akin to folly? When one man kisses his mistress's mole, or another is fascinated by the polyps in his sweetheart's nose, or the father of a cross-eyed son says that his eyes squint slightly, what, pray, is all that but unadulterated folly? Yes, all may brand it folly three and four times over. Yet it is this very folly that joins people in friendship and keeps them friends.

I am talking about ordinary mortals, none of whom is born without faults; the best one is the one least burdened with those faults. Among those "gods of wisdom," to be sure, friendship either never develops, or if it does, it is a disagreeable and glum sort;

and even that is quite rare, although I have scruples about saying it never occurs. For the great majority of humans are foolish. There is nobody who is not foolish in a great many ways; and close friendship is struck only between equals. If a certain friendliness comes about among these rigorous and severe thinkers, it is by no means steadfast and is not destined to endure, certainly not among somber men endowed with such eyesight that they observe the tiniest faults in their friends with the keen vision of an eagle or the Epidaurian[11] serpent, while being blind to their own defects and failing to notice the lump in the back of their coat. But man is so constituted that no character can be found which does not have its goodly share of faults. One must also bear in mind the great diversity in age and in education, also the variety of errors, mistakes, and accidents of human life. How can the joys of friendship last even one hour among those Arguses, unless it is accompanied by what the Greeks so appropriately call *euêtheia,* which you may render as "folly" or as "nonchalance." Why, is not even Cupid, the acknowledged source and instigator of every love affair, afflicted with shortsightedness, so that for him that seems to be beautiful which is not so at all? Similarly, among you humans, your object of affection always looks beautiful. "The old geezer dotes on the trollop, the knave on the wench." It is the same old story everywhere, and it provokes laughter everywhere, but, laughable as it may be, it is what cements and holds together all our pleasant social life.

What is true of friendship is even more applicable to marriage, a bond for life. God, what divorces or worse disasters would not happen everywhere if the marital relationship were not held together by flattery, joking, compromise, ignorance, and pretense— all of them members of my retinue, bear in mind! My, how few marriages would ever come off if the husband looked searchingly into all the affairs his apparently innocent and modest little woman had indulged in before they were wed. And how many marriages would survive beyond their beginning if the wife's carryings-on did not escape the husband's notice, either because of his oversight or his stupidity? Yet, for all these favors, it is Folly that is to be thanked. She sees to it that the wife pleases her husband, and the husband the wife, that the household is peaceful, that the marriage endures. One laughs, and the husband is called cuckoo or cuckold or whatever else, as he kisses away the tears of his philandering wife. Yet isn't it much better for him to be fooled this way than to be consumed by the torment of jealousy and to turn the whole situation into a domestic tragedy?

In short, without me no association or relationship in life could be either endurable or enduring. A nation will not put up with its ruler very long, nor a master with his servant, a teacher with his pupil, a friend with his friend, a wife with her husband, a landlord with his tenant, a partner with his partner, nor a boarder with his fellow, unless there are at times mistakes that are overlooked, compliments, ignoring of faults, or sweetening of all bitterness with the honey of flattery.

That may seem to have covered the subject rather completely, but you are going to hear still more. Let me ask you this: Will a person who hates himself ever love anybody else? Will one who cannot stand himself ever get along with another? Or will a person who is annoying and disagreeable to himself ever be pleasing to another? Nobody could answer any of these questions in the affirmative without being more foolish than folly. If you exclude me from things, no one will stand anyone else, everyone will smell bad to himself, the things he owns will disgust him, and he will find himself positively detestable. That is because Mother Nature is, in many respects, more of a stepmother. She has implanted into the hearts of men, especially of those who are at all critical, a germ of evil that makes each discontented with what is his, while admiring what belongs to another. The upshot of this is that all talent, taste, and elegance in life get tainted and spoiled. For what use is beauty, that greatest gift of the gods, if it succumbs to the ravages of decay? What is youth, if it is destroyed by the gloominess of old age? Finally, what activity in life, be it on a personal or a wider level, can you carry on with decorum—which is the criterion of everything you do—unless this lady, Philautia (Self-Love), stands beside you, deservedly representing me and performing my role? For what is as foolish as being pleased with yourself or admiring yourself? Yet if, on the other hand, you are not pleased with yourself, what can you possibly do that is pleasing, graceful, or decorous? Take this spice of life away, and the words of the orator leave the audience cold, the musician garners no applause for his tunes, the actor will be hissed off the stage, the poet and his works will be laughed at, the painter and his paintings will be dismissed as without worth, and the physician will starve in the midst of his medicines. Finally, without self-esteem you will look like a Thersites instead of a Nereus,[12] a Nestor instead of a Phaeon, a sow instead of Minerva, speechless instead of eloquent, a rustic yokel instead of an urbane man of the world. Everyone needs to sing his own praises and to applaud himself a bit before he will be applauded by others. After all, happiness depends to a great extent upon liking the way you are. My Philautia (Self-Love) sees to this directly, so that no one is ashamed of his looks, his personality, his home town, his work, or his native land. Thus no Irishman would change places with an Italian, no Thracian with an Athenian, and no Scythian with an inhabitant of the Blessed Isles. What marvelous solicitude nature shows in making all things equal amid such variety! When she has been less generous with her gifts, Philautia steps in and makes up the difference—although I admit I have said this in a most foolish way, because self-love is itself the greatest gift.

I would even go so far as to assert that no distinguished action is ever undertaken except at my instigation, and no outstanding arts are achieved without me as motivator. Now is not war the seedbed and source of all famous deeds? Yet what is more foolish than to start a war, for whatever reasons, when it brings more harm than good to all participants? No one mentions those who die. Take for instance the Megarians.[13] What good are those philosophers when the armored columns are drawn up for the fray and the bugle sounds the harsh call to war? Why, they are so worn out by their studies, and their blood is so thin and cold, that they hardly have enough strength to breathe. What it takes is big coarse chaps who, the stupider they are, the more courage they have, unless someone may favor the type of soldier represented by Demosthenes. He, following the advice of Archilochus, threw down his shield and ran as soon as he caught sight of the enemy—as cowardly as a soldier as he was eloquent as an orator. But they say that judgment and planning are of prime importance in war. As far as the general is concerned, I agree. But the kind of judgment needed is military, not philosophical. And the smart moves needed can be executed by parasites, pimps, thieves, assassins, bumpkins, blockheads, debtors, and similar dregs of humanity, but not by philosophers with lanterns. How little use philosophers are for the practical matters of everyday life is attested by the example of Socrates, who, while judged by the oracle of Apollo to be wise (not so wise a judgment), was laughed down by all when he tried to propose some public action or other. Yet the man was not completely devoid of wit, for he rejected the designation "wise," applying it to God alone, and expressed the opinion that a wise man should stay far away from affairs of state. Only he should perhaps have warned anyone to stay away from wisdom if he wanted to be considered a man. Furthermore, what was it but wisdom that drove the same man, when condemned, to take hemlock? For, while contemplating clouds and ideas, while measuring the feet of a flea, or admiring the song of a gnat, he failed to learn about things pertaining to everyday life. His pupil, Plato, stood by him during his trial for life but, stalwart defender that he was, was so scared by the noise of the crowd that he could hardly get half a sentence out. What can I say about Theophrastus, who, as soon as he started to speak in public, was struck dumb, as if suddenly finding himself face to face with a wolf? Yet that was a man who encouraged soldiers going into battle. Isocrates was so bashful by nature that he didn't even dare to open his mouth. And Cicero, the father of Roman oratory, always started his speeches like a schoolboy, sputtering with stage fright. Yet M. Fabius Quintilian interpreted this as the sign of a wise orator cognizant of the perils of his task. But does he not openly admit by this explanation that wisdom is an impediment to any successful undertaking? What would these men do if a matter had to be decided by weapons, if they are so transfixed with fear when the battle is fought with mere words?

Despite all this, that amazing statement of Plato's is often quoted with admiration, "Happy the states where philosophers rule or rulers philosophize." Well, if you consult historians, you will find there never were worse rulers of any state than when the rule fell to some would-be philosopher or someone addicted to literature. The two Catos seem to illustrate this quite adequately, for one of them disrupted the peace of the republic with mad denunciations, and the other completely undermined the freedom of the Roman people while supposedly defending it with all his wisdom. Add to this figures like Brutus, Cassius, the Gracchi, and even Cicero himself, who was no less deleterious to the republic of the Romans than Demosthenes had been to that of the Athenians. Later on Marcus Antoninus was a good emperor (although I could refute that too), yet he had a bad reputation and was hated by the citizens because he was such a philosopher. But, admitting for the sake of argument that he was a good one, he surely brought disaster to the Roman state by leaving a son who was far more detrimental than his father had been beneficial in his administration. It is usually true of people who have devoted themselves to the pursuit of wisdom that they are very unlucky in other things, especially in the children they sire. I believe that Nature provides that the evil of wisdom is not widely disseminated among mortals. Thus, it is known that Cicero had a degenerate son, and wise Socrates had children who took after their mother more than their father, that is, as someone has not too badly put it, they were stupid. But such things could be put up with if the people were merely as inept at performing public duties as an ass is at playing the lyre; but they are clearly even less apt at performing the ordinary functions of daily life.

Take a wise man to a banquet, and he'll ruin the occasion either by maintaining a deadly silence or by asking annoying, pedantic questions. Invite him to a dance and you'll learn how a camel dances. If you take him to the theater, he will ruin the enjoyment of the audience with his sour looks, and, if he can't get rid of his supercilious attitude, he'll be forced, like a latter-day Cato, to leave the theater. If he enters into a conversation, it will stop suddenly— the wolf in the fable all over again. If a purchase needs to be made or a contract signed, or any necessary matter of everyday life has to be seen to, you'll find the wise man to be a chunk of wood, not a human being. He's of no use to himself or his country, nor his family, because he has no experience in anything, being so shut off from what people are thinking and doing. Such an unusual style of life and such an alienated way of thinking must inevitably result in hatred of the man. For is there anything at all carried on by mortals that is not full of foolishness and done by fools in the midst of fools? If anybody wanted to clash with the everyday world completely, I'd urge him to follow the example of Timon and go out into the wilderness and enjoy his wisdom in solitude.

But to get back to my topic: What force has compelled rough, rocky, barbarous men to join together in a civilized society except blandishment? That's what the lyre of Amphion[14] or of Orpheus symbolizes. What brought the Roman rabble back to civic concord when it had been rushing madly toward the abyss of extreme discord? Some philosophical oration? Not exactly. It was a humorous, childish story of the stomach and the other parts of the body. And a tale by Themistocles about the fox and the hedgehog had the same effect. What speech of a wise man could have achieved as much as Sertorius' legendary deer? or Lycurgus' tale of the two dogs,[15] or the one about pulling the hairs out of the horses' tails? I shall not speak about Minor and Numa, each of whom kept the stupid masses in check by stories they made up. That great, powerful beast, the People, is controlled by means of trifles of this sort. But then, what state ever adopted the laws of Plato or Aristotle, or the principles of Socrates? And what was it that moved the Decians to consecrate themselves willingly to the gods of the underworld? What else but empty glory lured, siren-like, Quintus Curtius to hurl himself into the abyss? But it is amazing that this was soundly condemned by the wise men. For, as they say, what is more stupid than for a candidate for office to flatter the people, to buy favors with gifts, to woo the applause of so many fools, to be very pleased with himself at public acclamation, to be carried around in triumph like a trophy to be viewed by the people, and to have a bronze statue of himself set up in the marketplace? Add to this the assumption of new names and surnames. Add the godlike honors bestowed on some wretched little man, add even the most criminal tyrants exalted to the rank of gods in public ceremonies. These are the most stupid things imaginable, and *one* Democritus will not suffice to ridicule them. Who can deny this? Yet of such a source are born the deeds of brave heroes who are praised to the heavens in the writings of eloquent authors. This sort of folly founds states, by her empires are established, also the magistracy, religion, the decisions of councils, the verdicts of courts—in fact, all human life is nothing more than some game of folly's.

But I shall say something about the arts too. What, in the last analysis, has moved the talents of mankind to devise and pass on to posterity such outstanding fields of artistic activity (as they think) but the thirst for fame? Men in their highest folly have thought they could buy fame with so many sleepless nights and so much sweat; I can't imagine anything more inane. Meanwhile, you have Folly to thank for so many marvelous comforts of life and, what is by far the most delightful part of it, you can benefit from the insanity of others. Therefore, after I have claimed for myself the palm of courage and diligence, what should stop me from claiming that of good sense too? But someone may say that's like mixing fire and water. But I believe I can succeed in this matter too, if you will hear me with the same courteous attention you have shown me up to now. If good sense comes primarily from experience, who deserves the honor of that title more: the wise man who, partly out of shame, partly from fearfulness, never undertakes anything at all, or the foolish man whom neither shame, of which he is devoid, nor danger, which he disregards, can ever deter from anything? The wise man takes refuge in the book of the ancients, from which he merely learns subtleties of words. The fool, though, just jumps in and chances everything, and as a result, if I am not mistaken, he gains true sense. Homer, though blind, seems to have seen this, for he says, "Even the fool is wise after the fact." There are two particular obstacles to acquiring an understanding of things: shame, which befogs the mind, and fear, which, calling attention to danger, dissuades us from action. But Folly magnificently frees you from both. Few mortals realize to how many other benefits it will lead if we are never ashamed and never afraid. If, though, people prefer to accept that good sense consists of a power of judgment, please hear how far those are from that power who boast of having it. It is well established that all things in life have two sides, like the Sileni of Alcibiades,[16] each side the reverse of the other. What looks like death turns out to be life, on close examination, and vice versa. And so it goes, the beautiful proves to be ugly, the rich, poor, infamous—glorious, learned—ignorant, strong—weak, noble—base, happy—sad, lucky—unlucky, friendly—hostile, healthy—poisonous. In short, when you open up a Silenus, you suddenly find everything reversed. If that seems too philosophically put for some, I shall make it plainer with a "fat Minerva,"[17] as they say. Who would not admit that a king is rich and lordly? Yet, if he is blessed with no gifts of the mind, nothing is enough for him, and he is obviously poor. Or he may have a mind addicted to a number of vices, in which case he is a base slave. The same reasoning could be followed in other cases. But it is sufficient to let this serve as an example to represent all. Now someone may ask, "What's all this leading to?" Listen, and you shall find out what I am leading to. If someone were to try to tear the masks off the actors on the stage and to reveal their true visages to the spectators, would he not simply ruin the entire play, and would he not deserve to be chased out of the theater with stones, like a madman? For suddenly everything would take on a new look. One playing the part of a woman a moment ago turns out to be a man. One who was a youth is an old man. A king is suddenly Horace's Dama,[18] and one who was a god a short while ago is unmasked as a miserable little runt of a man. To take away the illusion is to wreck the entire play. The figment and deception is just what holds the audience spellbound. For what is the life of man but a play in which some masked characters precede others on stage and each acts his part until the Director makes him take his exit. Frequently, the same actor is ordered to return in a different costume, so that one who has just played the king in royal scarlet now acts the slave in shreds and patches. Everything is, of course, shadowy irreality, but this drama will not be presented in any other way. Still, what if some wise man, suddenly dropping down from the sky, were to appear to me now and cry out that this man to whom all look up as lord and god is not even a man, being driven by his passions like cattle, but is really the lowliest slave, since he voluntarily serves so many vile masters? Or what if he commanded someone mourning the death of his father to laugh, because the father had just begun to live, since this life is nothing but a kind of death? Or what if he called a man glorying in his ancestry a baseborn bastard, because he has departed far from the moral worth that is the only fount of nobility? He could talk the same way about everybody else. But, I ask, what would he have accomplished other than looking like a raving maniac? Just as nothing is more stupid than misplaced wisdom, so too is nothing more imprudent than wrongly applied prudence. Anyone acts amiss who does not adapt himself to the prevailing circumstances, nor follow the practice of the forum, nor even bear in mind the rule of the drinking party, "Drink or get lost," and demands that the play not be a play. Conversely, it is really smart, since you are among human beings, not to want to know more than you are supposed to, and to be willing, along with the crowd, to overlook some things or even gladly join in with them in being deceived. But that, they say, is the sign of folly. I'll not deny that; but let them, for their part, admit that it is also acting the play of life. Ye gods, should I mention the next subject, or should I keep silent? Yet why should I keep silent, when it is truer than true? Still, it might be more fitting in such an important matter to summon the Muses from Helicon whom the gods are frequently accustomed to invoke in mere trivialities. Therefore, O daughters of Jove, be present a short while, as I prove that no one has access to that famous wisdom and, as they call it, the citadel of happiness, without Folly as guide.

Well, first of all, it is an accepted fact that all emotions belong to Folly. Indeed, one distinguishes a wise man from a fool by this: the former is governed by reason, the latter by emotions. Therefore the Stoics deny all passionate emotions to a wise man, as if they were diseases. Yet these very passions not only act as tutors of those striving toward the portals of wisdom, but also as a stimulus and spur in every exercise of virtue, as well as driving them to do right. Of course, that super-stoic Seneca disallows any emotion at all for a wise man. But by so doing he not only abandons him as a man but even creates a new sort of deity, the demiurge, that never existed and never will. In fact, to speak frankly, he has set up a marble statue of a man, dull and remote from any human feeling whatsoever. Let them enjoy this wise man of theirs; let them love him with a love that brooks no rival; let them take up residence with him in Plato's Republic; or, if it suits them better, in the Realm of Ideas, or in the Gardens of Tantalus. Yet who would not dread and shrink in terror from such a man, as they would a ghost or phantom, a creature insensible to all natural feelings and unmoved by any passions, either love or pity, as if made of hard flintstone or Vergil's Marpesian rock,[19] one whom no one escapes, who does not err, who sees through everything like a Lynceus,[20] who measures everything by the most exacting standard, who accepts no excuses, who is satisfied with himself alone, who alone is rich, is sane, is king, is free, who, in short, alone is everything, albeit only in his own opinion; who cares for no friend, for he himself is a friend to no man; who does not hesitate to tell the gods themselves to go hang; and who condemns and ridicules everything in life as madness. That's the kind of animal the perfect wise man is. I ask you, if it came to a vote, what city would choose such a one as magistrate, what army would want a man like that for a general? In fact, what woman would want him as a husband, or what host would want him as a guest, what servant would want a master with habits like his, or which of these could stand him at all? Who would not prefer somebody from the common herd of most stupid men who, being a fool himself, could command or obey fools and would, for the most part, please the likes of himself, who would be considerate of his wife, popular with friends, a fine table companion, and who would regard nothing human as alien to himself? But I've been fed up with that wise fellow for a long time. Our speech will now be directed to other, more agreeable topics.

Well then, if someone were to look down from a lofty watch-tower, as poets claim Jupiter does, he would see in what bound-less calamities the life of man is entangled, how sordid and painful his birth, how arduous his upbringing, how numerous the injus-tices to which his childhood is exposed, how difficult the problems of youth, how burdensome old age, how harsh the inevitability of death, what endless series of illnesses assail man, how many acci-dents menace, how many troubles attack, how tinged with gall everything is. I shall not mention all the evils man inflicts on man, such as poverty, imprisonment, disgrace, shame, torture, plots, be-trayal, slander, lawsuits, fraud. But I am obviously starting to count the sands. It is not fitting for me on this occasion to discuss the crimes men have committed to deserve all this, or what angry god has compelled them to be born into such miseries. But if we care-fully weighed all these, would we not have to admit that the ac-tion of the Milesian virgins,[21] lamentable as it was, was right? Did they not bring their fate upon themselves, chiefly because they were tired of living? Were they not akin to the wise? I shall not mention Diogenes, Xenocrates, the Catos, Cassius, and Brutus, who belong to this category, but I would merely like to cite Chiron, who vol-untarily chose death, although he could have been immortal. I be-lieve you can see what the result would be if all men everywhere became wise; there would be need for more clay and for a new Prometheus as potter. But I come to men's aid in all such ills, partly with ignorance or thoughtlessness, sometimes by forgetting evils, once in a while through the hope of a change for the better, occasionally sprinkling things with honeyed pleasures, so that men are not willing to part with life, even when the fates have already spun their life's thread and life itself has been slipping from them for some time. The less reason they have for remaining alive, the fonder they are of living. They are far from being tired of life. It is certainly because of my benevolence that you see men of Nestor's age all over the place who scarcely preserve even the semblance of a man, babbling, senile, toothless, white-haired, bald— or, to describe them better in the words of Aristophanes,[22] dirty, stooped, wrinkled, bald, toothless, without a sex drive, yet clinging to life and acting so youthfully that one gets his hair dyed, another hides his bald head under a wig, a third has false teeth acquired somewhere, another falls desperately in love with a young girl and surpasses any youth in the absurdity of his amorous actions. Already candidates for the coffins, these old fossils will marry some young wife without a dowry, and her favors will be bestowed on others, and this has become such a common practice as to be almost applauded.

But a still more delightfully amusing sight is provided by old women who, old enough to be dead, and looking so much like corpses as to appear to have come back from the grave, nevertheless still have the song "Enjoy Life!" on their lips, are always in heat, and, as the Greeks say, are as lascivious as goats. They spare no expense to lure some husky Phaon. They constantly paint their faces, they cannot tear themselves away from the mirror, they trim their lower shrubbery and reveal their withered and flabby bosoms, trying to arouse their flagging libido with suggestive songs, by drinking, joining in the dance with young girls, and writing passionate love letters. Everybody laughs at these highly foolish goings-on, but the women are quite pleased with themselves, enjoy themselves to the utmost, and, thanks to me, anoint themselves all over with the honey of foolish delight. Now I would ask those who regard these things as ridiculous to consider whether it is better to sweeten their lives with this sort of foolishness or to hang themselves from the rafters. Furthermore, it makes no difference to my fools that this behavior is thought to be shameful by the public at large, for they have no sense of wrongdoing, or if they do have some, they simply ignore it. If a rock fell on their head, that would be bad to them. But shame, scandal, abuse, and curses harm them only when they can be felt. If feeling is not present, the evils do not exist. What is the harm if everybody hisses you, as long as you are perfectly satisfied with yourself? Folly alone offers you the license to do that. I seem to hear the philosophers contradicting me, saying that this very thing—being caught up in folly, erring, being deceived and not knowing—is real misery. Quite the contrary, that is being a man. And I fail to see why they call it misery, when you are born that way, constituted that way, made that way. That is the common lot of all of us. For nothing is miserable that remains true to character, unless, perhaps, someone is going to call man pitiable because he cannot fly like the birds, or run around on all fours like the rest of the animals, or is not armed with horns like a bull. Following that line of reasoning he would call the most beautiful horse miserable because he has not learned grammar and does not eat cake; and he would pity a bull because he is no good at gymnastics. Hence, just as a horse without knowledge of grammar is not wretched, so too is a foolish man by no means unfortunate, because that is in keeping with his nature.

But the word-mongers keep insisting: knowledge of arts and sciences is a special attribute of man, they say, since with the help of these he can provide artificially that which nature has denied him. As if there were any semblance of truth in assuming that nature, which has lavished so much care on gnats, plants, and flowers, was sleeping on the job while making man alone, so that he needs to resort to the arts which that deleterious inventor Theuth[23] devised—to the utter detriment of mankind, which, far from promoting happiness, actually impede the very happiness they were designed to aid, as is so neatly argued by that most astute king in Plato regarding the invention of the alphabet! Therefore, arts and sciences have crept into the fabric of life together with all the other plagues besetting it. And they stem from those who are the cause of all evils, namely demons, whose very name reflects this, because the Greek *daēmonas* means "knowing ones." In the golden age a simple folk, free of the armament of arts and sciences, lived in reliance on its natural instinct alone. What need was there of philology, when all spoke the same language and used speech only to communicate with one another? What use was there for dialectic when there was no conflict of opinions? What room was there for rhetoric when nobody wanted to sue anybody? What need was there for knowledge of the law, when there were no evil practices—indubitably the origin of good laws? People were too reverent, also, to investigate with impious curiosity the secrets of nature, to study the measurements, the motions, and the influence of the stars, or to look for the hidden origin of things, and it was regarded as sacrilegious for a mortal man to strive for more than his allotted share of knowledge. The madness of inquiring what was beyond the sky never even entered anyone's mind then. But as the pure brightness of the golden age gradually faded, the arts and sciences were invented by evil genuises, as I have said, but they were not numerous at first and were adopted by only a few. Later the superstition of the Chaldeans increased them six hundred fold, and the leisurely frivolity of the Greeks provided pure torture of the intellect, so that grammar alone will do for a lifetime of torment.

Among all these disciplines, however, the ones most highly prized are those coming closest to common sense, that is, folly. Theologians starve, scientists freeze, astronomers are laughed at, logicians are ignored. Only the physician is worth all the others put together, as Homer says. And within this group itself, the less learned a person is and the more audacious and ruthless, the greater is his esteem, even among nobles wearing insignia. For medicine, especially as now practiced by many, is nothing more than a branch of the art of currying favor, no less so, in fact, than rhetoric. The next place after doctors is occupied by lawyers—I am not sure I should not place them first, for, with general unanimity, philosophers ridicule the profession as asinine—not that I myself would pronounce such a judgment. Nevertheless, through the judgment of these asses, great and small transactions are managed. Their property holdings continue to increase, while the theologian, after plumbing the depths of all the treasure chests of divinity, chews beans and wages incessant warfare against bedbugs and lice.

Now, as those arts are more endurable that have the closest affinity to folly, similarly those people are happiest by far who abstain from any contact with the learned disciplines and follow nature alone as their guide; she never lets us down unless we try to transgress the limits set to the fate of a mortal. Nature abhors pretense, and that which is not spoiled by artifice turns out most felicitously. And do you not see that in every other variety of living creatures those have the happiest lives that are furthest from any arts and are guided by no other rule than that of nature? What is happier than bees, or more amazing? Yet they do not even possess all bodily senses. But what has architecture to show that can compete with their accomplishment in construction? What philosopher has ever designed a society like theirs? The horse, by contrast, being close to man in its senses, has come to be his companion and to share therefore human miseries. It not infrequently happens that, since a horse is ashamed to be beaten in a race, he strains and gets windbroken; and when he strives for triumph in war, he may be wounded and bite the dust with his rider. I'll not even mention the torturous bits, the stinging spurs, the prisonlike stable, the whips, clubs, and fetters, the rider, in short, that whole tragedy of servitude to which he voluntarily submits, imitating brave men and trying eagerly to take vengeance on the enemy. How much more desirable is the life of flies and birds. Birds live for the moment alone and follow the instincts of nature, as far as the treacherous snares of men permit it. When, however, birds are shut up in cages and get used to imitating the sounds of human speech, it is remarkable how they lose their natural brightness. In all respects, that which nature has created is happier than what art has counterfeited. Therefore, I cannot praise highly enough that Pythagorean rooster[24] who, while being one individual, had been all things, a philosopher (Pythagoras himself), a man, a woman, a king, a private citizen, a fish, a horse, a frog, and, I believe, even a sponge, yet found no animal more wretched than man, because all the others were content with the limitations imposed on them by nature, while man alone tried to exceed the boundaries set by fate. Among men, however, he gives preference to the simpleton over the learned and the great in many ways. That Gryllus[25] was quite a bit smarter than "many-counseled" Ulysses, because he preferred to grunt in a pigsty to being exposed with Ulysses to so many misadventures. Homer, the father of nonsensical trifles, seems to me not to hold a very different view from the above, for he not only repeatedly calls all mortals wretched and tiresome, but he often calls Ulysses, his example of a wise man, miserable too. Yet he never says that of Paris, Ajax, or Achilles. Why should that be so? For any reason other than that this wily and artful man did nothing except on the advice of Pallas? And he knew too much and had departed too far from the guidance of nature. As those are the least happy among mortals who strive for wisdom, those are doubly foolish who, born men, nevertheless, forgetful of their human role, yearn to emulate the life of the immortal gods and, following the example of the giants, declare war upon nature, using their arts and sciences as weapons. But those seem least wretched who come closest to the stupid state of beasts and never seek to do what is beyond men.

We may attempt to prove this, not with the lines of reasoning of the Stoics, but by means of a straightforward example. By the immortal gods, is there any happier type of humans than the ones commonly called morons, fools, nitwits, and idiots—all of which names have a beautiful sound to me? At first glance, this statement may appear foolish and absurd, but it is in reality very true. In the first place, they have no fear of death—no mean thing, by Jove. Then they are free of pangs of conscience. They are not frightened by ghost stories nor scared by goblins and phantoms. They are neither tormented by the fear of impending evils nor puffed up with the expectation of good things to come. In short, they are not devastated by the thousand cares that plague this life. They know no shame nor fear, nor ambition, nor envy, nor love. Finally, if they were to approach the state of ignorance of dumb beasts a bit closer, they would not be capable of sinning, as the theologians teach. Now I wish you would list for me, you foolish wise man, all the worries by which your mind is tortured day and night, and that you would gather together in a heap all the troubles of your life; then you would realize how many evils I have protected my fools from. Add to this that they not only are always happy, playing, singing, laughing but also spread pleasure, joy, fun, and laughter to others wherever they turn up, as if they had been intended by the grace of the gods to brighten the sorrows of human life. Thus it happens that, whereas other people act differently toward each other, all act as one toward these folk. They seek them out, feed them, care for them lovingly, embrace them, come to their aid if anything happens to them, and allow them to say or do anything they please with impunity. No one wants to do them any harm, and even wild animals leave them unscathed, as if through some natural sense of their innocence. They are, so to speak, sacred to the gods, especially me; for which reason all show them that honor, and rightly so. They provide so much pleasure, even to kings, that many of the latter will neither eat, nor make public appearances, nor pass one single hour without the presence of their fools. Sometimes they even prefer them to their somber philosophers—on whom they still bestow honor and favor. The reason for this preference seems to me to be quite clear and not at all surprising, for the philosophers communicate nothing but bad news to the rulers and, relying on their learning, do not shrink at times from hurting tender ears with biting truth, while fools offer only that which the rulers are aching to hear from any source whatever: jokes, humor, fun, and laughter. Observe also that these fools have one gift that is not to be scorned, namely that they alone are straightforward and speak the truth. What is more praiseworthy than that? Now, although the proverb of Alcibiades quoted in Plato ascribes truth to wine and children, all credit for this is really mine, as Euripides indicates in his famous statement, "A fool speaks folly." Whatever a fool has in his heart he also expresses on his face and speaks with his lips. But wise men have two tongues, as Euripides mentions, with one of which they speak the truth, with the other what seems most expedient at the time. They are capable of turning black into white, of blowing hot and cold[26] with the same breath, and of nurturing something in their heart that is quite at variance with the speech formed by their lips. But for all their supposed happiness, princes seem to me to be actually most unhappy for the reason that there is no one to tell them the truth, and they are forced to look at sycophants as if they were friends. But someone will say that the ears of princes shrink from the truth and for that very reason shun the wise, fearing that somebody more outspoken than the rest may dare to tell them more truth than they care to hear. There is much to the claim that truth is detestable to kings. Yet, despite this, it is a remarkable thing about my company of fools that, from them, not only truths but even outright insults are accepted with pleasure. It goes so far, in fact, that the same statement from the mouth of a wise man would be a capital offense but would, when coming from a fool, cause unbelievable amusement. For truth, you know, has a certain innate force that gives pleasure, provided it keeps clear of calumny. This truth, however, is something the gods have given to fools alone. And for similar reasons women are crazy about men of this type, being more disposed to fun and trifles. Moreover, whatever their involvement is with these fools, if it ever threatens to get too serious, they explain it away as being a joke, for that sex is ingenious, especially in covering up their own transgressions. But to get back to the subject of the happiness of fools: After spending a life in pleasure, and having no fear or even awareness of death, they go straight to the Elysian Fields where they delight the pious and leisurely souls with their playful doings. Let us proceed now to compare the lot of a wise man with that of a fool. Suppose we set some model of wisdom as a contrast to the fool, taking some man who has spent his childhood and youth in study and has wasted the best years of his life in burning the midnight oil, in worries, and in laborious cramming and, for the rest of his life, has never allowed himself a bit of pleasure, being always frugal, poor, sorrowful, gloomy, strict and unfair to himself, severe and detestable to others, pale, emaciated, sickly, bleary-eyed, old and white-haired before his time, and departing this life before his time too. Yet what difference does it make when such a man dies, since he has never really lived? Well, there you have an excellent picture of your wise man. But the Stoic frogs are croaking at me once more, saying that nothing is more miserable than madness, and that excessive folly comes very close to madness, or even is identical with it. For what else is madness but wandering of the mind? Yet they themselves wander all the way. Come, let us demolish this syllogism with the benevolent help of the Muses. Very astutely, as Plato teaches in the works of Socrates, they have made two Venuses out of one and have cut up Cupid and made two of him also;[27] yet those dialecticians ought to distinguish one insanity from another, if they want to appear sane themselves. For not all insanity is disastrous by any means, otherwise Horace would hardly have said, "Am I moved by divine madness?" Nor would Plato have counted the divine madness of poets, seers, and lovers among the greatest blessings of life. Nor would that Sibyl have called the labors of Aeneas mad. There really are two kinds of madness. One is that which the vengeful goddesses send up from the underworld when, with their snaky tresses loosened, they inflict on mortals the bitterness of war, the insatiable thirst for gold, or illicit love, or parricide, incest, sacrilege, or other evil of that sort, or when they assail the guilty, conscience-stricken soul with fury and the torches of demons. The other type, quite different and much sought after, no doubt because it comes from me, occurs whenever a pleasant wandering of the mind frees the spirit from cares and anxieties, steeping it in manifold delight. This sort of wandering Cicero said, in a letter to Atticus, he wished for himself as a great gift from the gods and as something to take from him the awareness of the numerous evils of life. And that Argive[28] in Horace was not wide of the mark when he assumed this posture: sitting all alone in the theater day after day, laughing, applauding, and enjoying himself under the impression that marvelous plays were being performed, while nothing was going on at all. Yet in other activities he acted quite rationally, was popular with friends, considerate of his wife, and easygoing with his servants and not given to flying into a rage over a broken wine jug. After his relatives had succeeded in having him cured of this affliction by the use of medicines and he was completely restored to normality, he protested, saying, "By Pollux, you've killed me, friends, not saved me, by taking away my pleasure like this and destroying an illusion that was most enjoyable to me." And he was right. Because they were the disturbed ones and had greater need of a dose of hellebore than he did, in thinking that such a happy and pleasant madness was an evil to be driven out with potions.

I have not, however, established that every disturbance of mind or emotions should be called madness. If a man with poor eyesight thinks a mule is an ass, or if someone admires a botched piece of verse as a poetic masterpiece, these people are not to be regarded as out of their minds. If, however, someone is deceived, not only in his senses but also in the judgment of his mind, and is constantly at odds with accepted opinion, he will then be regarded as close to madness. If, for example, every time he hears a donkey bray, he thinks he is hearing wonderful symphonies, or if a poor beggar of humble origin believes he is King Croesus of Lydia, he is called mad. Yet this kind of madness, provided it results in pleasure, as it usually does, causes no mean delight in those who are assailed by it and also in those who witness it. For this sort of madness is far more prevalent than is generally realized. One madman laughs at another, and they afford each other enjoyment.

Often enough you will behold the spectacle of the greater madman laughing at the lesser one.

In fact, the more ways a man is mad, the greater is his happiness, in the opinion of Folly, only he must remain with that kind of madness that is peculiarly mine. It is so widespread that you would hardly know how to find any person in the whole of mankind who has his wits at all times and is not affected by some sort of delusion. If someone sees a pumpkin and thinks it is a woman, they call him insane, because this deviates from common experience. But if a man swears that his wife, whom he shares with several others, surpasses Penelope in virtue and thus flatters himself in blissful error, nobody calls him insane, because this frequently happens to husbands.

To this species belong also those who neglect everything else in order to go hunting and who maintain that they experience incredible pleasure every time they hear the harsh sound of the horn or the baying of the hounds. I would almost think that the dogs' excrement had the odor of cinnamon for them. And what delight they take in butchering a beast! The slaughtering of oxen and sheep is left to the common people, but it is wrong for game to be cut up by anyone but a nobleman. Bareheaded and kneeling, with a hunting knife destined for this purpose alone—it would be a sin to use any other—with prescribed gestures he cuts the designated parts of the animal in proper sequence, ritualistically determined. The retinue stand around him in silence, looking on at the spectacle as if seeing it for the first time, whereas they have already witnessed it a thousand times. Any person permitted to taste a piece of the animal feels himself practically exalted to the nobility. And while the folk, with their constant killing and devouring of wild animals, are actually degenerating to the wild state themselves, they think they are living the life of a king.

Quite similar to the hunters are those people who are mad about building. Sometimes they change round structures into square ones, or square into round. There is no end or limit to their activities, but when they are consequently reduced to poverty, they have no place to eat or sleep. What do they have for all this? Well, they have spent many years quite happy. Very closely akin to them seem to be, to me, those who endeavor to turn things around by new and secret arts, and who hunt on land and sea for a magical "fifth essence." Lured on by a deceptively honeyed hope, they never regret these efforts nor begrudge the amount spent on them. With marvelous ingenuity they are always thinking up something new with which they deceive themselves. They continue in this pleasant self-deception until they are devoid of all possessions and cannot even afford to construct a little stove. Yet they still never cease to dream their pleasant dreams and to urge others to pursue the same sort of bliss. And when all hope is gone, there still remains one great belief and one tremendous consolation. In grandiose matters it is sufficient merely to have wanted to succeed; they complain about the shortness of life, though, which did not allow them the time to finish a project of such magnitude.

I am uncertain whether gamblers should be included in our category or not. But it is a foolish and utterly ridiculous sight to see some so addicted to the vice that, as soon as they hear the dice rattle, their hearts leap and beat faster. Then, lured by the unshakable hope of winning, after they have lost everything they own and have wrecked the ship of their existence on dice-rock, which is considerably more formidable than the Malean promontory, and they hardly manage to keep the shirt on their back, they will cheat everybody but the winner in order to preserve the semblance of honorable men. And what about them when they are old and half blind and have to wear glasses in order to see when they play? Finally, when a thoroughgoing case of gout strikes their joints, they hire someone to play for them at the gaming table and to throw the dice in their stead. A nice state of affairs indeed, except that this game very often tends to turn into an angry brawl, and, as such, to belong in the domain of the Furies, not me.

But another type of man is my cup of tea entirely, namely those who delight in marvelous lies and tall stories, whether on the hearing or the telling side. They are positively insatiable, whenever someone tells tales of horror, of phantoms, ghosts, goblins, devils, or the myriad phenomena of that kind. And the farther these stories are from the truth, the more gullibly they are believed and the more delightfully they titillate the ears. They are used not only to lighten the boredom of tedious hours, but also to earn money, especially in the case of clerics and priests.

Closely akin to them are the ones who give themselves over to the foolish but pleasing notion that if they look at a picture of

Polyphemus-Christopher they will not die that day; or that one who looks at a carved figure of Barbara and mumbles a prescribed formula will emerge unscathed from battle; or that one will get rich if on certain days he invokes Erasmus with certain candles and certain little prayers. Indeed they have found in George a new Hercules and have made another Hippolytus [29] of him. They reverently adorn his horse with breast trappings and bosses and not only pray to it but also seek to win its favor by means of some new little gift. Swearing by St. George's brass helmet is regarded as exceedingly regal.

What can I say about those who are happily deluded with forged indulgences for their sins, and precisely compute the duration of their future stay in purgatory, as if mathematically by means of hourglasses, by centuries, years, months, days, and hours, beyond any possibility of error? Or about those who, enamored of magic spells and prayers devised by some pious cheat for his soul's sake or the love of money, promising themselves as a result wealth, honor, pleasure, plenty, health, and long life, a thriving old age, and a seat next to Christ in heaven, but not anxious to occupy it until the latest possible time—that is, after the enjoyments of this life have left them—against their will and with their violent opposition, to be followed then by the delights of heaven. In other words, any merchant, soldier, or judge who donates one small coin out of all the amounts he has stolen believes that with this the whole filthy Lernan swamp of his life has been cleaned up, and all the perjury, lust, drunkenness, brawling, killing, fraud, treachery, and betrayal have been paid for, as if by contract, and he is free to start out with a clean slate on a new round of misdeeds.

Who are more foolish, but at the same time happier, than those who by reciting every day those seven verses of the Psalms promise themselves the supreme fortune? It is believed that some humorous devil, more loquacious than clever, gave these magic verses to St. Bernard [30] after the poor wretch was fooled by a trick of the saint. Yet these things are so foolish that I'm almost ashamed of them myself, but in spite of that, they are approved not only by the common herd but even by teachers of theology.

To this sort of foolishness also belongs the practice of every region's claiming its own special saint. Special powers are then attributed to each of them, and each is assigned his special rites and functions. Thus one helps to relieve toothache, another aids at childbirth, another recovers stolen goods, another protects against shipwreck, still another watches over flocks. And so it goes, but it would lead us too far afield to enumerate all. There are some with power in several areas, especially the Virgin Mother, to whom the common people attribute almost more power than to the Son.

Yet what do people seek from these saints but that which is allied to folly? Come now, have you ever seen among all the consecrated gifts adorning the walls of various churches, and the ceiling too, even one that was there for an escape from foolishness or to get one iota wiser? No; one was saved from drowning, another lived after being run through with the sword by an enemy, another saved himself in battle—no less luckily than bravely—and escaped, leaving the others to fight. Another with the help of a saint well disposed to thieves falls down from the gallows and proceeds to relieve those burdened with excessive wealth. Another succeeds in breaking out of jail. Another recovers from a fever to the chagrin of his doctor. Another one's poisoned drink fails to kill him, to the great displeasure of his wife, whose time and money were spent in vain. Another's wagon overturned, yet he drove the horses home unscathed. Another escaped with his life from a fallen building. Another is caught by an enraged husband but manages to get away. But nobody ever leaves a thank offering for recovering from foolishness. To know nothing is such a pleasant thing that mortals pray to escape from everything except folly. But why do I risk my life on this sea of superstitions? "If I had a hundred tongues and a hundred mouths, and a voice of iron, I would never be able to enumerate all the forms of folly nor to run through all its names." [31] Now the whole of Christendom is teeming with mad things like these, and even priests encourage and foster them, being well aware of how much profit derives from them. If, in the midst of all this, some pestiferous sage were to arise and proclaim, "You shall not have a bad death if you live a good life," which is true, or "You will atone for your sins if you add to your coin the hatred of evil, and also will add tears, vigils, prayers, and fasting, and if you change your whole way of life; a saint will favor you, if you make his life a model for your own"—if that wise man were to shout

out such and similar things, think how much happiness he would suddenly deprive human souls of, and in what a turmoil he would involve them.

Those also belong in the category of madmen who, while living, take great pains to arrange for their funeral ceremonies, going so far as to prescribe exactly how many torches, mourners, singers, and hired lamenters they want, as if they were going to witness the spectacle in person somehow and would be embarrassed if their body were not given a magnificent burial. They put as much effort into this as if they had been elected ediles and were responsible for arranging public games or banquets.

Even though I must move on with some speed, I cannot pass over in silence those who are boundlessly flattered by empty titles of nobility, while differing not one bit from the humblest artisan. One traces his family tree back to Aeneas, another to Brutus, a third to King Arthur. They put up busts and pictures of their ancestors all over the place; they enumerate their grandfathers and great-grandfathers, and know by heart their ancient titles of honor, while hardly yielding to any statue in their own obtuseness and perhaps being worth less themselves than one of those they exhibit. Yet because of lovely Philautia (Self-Love) they have a positively pleasant life. Nor is there any lack of those stupid ones who look up to this class of creatures as if they were gods. But why do I confine my remarks to one kind or another, while Self-Love, with her marvelous resources, causes the greatest number to be most happy? A man may be uglier than an ape, yet to himself he seems a veritable Nireus. And another, hardly capable of drawing three arcs with a compass, fancies himself a Euclid. One who is like the "ass with a lyre" and sounds worse than a rooster while treading a hen, nevertheless hears himself as a second Hermogenes.[32] But by far the sweetest kind of madness is that which makes someone glory in the talent of his relatives as if they were his own. Such a one was that twice blessed wealthy man in Seneca who, when he was going to tell some little story, had to have servants standing by to feed him the names he needed in telling it. A man so weak that he hardly seemed to be alive, he would not hesitate to challenge someone to a fist fight, trusting in the fact that he had so many sturdy slaves at home.

What is it necessary to say about the practitioners of the arts and sciences, when self-love is so characteristic of all of them that you'll sooner find one who will part with his inheritance than with his tiny bit of talent? This is especially true of actors, singers, orators, and poets. And the more untrained one of them is, the more brazenly he will vaunt his self-satisfaction, the more he will throw his weight around and spread himself. Every mouth finds its own cup of tea. The more inept something is, the more admirers it will attract, just as the worst things delight the greatest number, because most people, as we have said, are smitten with folly. If then, a less endowed man is more pleasing to himself and also has the admiration of many more admirers, what incentive is there for him to choose a real education, which is very expensive and renders him more affected and pedantic and, as a result, pleasing to fewer people?

I also note that nature has implanted a special self-esteem, not only in individuals, but also in nations, and even in individual cities. Thus it is that the British claim for themselves good looks, music, and fine food, the Scots boast of their nobility and royal connections, as well as skill in philosophy; the French claim courtesy as their province, with the Parisians presumptuously claiming the prize for theology, almost exclusively. The Italians award themselves the first prize for belles lettres and oratorical eloquence, and they also flatter themselves as being the only people on earth not barbarian. The Romans have taken first place in this complacency and are still dreaming pleasant dreams of ancient Rome. The Venetians are happy in their belief in their own nobility. The Greeks, as founders of the learned disciplines, peddle the notion of the excellent names of their highly lauded heroes of old. The Turks and all that rabble of really barbarous folk claim a superiority in religion and laugh at the Christians for their superstitions. Much more agreeably, the Jews are still waiting for their Messiah and still cling tenaciously to their Moses even today. The Spaniards yield to nobody in their military superiority. The Germans are proud of their great stature and their knowledge of magic. But, to avoid dwelling on details, I believe you can see how much pleasure Self-Love provides both to individuals and to all mankind, and almost equal to her is her sister, Flattery. For self-esteem is nothing less than caressing oneself. If you do this to someone else, it is Kolakia/Flattery. Yet flattery is in ill repute nowadays, but only among people who are more affected by the names of things than by the things themselves. They believe flattery to be closely linked to bad faith. Yet they can learn from the example of dumb animals how wide of the mark they are. What animal is more flattering than a dog? Yet what one is more faithful? What acts more cajolingly than a squirrel? But what is friendlier to man? Or are ferocious lions, or wild tigers, or fierce panthers more appropriate to the life of man? There is, to be sure, a pernicious sort of flattery with which some scoffers and mockers bring disaster upon poor victims. Yet this flattery of mine stems from a kindness of disposition and a candor of mind and is much closer to a virtue than to its opposite, harsh severity and, as Horace says, repulsive, heavy moroseness. Mine raises drooping spirits, soothes saddened ones, revives the faint, livens up the slow-witted, eases the suffering, tames the ferocious, and reconciles lovers and keeps them together. It entices the young to study literature, it cheers up the aged. Under the guise of praise it instructs and admonishes rulers without offending. In short, it makes everyone more pleasant and dearer to himself, which is certainly a great part of happiness. What is more pleasant than when one mule scratches the other, as the saying goes? I shall refrain from saying that this plays a leading role in that highly praised eloquence of yours, a still greater one in medicine, and the greatest of all in poetry, which is the honey and spice of all human relationship.

But being deceived is a wretched thing, it is said. On the contrary, *not* being deceived is the most wretched of all. Those who believe that man's happiness resides in things themselves are exceedingly unwise. It depends upon opinions. For there is such great obscurity and diversity in human affairs that nothing can be known with clarity, as has been correctly stated by my academicians, who are the least overweening among the philosophers. But when a clear recognition *is* possible, it not infrequently militates against the enjoyment of life. But the spirit of man is so constituted that it is more fascinated by appearances than by reality. If anyone wants definite, tangible proof of this, let him go to church and listen to the sermon. Whenever anything of a serious nature is preached, everybody sleeps or yawns or feels squeamish. But if the loud-mouthed screecher (sorry, I meant preacher) brings up some stupid old chestnut, as often happens, they all wake up, sit up

straight, and listen wide-eyed. And if some saint is more surrounded by a cloud of legend or is a more poetic figure than others, for example, St. George, St. Christopher, or St. Barbara, you'll
find that he is far more devoutly revered than Peter or Paul or
Christ Himself. But these things are out of place here. Yet how
much less this way to happiness costs! Whereas, to get at the real
essence of things, even the slightest, like grammar, sometimes requires the expenditure of great effort. But imagination can be had
for very little expense and leads to just as much happiness, if not
more. Now, if somebody eats stinking pickled fish, the odor of
which another cannot stand, yet it tastes like ambrosia to him,
how does that affect happiness? On the other hand, if a fine stur-
geon makes someone feel nauseated, how can it help the enjoyment of life? If some man's wife is extraordinarily ugly, yet to him
appears a match for Venus herself, is it not the same as if she
actually were a beauty? If someone beholds a painting that is a
smear of red lead and yellow mud and admires it, persuaded that
it is a picture by Appelles or Zeuxis, isn't he happier than the one
who has bought the works of those artists at great price but derives less pleasure from them? I know someone of the same name
as myself[33] who gave his new bride a present of some imitation
jewels and convinced her, clever joker that he was, that they were
genuine and, more than that, very rare and of priceless worth. I
ask you, what difference did it make to the young woman to be
feasting her eyes and delighting her heart on glass, as she carefully
guarded the spurious gems like some precious treasure, and hiding
them near her. Meanwhile her husband avoided paying a high price
and had some fun fooling his wife, and she was as devotedly in
his debt as if he had really given her expensive jewels.

What difference do you see between those people in Plato's cave
who admire the shadows and images of things and, in so doing,
are completely happy and self-satisfied, and that wise man who
leaves the cave and sees real things? If Lucian's Mycillus had been
allowed to keep on dreaming his golden dream of wealth forever,
there would have been no need for him to desire any other happiness. Therefore there either is no difference in these cases or, if
there is, the condition of fools is superior. Thus happiness, first of
all, costs the least, only a few little illusions. And they are enjoyed
in common with very many people, for, as with all good things in

life, enjoyment of possession occurs only when they are shared. And who does not know how scarce the wise men are, if indeed any can be found at all. In all the centuries the Greeks counted only seven, but I'll be hanged if a more accurate count would have found one-half a wise man, or even a third of one. Among the many blessings of Bacchus, the one for which he is most highly and fittingly praised is that he washes away cares—only for a short time, to be sure, for as soon as you have slept off the effects of his wine, the worries of your mind come rushing back, as they say, "on four white horses." How much fuller is the blessing I bestow, and much more effective and more lasting, since I fill the mind, in a sort of permanent intoxication, with joys, delights, and fantasies, while demanding nothing in return. And I exclude no mortal whatsoever from the favor of my gifts, whereas those of the other divinities are dispensed only to specially favored persons. Not everywhere, for example, is that mild, noble wine produced which drives away care and richly supports our fondest hopes. Few have been allotted that beauty which is the gift of Venus, and still fewer the eloquence which comes from Mercury. Nor have many been endowed with gifts by Hercules. And Homer's Jupiter has not lent the power of ruling to everyone. Mars all too often favors neither side in battle. Many leave Apollo's tripod sadly disappointed. Saturnine Jupiter often hurls his thunderbolts. Phoebus at times sends pestilence with his javelins. Neptune drowns more than he saves. Meanwhile I regard avenging Veiovis,[34] and also Pluto, Ate, Poena, Febris, and all that lot, as executioners rather than gods. I am the one Folly indivisible that embraces all with equal favor. I don't bother with vows, I am never provoked, and I demand no expiation if some ritual has been neglected. Nor do I confound heaven and earth with petulance if the other gods receive an invitation to enjoy the odor of burning sacrifices while I am left at home. In fact, the gods are so touching that it pays—and is safer—to disregard them rather than to worship them. There are also humans like that—so sensitive and difficult that it is best to avoid any association with them whatsoever. But, people will say, nobody sacrifices to Folly, and nobody erects a temple to her. I have been surprised a bit myself at this ingratitude, as I have said. Yet, in keeping with my easygoing nature, I view this in a positive way. Who needs such things? What do I need incense for, or a sacrificial meal, or a goat, or a pig, when humans show me such devotion as even theologians approve? Perhaps I ought to envy Diana, because human blood is sacrificed to her. Yet I regard myself as most devoutly worshipped when people take me to their hearts, as they do everywhere, reflect me in all of their habits, and represent me in their way of life. This sort of adoration of saints is not common even among Christians. How many of them will light a candle to the Virgin, even at noon, when there is no need! But how few of them burn with a desire to emulate her in life with respect to chastity, modesty, and love of heavenly things? For that, after all, is true worship and most pleasing by far to those on high. Therefore, why should I want a temple, when the whole world is my temple, and, if I am not deceived, a most beautiful one? And I shall have no lack of priests as long as there is no lack of human beings. I am not so stupid as to ask for painted stone images which often enough impede our worship, since the symbols themselves are worshipped by those dense fatheads as if they were the deities themselves. The result is that the divinities are crowded out by these substitutes, and that is what would happen to me. In my estimation there are as many statues erected to me as there are people who carry my likeness around with them, even involuntarily. Therefore, there is no reason for me to envy the other gods at all, if some people in some remote corners of the world celebrate one god or another on certain days—for instance, Phoebus in Rhodes, Venus on Cyprus, Juno at Argos, Minerva at Athens, Jupiter on Olympus, Neptune at Tarentum, Priapus at Lampsacus— as long as the whole world unceasingly offers far more appropriate sacrifices to me.

If I seem to be speaking with more daring than truthfulness, let us take a closer look at the lives of men, so that it may become clear how much they owe me, and how many follow me, of both high and low estate. But we will not go into the life of each one of these in detail, because that would lead too far afield, only into the outstanding lives, and from these an opinion about the others may easily be formed. For why should one take the time to discuss ordinary folks, all of whom belong beyond any dispute wholly to me? For they abound with so many forms of folly everywhere that not even a thousand Democrituses would suffice to ridicule them all. And, in turn, another Democritus would be required to ridicule all of those Democrituses. It is unbelievable how much sport and amusement these little men provide the gods every day. You see, the gods spend the sober morning hours in resolving disputes and hearing prayers. Apart from that, when they have had enough nectar to drink and don't feel like doing anything serious, they gather at the big bay window in the sky and, craning their necks, look at what men are doing. There is no show they enjoy more. God almighty, what a spectacle! What a confused, mixed-up bunch of fools in action! For I occasionally join the gods of the poets and watch too. One man is madly in love with a little woman, and the less she loves him, the more desperate is his love. Another marries a dowry, not a wife. Another rents out his wife as a prostitute. Still another, a jealous husband, watches like an Argus. Then a man in mourning says and does such foolish things! He acts as if he had hired the players to put on a tragedy. Another weeps at the grave of his stepmother. Another crams into his belly whatever he can gather together but a short time later will be starving. Another thinks nothing more enjoyable than sleep and idleness. Some are so involved in managing the affairs of others that they neglect their own. Then there is one who, living off money borrowed from others, thinks he is wealthy but will soon go bankrupt. Another finds nothing more enjoyable than living like a pauper so that he can leave his heir a fortune. This other one, on the trail of slight and uncertain gain, sails all the seven seas, entrusting to the winds and waves the life that no money could ever buy back. That one prefers to seek riches through warfare rather than to pursue a life of safety and comfort at home. There are some who think they can most expeditiously come into wealth by making a fuss of childless old men. Others prefer to try the same thing by making love to rich old women. But all of these cause the most exquisite enjoyment to the gods looking on when they are fooled by their intended victims. But the most foolish and shabbiest bunch of all are the businessmen. They carry on the shabbiest business by the shabbiest means. For while they resort to lying, stealing, cheating, and pulling the wool over the eyes of the public, they at the same time act as if they were the most exalted of all people because they have gold rings on their fingers. Nor are flattering brothers lacking to bow down to them and do them honor in public, so that some little crumbs of their ill-gotten gain may fall to them.

Elsewhere you will notice those Pythagoreans, by whom all things are so firmly regarded as common property that whenever they find anything left unguarded, they coolly take it, as if it were left them as an inheritance. Others are wealthy only in their desires, and they invent beautiful daydreams and regard that as sufficient for happiness. Some get pleasure out of being taken for wealthy men when away from home, yet at home they starve wretchedly. One hastens to spend whatever he has, another keeps hoarding without end. One continues to run for public office, another prefers to stay at home. A goodly percentage of them institute lawsuits which are destined never to be decided; but they try to outdo each other in suing, and they meanwhile enrich the judge who postpones the case and the lawyer who is in league with him. This one is interested in revolutionary activity; that one is working on some great plan. One may go on a pilgrimage to Jerusalem or Rome or Santiago (de Compostela), where he has no business to transact, abandoning wife and children at home. In short, if you viewed the countless feverish activities of mortals from the moon, as Menippus once did, you would think you saw a swarm of flies or fleas squabbling and fighting with one another, plotting against each other, robbing, playing, carrying on lasciviously, being born, declining, and dying. It is almost incredible what disturbances and tragic involvements such as a tiny little animal, destined so soon to die, can set in motion. For the disturbance of a minor war or the wind of pestilence can often take away the lives of thousands at once. But I would be the most foolish of all, and eminently deserving of the multiple ridicule of a Democritus, if I were to continue to enumerate the varieties of foolishness and insanity prevalent among people.

I shall now turn my attention to those who have a reputation for wisdom among mortals and who search for the golden bough,[35] as they say. Among these, the grammarians occupy first place. This class of men would be more calamitous, miserable, and more detestable to the gods than any other if I had not mitigated the sufferings of that most wretched profession with a certain pleasant sort of madness. For they are subject, not only to the five curses, as the Greek epigram[36] has it, but to six hundred. They are always starved and unkempt in their schools—I say "their schools," but their torture chambers and treadmills would be more like it—

among their crowds of boys, they grow old in their labors, deaf from the shouts, ill from the stench and the filth; it is only through my beneficent influence that they seem to themselves to be in the top rank of humanity. Indeed, they are delighted with themselves when they terrify the timorous mass with their menacing looks and voices, when they thrash their poor pupils with whips, canes, and straps, and when they rage in all sorts of violent ways as the spirit moves them, like the Cumanian[37] donkey. Yet for all that, the squalor seems to them to be spotless cleanliness, the filth smells like marjoram, their wretched servitude is thought by them to be a royal reign, and they would not exchange their tyranny for the empire of Phalaris or Dionysius. But they are happier by far when they are able to make some new scholarly contribution to learning. While they inculcate their schoolboys with sheer nonsense— what Palemon or Donatus—ye gods!—do they not scorn in comparison with themselves? And they bring it off so successfully with I know not what magical tricks that they seem to the stupid mothers and idiotic fathers to be what they make themselves out to be.

Add to that this kind of pleasure: If one of them has gleaned from some musty old manuscript the name of Anchises' mother, or a word not generally known, such as *bubsequa* for shepherd, or *bovinator* for brawler, or *manticulator* for purse snatcher, or if one digs up a fragment of an old stone somewhere with remnants of an inscription, by Jove, what exultation, what triumphs, what encomia there are! It is almost as if they had conquered Africa, or captured Babylon. And how about their constant reciting of their piddling dull insipid verses—and people who admire them are not lacking—when they evidently believe that the soul of P. Vergilius Maro has entered their own breasts. But there is nothing more amusing in all of this than to behold them praising and admiring each other and scratching each other's backs. For if anyone commits an error in a single word and by chance some keener one spots it, by Jove, what a to-do there is at once, what fighting, what insults, and what vituperations are heard! May all the ill-will of the grammarians fall upon my head if I am lying. I know a sixty-year-old polymath who mastered Greek, Latin, mathematics, philosophy, and medicine. Bothering with nothing else, he plagued himself for forty years learning grammar, thinking he would be perfectly happy if he were allowed to live long enough to find

out for sure how to distinguish the eight parts of speech, something none of the Greeks or Romans had been able to do satisfactorily. It almost turns into an act of war if someone wants to
include conjunctions within the domain of adverbs. Thanks to that,
there are as many grammars as there are grammarians—in fact,
far more, because my friend Aldus[38] alone has brought out a
grammar more than five times. He overlooks none of the others,
no matter how poorly or atrociously written, and he reads and
analyzes each one. He is jealous of anyone else working in the
same field, no matter how ineptly, wretchedly fearing that such a
person may snatch the glory from him and cause the work of a
lifetime to go down the drain. Would you prefer to call that madness or folly? It doesn't matter much to me; but you will admit
that this most miserable animal of all owes the feeling of happiness he has to me alone and would not change places with the
king of Persia.

Poets are less indebted to me, although they are admittedly
members of my faction, for as a "free" breed of man, they devote
all their effort to blandishing the ears of fools with utter trivia and
ridiculous little stories. Yet, strange to say, on the strength of these
things they promise themselves, and others too, immortality and a
life of the quality of that of the gods. Philautia (Self-Love) and
Kolakia (Adulation) are more characteristically associated with this
group than are others. And I am not worshipped more faithfully
and truly by any other breed of men than by them.

Now the rhetoricians, although sometimes straddling the fence
and at times verging close on the area of the philosophers, can be
argued on many grounds to belong to my party, chiefly for this
reason: that, in addition to other trifles, they have written copiously and thoroughly on the essence of humor. And whoever the
rhetorician was who wrote on the art of eloquence for Herennius,
he counted folly itself among the types of humor, and in Quintilian, far and away the leading one of this class, there is a chapter
on laughter that is longer than the *Iliad*. So much value is assigned
to folly that very often that which cannot be refuted by arguments
can be by laughter, although some may think that it is not part of
the function of folly to induce laughter by means of humorous
remarks intentionally made.

Writers who strive for immortality by turning out books are

tarred with the same brush. Now, although all are deeply indebted to me, those are most decidedly so who blacken the paper with sheer nonsense. For those who write learnedly for the judgment of a few scholars, shunning the verdict of neither a Persius nor a Laelius, seem to me rather pitiful than happy, as they perpetually torment themselves, making additions and alterations, crossing out, putting back in, rewriting, rephrasing, explicating, and after brooding over it for nine years are still not satisfied with their work. They buy a worthless reward, praise, for such a high price, and praise of a paltry few at that. They buy it for the price of so many late hours, of loss of sleep—that sweetest of all things—of such sacrifice, sweat, torments, loss of health and good looks, weakness of eyes or even blindness, poverty, envy, abstention from pleasures, premature aging, early death, and whatever other things of that sort there may be. The learned man considers himself compensated for such evils if he enjoys the approval of one or two other nearsighted drudges. But my kind of writer is far better off in his madness. Without extensive preliminary cogitation he quickly writes down whatever has popped into his head or has come to his pen. Even his dreams are turned into writing, and, little worried about waste of paper, he knows that if the things he writes are bad enough, the vast majority of readers—fools and ignoramuses—will approve. What does it matter if a couple of scholars happen to read the work and dismiss it as junk? Or what does the adverse criticism of a few learned readers count against the huge means of those shouting acclaim?

Still more clever are those who publish the works of others as their own. With a few words they turn to their own benefit the fame resulting from lengthy toil by someone else and expect to enjoy temporary benefit from this, even if they are eventually convicted of plagiarism. It is worth the trouble to see how pleased they are with themselves when they are praised by the public, when somebody in the crowd points to them saying, "There goes the famous So-and-So!" Their works are prominently displayed in the bookstores. On every page a few words are featured, preferably foreign ones, with the effect of magic spells. But how many people will see them, considering the vastness of the world? And by how many fewer will they be praised, since the tastes of the unlearned are so fickle? Not infrequently, their names are invented or taken from the books of the ancients. One enjoys calling himself Telemachus, another Stelenus or Laertes; this one is Polycrates, that one Thrasymachus, so that it makes no difference now whether you attribute your book to a chameleon or a pumpkin or simply to Alpha or Beta, in the fashion of the philosophers.

The most exquisite amusement is provided by the practice of complimenting each other in scores of letters, in poems, encomia, blurbs, etc., as the stupid praise the stupid, the unlearned the unlearned. One emerges as an Alcaeus after such evaluation, another as a Callimachus;[39] this one is judged superior to M. Tullius Cicero, that one is called more learned than Plato. Sometimes they purposely seek a competitor in order to increase their fame through that rivalry. In the unstable public sides are soon taken, and, when the battle is over, each contender proclaims himself the winner and holds a victory parade. Who can deny it? But in the meantime they profit from my assistance and enjoy a nice life and would not change their triumphs for those of the Scipios. Meanwhile even the learned enjoy a hearty laugh at these goings-on and are mightily amused at the madness of others; hence they too are indebted to me not a little, something they cannot deny without being the most ungrateful of all men.

Among learned men the lawyers claim first place for themselves, and no others equal them in self-satisfaction, as they incessantly roll the stone of Sisyphus, find six hundred laws in one breath, no matter how irrelevant, and pile gloss on gloss or opinion on opinion, thus creating the impression that their field is the most difficult of all. For they consider that which is tedious to be positively brilliant. We may group them with the logicians and the sophists, a brand of man that is more loquacious than the brass kettles of Dodona, for any one of them could hold his own in a talking competition with twenty choice women. They would be still happier if they were merely talkative and not so disputatious. For, with hard-bitten tenacity, they can argue about a bit of goat's wool and most of the time lose the truth in the midst of the squabbling. Yet their self-esteem makes them happy, while, armed with their syllogisms, they take on all comers in fighting over anything. Besides this, their pertinacity renders them invincible, even if you put up a Stentor[40] against them.

They are closely followed by the philosophers, venerable by virtue of beard and white fur, who maintain that they alone are wise and that all other mortals flit by like shadows. In what sweet madness they rave, as they construct countless worlds and measure sun, moon, stars, and spheres with thumb and thread and explain the causes of lightning, winds, eclipses, and other inexplicable phenomena, never hesitating for a moment, as if they had peered into the secrets of Mother Nature, creator of things, or as if they had come to us from the council of the gods. Meanwhile nature has a good laugh at them and their conjectures. That they really know nothing at all is amply proved by the fact that there is an irresoluble difference of opinion among them on every single issue. Knowing nothing, they profess to know everything. Yet they do not know themselves and, in their shortsightedness, or absentmindedness, often fail to see a ditch or a rock ahead of them. They claim they see ideas, universals, forms devoid of matter, quiddities and ecceities, things so tenuous that I don't believe Lynceus could even perceive them. They look down on the common people with disdain, as they draw their triangles, quadrangles, circles, and similar mathematical figures, laying one on top of the other in great confusion, providing them with letters drawn up as if in battle array, then rearranging them in another order, and befog the uninitiated. Nor does this group lack those who predict the future by consulting the stars and promise still more astounding miracles; they are even fortunate enough to find people to believe these things.

It would perhaps be best to pass over the theologians in silence and not to stir up the foul Camarina[41] swamp or to touch the herb *anagyris*. This arrogant and sullen crew might attack me in troops with six hundred conclusions and force me to recant, and if I were to refuse, to proclaim me a heretic on the spot. With the thunderbolt of that condemnation they terrify anyone to whom they are ill disposed. Now, although no others are less willing to acknowledge my favor to them, nevertheless they too are indebted to me with no mean obligation as, blissful in their self-love and as if inhabiting the third heaven, they look down from their lofty height upon all other humans as if they were animals creeping on the ground and almost pity them. Fortified by a battle line of didactic definitions, conclusions, corollaries, and simple and complex premises, they have such an abundance of hiding places that they could not be caught even in the chains of Vulcan, for they can slip out of their definitions, with which they so easily cut through all knots, so that the famed double-edged axe of Tenedos could not do it better; they abound with recently coined terms and tremendous words. Moreover, they explain arcane mysteries as suits them, e.g. how the world was created and organized, by what channels the defect of original sin has been transmitted to posterity, by what measures and means, how long Christ was in the womb of the Virgin, how accidents may subsist in the Eucharist without residing there. But these are run-of-the-mill matters. They regard different things entirely as worthy of a great and, in their opinion, illuminated theologian. They perk up when such subjects are brought up as: Was there an instant in the divine creation? Are there several "sonships" in Christ? Is the proposition "The Father hates the Son" possible? Could God have assumed the form of a woman, the Devil, an ass, a cucumber, a stone? If so, how could the cucumber have preached, worked miracles, been crucified? And what would Peter have consecrated if he had administered the sacrament while the body of Christ hung on the cross? And could Christ have been called man at the same time? And would it be permitted for us to eat and drink after the resurrection? (At least they are trying to protect us from hunger and thirst.) There are countless other hair-splitting trifles, much subtler than these, concerning moments, opinions, relationships, accidents, quiddities, ecceities, which no one can perceive with his eyes, unless he is a Lynceus, able to see in the deepest darkness things that are not there. Add to these those propositions which are so contradictory that the pronouncements usually called paradoxes appear clear as day by contrast: for instance, the assertion that it is a lesser crime to cut the throats of a thousand men than to sew a poor man's shoes on the Lord's Day, or that it is better for the whole world to perish, the whole kit and kaboodle, as they say, than for someone to tell a lie, even the most inconsequential one. These subtlest subtleties are rendered still more so by the procedures of the Scholastics, so that you could more easily extricate yourself from a labyrinth than from the entanglements of the Realists, Nominalists, Albertists, Occamists, Scotists[42]—and I have not named them all, simply some of the most conspicuous ones. In all of them there is so much pedantic erudition and so much complexity that I would think the Apostles themselves would need a whole different spirit if they hoped to come to grips with these topics and to debate them with this new breed of theologians. Paul[43] was able to exemplify faith, but when he said, "Faith is the substance of things hoped for, the evidence of things unseen," he did not define it with the requisite learning. The same Paul excellently exemplified charity in his own life, but in 1 Corinthians 13 he analyzed and defined it with very little dialectical skill. The Apostles consecrated the Eucharist with pious intent, but I don't believe they would have answered with the same acuteness as the Scotists use in discussing and defining these matters, or when questioned about the *terminus ab quo* and the *terminus ad quem,* about Transubstantiation, about the way the same body can be in different places at the same time, about the difference between the body of Christ in heaven, on the cross, and in the Eucharist, or about the instant at which Transubstantiation takes place when the prayer that brings it about is a discrete quantity of time duration. They knew Jesus' mother, but who of them proved as philosophically as our theologians how she remained free of the original sin of Adam? Peter received the keys of heaven from Him who would not entrust them to an unworthy person, yet I am not sure that he understood—for he never achieved sophistication— how a man can have the key of wisdom without having wisdom himself. They baptized in a great number of places, yet they never taught the formal, material, effective, and ultimate cause of baptism, nor is its delible and indelible character mentioned anywhere in the Apostles. They worshipped, of course, but in spirit, following only that word of the Gospel that says, "God is a spirit, and those that worship him must worship him in spirit and in truth." Apparently it had never been revealed to them that a picture drawn in charcoal on a wall was to be worshipped with the same devotion as Christ Himself, provided he is represented as raising two fingers in blessing, with hair unshorn, and three rays in a halo stuck to the back of His head. For who can grasp all these things unless he has spent thirty-six whole years studying the physics and metaphysics of Aristotle and the Scotists? The Apostles also emphasized the importance of grace, but they never distinguished between grace freely given and grace that makes one deserving. They urge us to do good deeds, but do not make a distinction between deeds doing and deeds done. They constantly urge us to love, but do not discriminate between love bestowed and love acquired and fail to explain whether it is an accident or a substance, a thing created or one uncreated. They detest sin, but may I drop dead if they could give a scientific definition of what it is that we call sin, unless they happened to be trained by the spirit of the Scotists.

I can never be convinced that Paul, by whose erudition all the other Apostles may be judged, would have condemned all the questions, disputes, genealogies, and, as he calls them, "battles of words," if he himself had had a good mastery of those subtleties, especially since all arguments and disputations at that time were primitive and uncouth compared to the hyper-Chrysippean[44] subtleties of our professors. For, extremely modest men as they are, if something written by the Apostles proves to be stylistically infelicitous or somewhat unscholarly, they do not bluntly condemn it but interpret it in the right way. This is done, of course, out of deference to the antiquity and the fame of the Apostles. And, by Jove, it would not be fair to demand of them things the like of which they had never heard a word about from their Master. But if the same things turn up in Chrystomus, Basilius, or Jerome, they simply write "not binding." The Apostles also confuted the heathen and Jewish philosophers, who were, by nature, extremely obstinate, but they did so more by their way of life and through miracles than by syllogisms, for the former were men none of whom would have been capable of following one single *quodlibet* of Scotus. What heathen or heretic today would not immediately yield to such hair-splitting subtleties, unless he was so dull that he could not follow or so brazen as to hiss, or happened to be armed with such tricks and snares as to be able to stand up to them in single combat. Then it is like matching one Magus against another, or having a man armed with a miraculous sword fight another armed the same way; for then it is the story of Penelope's weaving all over again. In my opinion Christians would do well if, instead of using those huge forces of soldiers with which they have been fighting so long with so little success, they would send against the Turks and Saracens these noisy Scotists, stubborn Occamists, and invincible Albertists, together with the whole body of Sophists. I believe they would see the jolliest fight and the most unprecedented victory. For who is so apathetic as not to be inflamed by such keenness, who so stupid as not to be moved by such sophistries, who so sharp-eyed that he would not be enveloped by the densest shadows?

It no doubt looks to you as if I am saying all these things more or less in jest. But there are in fact among the theologians men better trained in letters who are sickened by the frivolous sophistries, as they think, of some theologians. There are those who abominate it as a sort of sacrilege and as the height of impiety to speak with such an unclean mouth about such mysteries, which are rather to be worshipped than investigated; to dispute by means of the profane subtleties of the heathens, to formulate things so arrogantly, and to defile the majesty of sacred theology with such hollow, sordid words and phrases. Yet they themselves (some theologians) are pleased with, and congratulate themselves in, their bliss, and are so busy night and day with their nice little trivia that they haven't a moment's time to open the Gospel or to read Paul's epistles. And while they talk their nonsense in the schools, they think they are supporting, with the props of their syllogisms, the Church Universal, just as Atlas, according to the poets, holds the heavens on his shoulders. Think how much pleasure it is for them to mold and remold the secret words, like wax, at will, while they insist on having their own conclusions, to which a few fellow Scholastics subscribe, regarded as superior to the laws of Solon and exalted even above papal decrees. And, as censors of the world, they insist on compelling retraction of anything that does not completely square with their own implicit and explicit conclusions. And they proclaim, as if speaking with oracular authority, "This proposition is scandalous; this one lacks reverence; this does not ring true." Thus, for them, neither baptism nor the Gospel, nor Peter and Paul, nor St. Jerome or Augustine, in fact, not even the Super-Aristotelian Thomas himself, can make a Christian without the vote of approval of the baccalaureate mob. Such is the exactness of their verdict. Who would have thought that a person who regards the sentences, "Pot, you stink," and "The pot stinks," as grammatically equivalent, or "The jar gets hot," and "It's hot in the jar," cannot be a Christian unless the wise men had informed us of that fact? Who would have freed the Church from these dark errors which nobody would have heard of if those wise men [45] had not issued them under the imposing seals (of their universities)? Indeed, they are happiest, are they not, while doing these things. For instance, when they depict all the things in the lower regions in as great detail as if they had spent several years in those parts. Or when they invent new worlds, as their whim moves them, adding that biggest and most beautiful one, so that the blessed souls may have no lack of space to take walks, or hold banquets, or even play ball. Their heads are crammed and stuffed with these and two thousand other trifles. I would think Jupiter's brain was not more pregnant when he asked Vulcan for his axe to aid at the birth of Pallas. Therefore, do not be surprised if you see the head of one of these fellows carefully wrapped in bandages when he participates in public debates, for otherwise it would certainly come apart. I myself occasionally have to laugh at this: The theologians seem to be greatest in their own eyes when they speak most barbarously and sloppily—in fact, when they babble so badly that no one but a babbler himself could understand them. That which the general public cannot grasp they call acumen. They also state that it is beneath the dignity of sacred writings to be compelled to obey the rules of the grammarians. It is a strangely splendid monopoly of the theologians that they alone are permitted to speak erroneously, a privilege which they share with many cobblers. Finally, they consider themselves very close to the gods whenever they greet each other, almost religiously, as "Our Masters," in which title they believe the kind of power inheres that was in the four letters of the ineffable name of the God of the Jews. And they claim it is wrong, therefore, to write MAGISTER NOSTER (our master) in anything but capital letters. If one were, perversely, to pronounce the title with small letters, he would at once ruin all the majesty of the entire realm of theology.

Closest to these in felicity are those who usually call themselves "religious" and "monks," each of which is a completely false designation, since most of them keep as far away from religion as possible and no people are seen more in public in all sorts of places. I doubt that any group would be more miserable than they, if I did not come to their aid in many ways. For although everybody curses them and regards it as an evil omen to meet one of them accidentally, they have a very high opinion of themselves. First, they deem it supreme piety if they shun learning to the point of not being able to read. Then, when they blare out in church with their donkey voices to sing the Psalms, they really imagine they are soothing the ears of the Lord (they have learned the words by rote, without knowing what they mean). Some of them make a great profit from their filthiness and their mendicancy, crying for bread as they go from door to door with much moaning and groaning. There are no inns, vehicles, or boats where they do not make great pests of themselves. They also make things very hard for the other beggars. Yet, in their own way, these funny chaps are, with their filth, ignorance, boorishness, and impudence, providing us with an example of the life of the Apostles—to listen to them. What is still more amusing is that they do everything according to prescribed rules, almost mathematical formulas. To fail to observe one such rule would be a sin. A sandal must have a certain number of knots; the shoelace must be of a certain color; the belt must be of a certain material and of a certain width; the cowl must be of a certain shape and volume; the tonsure must be a certain number of inches wide; and one must sleep a certain number of hours. Yet who can fail to see how unequal such equality must inevitably be, in view of the wide variation in physique and temperament? And yet, because of such piddling matters, they not only hold other folks to be worthless, but even despise each other, and men professing apostolic love can precipitate all kinds of rows because of a garment differently belted or a color that turns out to be a shade too red. Among these monks you may see some strictly religious ones who use nothing but a coarse Cilician outer garment, though inside it is lined with soft Milesian wool. Others wear linen on the outside and wool inside. You'll find some who avoid touching money as if it were poison, but they by no means avoid contact with wine or with women. In short, then, all orders of monks make a great effort to complicate their own way of life. That is not exactly an attempt to be like Christ, but to be different from each other. A great portion of their delight has to do with their names. Some take pleasure in calling themselves rope-wearers or Cordeliers, and among these some are Coletes, others Minorites, still others Minims, and others Button-wearers. Then there are Benedictines, and Bernardines, then Bridgetines and Augustinians; further, Williamists and Jacobines [46]—as if being simply called Christians were not enough. Most of them tend to their special ceremony and their petty little human traditions with such energy that one heaven cannot properly reward such labors. They fail to bear in mind that Christ looks down on all these things and will demand that His one commandment be observed: love. One monk will display his belly, swollen from all the varieties of fish he has consumed. Another will pour forth a hundred bushels of Psalms. Another will enumerate myriads of fasts and will account for his positively bursting belly by saying he has always broken each fast with one single dinner. Another will report such a heap of ceremonies that they could hardly be transported in seven freighters. Another will boast that for sixty years he has never touched money—except when wearing double gloves on his fingers. Another will wear such a filthy cowl that no sailor would think it fit to be worn. Another will call attention to the fact that he lived for more than eleven five-year periods attached to one place, like a sponge. Another will present a hoarse voice as evidence of his constant chanting, another will show the lethargy acquired during his life as a hermit, another a paralyzed tongue, the result of strict observance of a vow of silence. But Christ will interrupt this endless boasting, for fear it may never stop, and will ask, "Whence comes this new tribe of Israel? I acknowledge only one commandment as truly mine, and that is the only one I am not hearing a word about. I once promised, speaking plainly and without parables, the inheritance of my Father, not for cowls, little prayers, or fasts, but for deeds of love. I do not acknowledge those who keep on acknowledging their own deeds in the desire of appearing holier than I. Let them occupy the heavens of the servants of Abraxas,[47] if they like, or let them order a new heaven to be built by the ones whose petty little traditions they have placed above my commandments." When they hear and see that sailors and teamsters find more divine favor than they themselves, what sort of looks do you think they will have on their faces? Meanwhile, though, they are happy in the hope they enjoy through me. Although they hold no public office, nobody dares to slight them—especially the beggar monks—because they get hold of everybody's secrets through confessions, as they call them. Of course they consider it a sin to reveal these things, except when they are tipsy and feel like enjoying themselves with some entertaining storytelling; but they relate the matter only by hints, and with no mention of any names. But if anyone annoys these hornets, they will get even with them in their sermons, pointing out their enemies via indirect references and in such guarded innuendos that nobody will fail to understand except those who understand nothing. And they do not put an end to their snapping until you bribe them. Tell me, though, would you prefer to watch any comic or hawker when these monks preach their sermons, emoting most ridiculously, while still amusingly imitating the things that rhetoricians have handed down on the art of speaking? Heavens, how they gesticulate, modulate the voice, intone, throw themselves about, suddenly assume different facial expressions, and turn everything into one great pandemonium with their shouting! This kind of preaching is passed down from one friar to another as a secret art. I'm not allowed to know about it, being a female, yet I can come up with a few conjectures. First they start with an invocation, which they all take from the poets. Then they take their exordium from the River Nile, or, if they are to speak on the mystery of the Cross, they like to begin with the Babylonian dragon-god, Baal. If the subject they choose to discuss is fasting, they start with the twelve signs of the zodiac. If they are speaking about faith, they preface that with a lengthy discussion on squaring the circle. I myself have heard a certain loony—sorry, I meant learned man—who was going to explain the mystery of the Holy Trinity at a well-attended service. In order to display his extraordinary erudition and to please the ears of the theologians present, he embarked on a new course, starting with letters, syllables, and words. Then he spoke about the agreement of noun and verb, of adjective and noun. Most people looked amazed, and to some that phrase of Horace came to mind, as they muttered to themselves, "What is this crap leading to?"[48] He tried, at last, to make the point that he could show, in the rudiments of grammar, a symbol of the Holy Trinity which could not be more clearly drawn in the sand by any mathematician. And the super-divine had worked so hard for eight months that today he's blinder than a mole, because all the brilliance of his sight had been exhausted in lending an edge to his intellect. Yet he has no regrets, and the price seems trifling to him compared to the glory earned.

I have heard another one, an octogenarian, likewise a theologian, whom you would think was a second Scotus. In trying to explain the name of Jesus, he showed with remarkable acuity that

everything that could be said was inherent in the letters themselves. For the name can be inflected in three cases only. This was
obviously symbolic of the triune nature of God. Then, since the
first case *Jesus,* ends in *s,* the second, *Jesum,* in *m,* and the third,
Jesu, in *u,* the ineffable mystery is within the name, for He is the
highest (*s*ummus), the middle (*m*edius), and the end (*u*ltimus). Another, still more recondite mystery was vouchsafed: he divided the
name into two exactly equal parts, so that the letter *s* is in the
middle (*Je*|*s*|*us*). Then he told them that this letter is in Hebrew
called *sin* (שׁ). And, as he recalled, in the Scottish[49] language this
means *peccatum.* From this he was able to deduce and proclaim
that Jesus was He who took away the sins of the world. This
novel approach was admired with such gaping wonder by all, especially the theologians, that it would not have taken much for
them to repeat Niobe's experience. I myself came closer to acting
like that fig-wood Priapus who, to his own great detriment, witnessed the nocturnal ceremonies of Canidia and Sagana.[50] I would
not have been wrong, to be sure, for when did Democritus the
Greek or Cicero the Roman ever produce a rhetorical insinuation
like that? They considered that an introduction that was too remote from the main topic was defective; not even swineherds, with
mother nature leading them, start out that way. But these learned
scholars regard their preamble—that's what they call it—as the
ultimate in rhetorical excellence if it has no connection with the
rest of the sermon, so that the listener keeps wondering and mur-
muring to himself, "What's he driving at?"

In the third part, instead of the narration itself, they interpret
briefly and in passing some short passage from the gospels, which
really ought to have been the main topic of discussion. In the
fourth section they put on a different mask and attack a theological
question which many times hovers aimlessly between heaven and
earth, yet which they deem an appropriate part of their oratorical
art. Here, attaining the height of theological arrogance, they blare
at the ears of the congregation those imposing titles of Religious
Doctors, Subtle Doctors, Most Subtle Doctors, Seraphic Doctors,
Holy Doctors, and Irrefutable Doctors. Then they hurl at the un-
tutored multitude their syllogisms—greater and lesser—conclusions, corollaries, their utterly boring propositions, and their more
than Scholastic trivia. That leaves the fifth act, in which it would

be fitting to present the rhetorical art at its best. Here they drag out for us some stupid and brainless story taken from the *Speculum historiale* or the *Gesta Romanorum*,[51] I fancy, and interpret it allegorically, tropologically, and anagogically. And in that manner they let loose their monstrosity, the likes of which even Horace could not succeed in achieving when he wrote at the beginning of his *Ars poetica, humano capiti* ("human head"), etc.

They have heard from sources, I know not which, that the start of a speech must be calm, not loud, so they start so softly that they can hardly hear their own voice, as if it did any good to say something that nobody gets. They have also heard somewhere that one should use loud shouts to arouse the emotions. Therefore, in the midst of a softly spoken passage, they suddenly raise their voice to a loud roar, with no apparent reason. You would swear the man needed a dose of hellebore to treat his madness, although nothing would be likely to cure his shouting. Furthermore, since they have heard that a sermon ought constantly to increase in fervor as it goes on, you will note that, while starting with restrained voice in the first passages, they soon employ a marvelous vehemence of presentation, even when the topic is of no great significance. And then they stop, so that you would think they were out of breath. Finally, they have learned that in the words of the rhetoricians there is mention of laughter, so they endeavor to insert a few jokes into their speech, and these are so gracefully told and so appropriately introduced that you cannot help exclaiming, "The ass at the lyre again!" Occasionally they attempt a bit of satire, but it is so feeble that they can only tickle, not wound. And they are never more adulatory than when they try their best to appear outspoken. In fact, their whole behavior is such that you'd think they had learned it from wandering minstrels or strolling players in the marketplace, although such players are far superior to them. But they are so similar to each other that nobody would doubt that one group had learned its rhetoric from the other. Yet they find some people (my influence again!) who, on hearing them, think they are listening to a real Demosthenes or a genuine Cicero. This kind will usually be merchants and women, whose ears the preachers take special pains to please, because the merchants will be inclined to give them a nice share of their ill-gotten gains, if they are sufficiently flattered, and the women, while favoring this order (of monks) for several reasons, do so mainly because they weep on their shoulders when they are having squabbles with their husbands. I am sure you can see how much these fellows tyrannize over ordinary mortals with their little ceremonies and ridiculous nonsense, and loud shouts, as they believe themselves to be St. Paul or St. Anthony.

I now gladly take leave of those actors and pretenders who are just as ungrateful for my favors as they are wicked in their false pretensions to piety. And now I am happy to discuss those kings and princes a little, by whom I am worshipped purely and simply, as befits freeborn gentlemen. If they had as much as half an ounce of common sense in them, their life would be more sorrowful and more to be avoided than anyone's. For if anybody weighs in his mind how great a burden a man carries on his shoulders who tries truly to perform the role of prince, he will come to the conclusion that it is not worth committing perjury or parricide to obtain princely power. Whoever takes the helm of the ship of state must be prepared to pursue no private interests but to devote his entire attention to the public welfare, to deviate not one inch from the laws of which he himself is author and executor. He must be a model of integrity of administration for all officials and magistrates. He alone must constantly be exposed to the view of all. Like a favorable star, he can, by the uprightness of his conduct, bring a highly salubrious influence into human affairs. Or, like a fatal comet, he can inflict complete destruction. The vices of others are not perceived to the same extent, nor do they spread so far. A prince occupies such a position that if there is the slightest deviation from rectitude, it can creep like a plague into the lives of numerous people. Then how many things does the lot of a prince bring with it, tending to lead away from righteousness, such as pleasure, liberty, adulation, excess, because of which he must strive all the harder and watch all the more vigilantly in order not to fail in his duty as a result of these diversions. Finally, I shall not mention plots, hatred, and other dangers and fears, and shall merely point out that the king himself is always hovering over the head of the prince and will soon demand an accounting of him for the slightest transgression, and the greater the realm of the prince, the more severe will any penalty be. If the prince were to consider these and similar matters—and he would do so, if he were wise—

he would, in my opinion, not be able to enjoy sleeping or eating. But as it is, with my helping hand, the princes entrust all these worries to the gods and make life easy for themselves, lending an ear only to those who bear good news, so that they are assured peace of mind. They believe they play the role of a prince properly if they go hunting, keep fine horses, sell offices and titles at a profit to themselves, and think up new ways to fleece their subjects every day and to direct the state revenues into their private purses. This is done, of course, with propriety, with newly invented terms, so that even if it is a most unjust act, it may present some semblance of equity. They also take pains to add a little flattery to it, in order to win over the popular mind. Now imagine a person—such as occasionally is found—ignorant of the laws, practically an enemy of public well-being, intent only upon personal pleasures, a hater of learning, of freedom and truth, thinking about anything but the welfare of the republic, but measuring all things according to his own greed and his own gain. Then put on this man a golden chain, symbolizing the union of all virtues, then a crown studded with precious stones, which is supposed to remind him that he must surpass all others in heroic acts and in virtues. Then give him a scepter, the symbol of justice and of a completely uncorrupted heart, and finally a scarlet robe, the outward sign of his supreme love for the state. If a prince were to compare the implications of these insignia with his own life, I believe he would be ashamed of his decorations and fear that some impertinent observer might turn this whole tragic spectacle into laughter and farce. What shall I say about the high-born courtiers? They yield to no one in being venal, servile, stupid, and despicable, yet they want to be seen as the lords of creation. In one thing, however, they are as modest as can be; they are content with carrying on their person gold, jewels, scarlet, and other symbols of wisdom and virtue, but they leave to others all concern for those qualities themselves. They consider themselves boundlessly fortunate because they are allowed to call the king "Sir," because they've learned to greet people with three words, because they know how to use these polite titles from time to time: *Serenitas* ("Your Grace"), *Dominatio* ("Your Lordship"), and *Magnificentia* ("Your Majesty"), and because they abolish all show of shame and flatter as nicely as you please. For these are the accomplishments that become any true nobleman or courtier. Furthermore, if you were to look closely into the whole course of life you'd no doubt find sheer Phaecians, suitors of Penelope—you know the rest of the poem, which Echo could give you better than I. They sleep until noon; then a paid priest stands ready by their bed and rushes through the mass while they still lie there. Then it's breakfast time immediately, and hardly is that over when lunch summons. After that, there are games of dice, board games, cards, then jesters, fools, harlots, horseplay, coarse jokes, and so on. Meanwhile there'll be a serving or two of refreshments, then dinner, and after it, toasts—in the plural, by Jove. And so in this way hours, days, months, years, and centuries slip by without boredom. I myself sometimes go away well satisfied after merely seeing them perform their high jinks, when each lady believes she's closer to the gods the longer the train of her gown; when one nobleman elbows another out of the way so that he can be closer to that Zeus, the Prince; when every man is proud of wearing the heaviest chain possible around his neck, in order to show off his strength, not just his wealth.

Our popes, cardinals, and bishops have now for some time actively copied the customs of the princes and have almost surpassed them in splendor. A bishop might well bear in mind what the whiteness of his garb is supposed to admonish him to do, namely to lead a life completely free of blame. The two-horned miter with the two equal peaks held together by one knot means what? Probably a thorough knowledge of the Old and New Testaments. What does covering his hands with gloves mean but a pure administering of the sacraments, free of any contact with worldly matters? What the shepherd's crozier means, evidently, is most vigilant care of the flock entrusted to him. The cross borne in front of him symbolizes victory over all human passions. If one thinks of these matters and all similar ones, would it not seem that the bishop has a gloomy life filled with cares? But as it is, they do very well, for they feed themselves. As for the other function, caring for the sheep, they either entrust it to Christ or delegate it to the friars, as they call them (*fratres*), or to other deputies. They do not even recall the meaning of the name bishop,[52] which implies work, care, and supervision, except in the business of raking in money; there they really act the part of bishop, overlooking nothing. Similarly, if only the cardinals would reflect that they are the successors of the

Apostles and that the same things are demanded of them as were performed by the latter, namely that they are not to be masters but stewards of spiritual gifts, of which they must soon give a very accurate accounting. Yes, let them also think about their garb a little and reflect to themselves what the whiteness of their upper garment signifies. Is it not a life of the highest, most excellent purity? What does the crimson inside mean? Is it not the most fervent love of God? What, in turn, is the significance of the outer robe that flows down in a wealth of folds and covers the whole mule-sized form of his exalted Reverence, while having the capacity to cover a camel too? Does it not signify the love which extends far and wide to embrace and help all, that is to teach, exhort, chastise, admonish, settle wars, resist evil princes, and, indeed, willingly give their life's blood, not just their money, for their Christian flock. And why do they need all that money anyway, since they occupy the place of the poor Apostles? I tell you, if they thought it over, they would never bother to seek the office but would gladly let it alone—or they would lead a very difficult, troublesome life like that of the Apostles of old.

As for the popes, the supreme pontiffs, who are the representatives of Christ, if they were to try to emulate His life, i.e., His poverty, His labors, His teaching, His cross, His disdain of death; or if they pondered the name *papa* (father) or *sanctissimus* (most holy), what on earth would be a more afflicted life than theirs? Or who would buy the position for all the money in the world? Or who, having bought it, would defend it with sword, poison, and all his might? If wisdom were to descend upon them, of how much comfort it would deprive them! Did I say "wisdom?" Nay, even a grain of that salt that Christ mentioned! It would deprive them of all the wealth, all the honors, the power, the victories, the offices, dispensations, revenues, indulgences, horses, mules, retainers, and all their good times. You see how many markets, how many harvests, what a great ocean of goods I have included in a few words. And instead of all these it would bring vigils, fasts, tears, prayers, sermons, studies, sighs, and a thousand troublesome toils of that sort. Nor should one fail to mention that all the scribes, copyists, notaries, advocates, pimps—I almost substituted a milder word, but I'm afraid it might have a still harsher effect on the ears—in short, such an enormous mass of men that has been such a horror—excuse me, I meant "honor"—to the Roman See, would starve. Why, that would be an inhuman and abominable act, and it would be much more detestable still to have the highest princes of the Church themselves, and the luminaries of this world, consigned to the wanderer's staff and pouch. But now they usually turn over whatever work there is to Peter and Paul, who have plenty of leisure. But whatever splendor and pleasure there is they take for themselves. Thus it happens that with my aid almost no kind of men live more comfortably and freer of worries, and they think they have done their duty to Christ perfectly well if they play the role of bishop with mysterious hocus-pocus and practically theatrical splendor, and with titles of reverence and holiness, with blessings and curses. To perform miracles is an antiquated, obsolete practice that is not at all in keeping with these modern times. To teach the people is tiresome. Interpreting Holy Scripture is pedantic. Praying is a waste of time. Shedding tears is pitiable and unmanly. Living in poverty is sordid. To be defeated is a disgrace and unbecoming in a man who hardly admits the noblest kings to the ceremony of kissing his holy feet. Finally, to die is unpleasant, and to die on the cross is a disgrace.

Therefore they are left with only those weapons and mild benedictions of which Paul speaks, and they are very generous indeed in dispensing them: interdictions, excommunications, re-excommunications, anathematizations, depicted threats of vengeance, and the terrifying lightning bolt of the ban which with a mere nod casts the souls of men into outer darkness beyond hell. This the holy fathers in Christ and vicars of Christ apply to none more fiercely than to those who, at the instigation of the Devil, try to diminish and erode the patrimony of Peter. Although his words in the Gospel say, "We have left all and followed Thee," [53] they nevertheless apply the name of Peter's patrimony to lands, towns, tax revenues, harbor duties, and power and money. Inflamed with Christ's zeal, they fight for these things with fire and sword, not without spilling Christian blood; and they believe they are apostolically defending the Bride of Christ, which is what they call the Church, by bravely dispersing the enemies—as if there were any more destructive enemies of the Church than the unholy who allow Christ to be forgotten by their silence and who fetter Him with the chains of mercenary regulations and falsify Him with forced interpretations and slay Him with the corruptness of their own lives. Since the Church was founded on the blood, strengthened by the blood, and increased by the blood, it now looks as if Christ, who does defend His flock with His own means, had died, from the way they carry on the work by means of the sword. Now, although war is such a monstrous thing that it is fit for wild beasts but not for humans, and such a madness that the poets say it was released by the Furies, and such a pestilence that it inflicts a universal deterioration of morals, such an unjust thing that it is usually directed by the worst bandits, and so unholy a thing that it has nothing to do with Christ—they nevertheless pursue it to the neglect of everything else. Here you may see decrepit old men acting as if with the vigor of youth and not averse to throwing law, religion, peace, and all human activities into confusion and disorder. There is also no lack of learned sycophants who, in referring to this obvious madness, use names like zeal, piety, and valor, and devise ways for a man to draw the death-dealing sword and plunge it into his brother's viscera, while at the same time supposedly dwelling in that love which, according to Christ's highest teaching, a Christian owes to his neighbor. Now I am not sure whether certain German bishops provided these popes with an example in such matters or whether they took an example from them; they quite simply abandoned garb, benedictions, and all other ceremonies, and just acted the part of satraps, so that they deemed it positively cowardly and unworthy for a bishop to return his brave soul to God anywhere but in battle. Indeed, the common mob of priests, regarding it as a sin to lag behind their superiors in holiness, wage war in great military style when fighting for their right to tithes, using swords, spears, stones, and every possible weapon. What eagle eyes they have when it comes to finding something in the writings of the ancients which they can use to terrify the common people and convince them that they owe more than a simple tithe! But it never enters their minds how many things can be found throughout the scriptures about their own duties, which they, in turn, must discharge for the people. Their tonsure does not remind them in the slightest that a priest must be free of the desires of this world and think of nothing but heavenly things. But these fine fellows say they have properly performed their duty if they just mumble those little prayers of theirs;

but, by Jove, I wonder whether any God hears them or understands them, when they neither hear nor understand them themselves as they speak them with their mouths. But priests have one
thing in common with laymen; that is, they all eagerly take care
of reaping the benefits coming to them and all are well versed in
the laws governing that topic. Also, if there is any burden to be
borne, they cleverly cast it onto the shoulders of somebody else
and pass it, like a ball, from hand to hand. And just as lay princes
delegate part of the administration of their realm of ministers, and
these in turn to others, they, out of sheer modesty, turn over the
function of piety to the common people. The people themselves
hand that function over to the ones they call "ecclesiastics," as if
they themselves had nothing to do with the Church and as if their
baptismal vows had had no effect whatever. Those priests who
call themselves secular, as if destined for the world, not for Christ,
shift the burden to the *regulares*. The regulars pass it on to the
monks; the freer monks to the stricter ones; and both shift it onto
the mendicant monks, who pass it on to the Carthusians, with
whom piety lies buried, so deeply in fact that it is hard to find.
Similarly, the popes, who are most exacting in reaping the harvest
of money, delegate the tasks that are too apostolic to the bishops;
the bishops pass them on to the pastors, the pastors to the vicars,
and the vicars to the mendicant friars. These, in turn, pass them
back to those by whom the wool is shorn from the sheep.

But it is not my intent to investigate the lives of priests and
popes, or I might seem to be composing a satire instead of speaking an encomium. And nobody should think that I am reproaching
good princes while praising bad ones. I have merely touched upon
this theme lightly to make it clear that no mortal can have a happy
life without being admitted to my rituals and without enjoying my
favor. How could it be otherwise, when Nemesis herself, who di-
rects the fortunes of humans, is of the same opinion as myself in
this, so that she always has been most unfriendly to the wise but
has, on the other hand, kept on bestowing gifts on fools, even in
their sleep. You must know about Timotheus,[54] who has a nickname and a saying, "He catches (fish) in his net while sleeping."
Or there's another saying, "The owl flies."[55] Opposed to these are
the sayings applied to the wise, such as, "He was born in the
fourth moon," and "He has Seius' horse,"[56] or "The gold of Tou-

louse." [57] But I shall stop quoting proverbs, or it will look as if I am pillaging the *Adagia* [58] of my friend Erasmus.

To return to the subject, Fortune loves those who are not too prudent, those who are a little rash, and those who like the saying, "The die is cast." But wisdom makes folks fainthearted, and you generally see the wise involved with poverty, hunger, and soot; they are neglected, disreputable, and detested; but you see fools flush with money, the offices of state fall to them, and, in short, they flourish in every way. For if anyone deems it bliss to kowtow to highborn men and to associate with my foolish characters and gem-bedecked gods, what is more useless than wisdom? In fact, what is more damned in the eyes of such people? If it is a matter of amassing wealth, how much money would a merchant make if, following wisdom, he worried about a bit of perjury or blushed when caught in a lie, or if he paid the slightest attention to the scruples of the wise against theft and usury? If anyone aims for ecclesiastical honors or wealth, why a donkey or a buffalo will achieve them sooner than a wise man. If you are concerned with the pleasures of love, the girls—an important part of the game—surrender their hearts completely to fools but are repelled by a wise man and avoid him like a scorpion. And people who have a mind to lead a life with a bit of fun and enjoyment will bar wise men from their society more than anyone else, and would sooner accept any animal. In short, wherever you turn, among popes, princes, judges, officials, friends, enemies, the high and the low, it is only hard cash that gets anything done; and since the wise man shuns this, people normally do their best to keep away from him.

Now, although there is no bound or limit to my praises, this speech has got to end sometime. Therefore I shall stop, but before doing so I shall briefly point out that many authors have given examples of me both in their writings and in their deeds. I do not want it to look as if I foolishly only pat myself on the back, and I do not want legalistic chaps to raise the false accusation against me that I do not cite references. Therefore, taking an example of their own, I shall give a reference that has "nothing to do with the case." In the first place all people seem to agree with the well-known saying, "If the thing is not present, it is best to have a facsimile of it." Thus it is right for us to teach children the maxim, "To pretend to be a fool at the right time is the highest wisdom."

Consider then how valuable a thing folly is, the mere imitation and semblance of which finds so much acceptance among learned men. But that sleek fat hog from Epicurus' herd [59] much more frankly recommends mixing a portion of folly in all deliberations, not too wisely adding, however, "a slight portion." Similarly, we read elsewhere, "It is fine to play the fool at the right time." In still another place we find, "He prefers to look mad and foolish to being wise and gnashing his teeth." Then, in Homer, Telemachus, whom the poet praises at every opportunity, is called silly, and the authors of tragedy like to use the same adjective for boys and youths, as if it were a good-luck omen. For what does that sacred poem, the *Iliad,* contain but the angry fights of foolish kings and peoples? Then how limitless is Cicero's praise, "All things are saturated with folly." Who does not know that the more widespread something is, the more excellent it is? But perhaps the authority of these writers is slight among Christians. Therefore let us try to bolster our praise with the evidence of sacred writings, if you will, or, as the learned are accustomed to do, first asking forgiveness of the theologians for that which has been said, so that they may give us their imprimatur, also because we are approaching a serious subject, and it might be improper to summon the Muses all the way from Helicon again, especially since the matter is a bit remote from their field. And perhaps it would be still more fitting, since I am playing theologian for a while and am treading that thorny path, if the soul of Scotus, more prickly than any porcupine or hedgehog, would descend from his Sorbonne and enter my breast. After a little while it may go back wherever it pleases— to the Devil for all I care. I wish it were possible for me to put on another face and appear in the garb of a full-fledged divine! But I am afraid someone would accuse me of theft, as if I had secretly pillaged the files of our master, since I possess so much theological lore. But it really should not be surprising if, after such long and close association with the theologians, I have picked up a few things, just as old fig-wood Priapus learned a Greek word or two from hearing his master read them. And Lucian's rooster, after years of association with humans, learned to handle human speech remarkably well.

But to return to the subject, with favoring auguries, Ecclesiastes writes in the first chapter, "The number of fools is infinite." [60]

Since he calls the number "infinite," does he not seem to include all mortals, except perhaps a few rare ones—but I don't know who has ever had the luck to find them. Jeremiah remarks, much more frankly, saying, in the tenth chapter,[61] "Every man is made foolish by his wisdom." He attributes wisdom to God alone, leaving foolishness to all men. A little before this he says, "Let man not glory in his wisdom."[62] Why do you not want a man to glory in his wisdom, excellent Jeremiah? Why, because he has none, would be the answer. But I return to Ecclesiastes. What do you think he means when he exclaims, "Vanity of vanities, all is vanity"?[63] other than, as I have just said, that the life of man is nothing but a game of folly? He votes affirmatively in favor of what Cicero said, as cited above: "Everything is saturated with folly." And when the wise Ecclesiasticus[64] said, "The fool changes like the moon, the wise man is steadfast like the sun," what else did he mean but that the whole of mankind is foolish and only God deserves the name of wise? In truth, if they interpret the moon as representing human nature, the sun, the source of all light, is God. And that is in keeping with what Christ says in the gospels, when He claims that no one must be called good but God alone. If, then, he who is not wise is stupid, and if whoever is good is also wise, according to the Stoics all mortals must necessarily be subsumed under the heading of Folly. Further, Solomon[65] says, Chapter 15, "A fool delights in his folly," which clearly attests that nothing is pleasurable without foolishness. And that agrees with the statement that "He that increaseth knowledge increaseth sorrow, and in much wisdom is much grief."[66] Does not the excellent Preacher say the same thing in Chapter 7, "The heart of the wise is where sadness is, but the heart of fools follows mirth"?[67] By this he maintained that it is not enough to have learned wisdom without also adding knowledge of me. If you do not have much trust in me, listen to his words in Chapter 1,[68] in which he wrote, "I gave my heart to know wisdom, and to know madness and folly." In this quotation it is to be noted that the prize belongs to folly, since he puts it last. Ecclesiastes wrote this, and you know that the ecclesiastical order puts the one last that is first in importance, which indeed accords with the teaching of the gospel. But that folly is superior to wisdom, Ecclesiasticus asserts (whoever he was) perfectly clearly in Chapter 44. But I shall not quote his words now until you have accorded my introduction of the topic a fa-vorable reaction, as those do in Plato who discourse with Socrates. Which is it more reasonable to hide, the things that are rare and precious or those that are ordinary and cheap? Why are you si-lent? Even if you are dissembling, the Greek saying will answer for you, "One leaves a bucket at the door." Before you sneer at that, permit me to say that Aristotle, the god of our masters, quotes it. Now who of you is foolish enough to leave gold and precious jewels in the street? No one, I'm sure. You put them in the most secret corners of well-guarded strong boxes, while you put trash outdoors. If, then, valuables are hidden away and cheap stuff is left out in the open, is it not obvious that wisdom, which he for-bids us to hide, is cheaper than folly, which he orders hidden? Hear now the words of the passage referred to: "Better is the man that hideth his folly than he that hideth his wisdom." [69] Then why do the Holy Scriptures attribute humility of soul to the fool, whereas the wise man thinks no one to be his equal? For that's how I interpret what Ecclesiastes writes in Chapter 10: "A fool walking along the road, being a fool himself, thinks all men are fools." [70] [King James: "When he that is a fool walketh by the way, his wisdom faileth him, and he saith to everyone that he is a fool."] Is that not a special kind of honesty to consider all others your equals, and when everyone feels his own magnificence, to share the praise with all? For even the great king was not ashamed of this name, when he said in Chapter 30, "I am the most foolish of men." [71] Also Paul, the teacher of the Gentiles, writing to the Corinthians, accepts the name of fool: "I speak as a fool. I am more," [72] as if it were shameful to be surpassed in folly. But some would-be Greek scholars will no doubt roar objections at me. They are eager to give modern theologians a dose of their own medicine, as they pour their own annotations over other people's like smoke. Of this group my friend Erasmus, whom I often men-tion approvingly, is, if not the Alpha, at least the Beta. "What a foolish citation," they say, "and worthy of Folly herself. The Apostle meant something quite different from what you imagine. For he did not mean by those words that he was to be considered more foolish than others; but when he said, 'Are they ministers of Christ? So am I,' boasting that he was equal to others in this re-spect, he added, by way of emendation, *plus ego* ('I am more'), meaning that he was not merely equal to the rest of the Apostles in the ministry of the Gospel, but that he was a bit superior to them. And while he really wanted to appear so, in order not to give offense to their ears by speaking too arrogantly he protected himself with the pretext of folly, 'I speak as a fool,' implying that it is the privilege of fools alone to be able to speak the truth without causing resentment." What Paul may really have had in mind when speaking these words, I leave to them to argue about. I myself side with the big, fat, dull, coarse, and generally approved theologians, with whom a great percentage of the learned prefer to err, by God, than to give the correct interpretation of those scholars learned in three languages. And none of them would consider those pseudo-Greek scholars to be anything but cackling jackdaws, especially when a highly praised theologian, who shall be nameless [73] (so that those would-be Greek scholars of ours will not bring up the old Greek chestnut of the ass and the lyre against him), magisterially and theologically citing this passage, starting with the words, "I speak as a fool, I am more," writes a new chapter and adds a new section, which he could not have done without a mastery of the highest kind of dialectics, and then interpreted it in this way (I shall give his own words, both in form and subject matter): " 'I speak as a fool,' that is, if I seem foolish to you for equating myself with the pseudo-apostles, I will seem even more so if I set myself up as superior to them." Despite this, the same theologian a little further on, apparently forgetting his own words, slips into another interpretation.

But why do I so anxiously defend myself by means of the example of one single person, when it has become the accepted right of theologians to stretch heaven, that is, the Scriptures, like a sheepskin? If any credence is to be placed in Jerome, that master of five languages, the words of the scriptures are contradictory in Paul, although in context they are not contradictory at all. For, at Athens, he took the inscription he saw on the altar and twisted it into an argument for the Christian religion by passing over the words that would militate against his case and picking out only a couple toward the end, "To the unknown God," and he even changed those, because the whole inscription read, "To the gods of Asia, Europe, and Africa, to the unknown gods and the foreign ones." Following his example, I believe, the sons of the theologians pick out four or five words here and there and, if necessary, distort their meaning and adapt them to their own use; yet the words preceding and following these words may either have nothing to do with the case or may actually refute it. They do this so brazenly and so skillfully that lawyers often envy the theologians. And to what lengths do they not go! That great man (I nearly slipped and said his name, but then I stopped for fear of that Greek proverb) has managed to squeeze a meaning out of Luke's words that is about as compatible with the spirit of Christ as fire is with water. For at a time when extreme danger was threatening—a time when loyal followers ordinarily keep close to their protectors and get set to do battle with all the resources they can muster—Christ, with the intent of removing from the minds of His followers any trust in help of that kind, asked His disciples whether they had ever lacked anything, for He had sent them out unprovided with the needs of travel, without even so much as shoes on their feet to protect them from thorns and stones, or a pouch to safeguard them from hunger. When they replied that they had lacked nothing at all, He responded, "But now, he who has a pouch, let him take it, likewise a wallet. And let him who has no sword sell his coat and buy one." [74] Since Christ's whole teaching emphasizes only mildness, tolerance, and disdain for life, who will not realize at once what He means in this passage? Namely that He was now disarming His disciples even more, so that they would not only have no shoes or wallet but would even throw away their coat also and, naked and completely unimpeded, would proceed to the work of the Gospel and would provide themselves with nothing but a sword, not the kind that robbers and murderers carry, but the sword of the spirit, which penetrates to the deepest recesses of the heart and with one stroke severs all passions so that nothing remains in the heart but piety. But please observe how that celebrated theologian has twisted these words. He explains the sword as being protection against persecution; the bag as sufficient provisions, as if Christ had all at once changed His mind and done an about-face, renouncing His previous teaching, because He had sent out his followers inadequately equipped, that is, as if He had forgotten that He had said they would be blessed when they were afflicted with reproaches, humiliations, and punishments, and had forbidden them to resist evil, saying that He had invoked the example of the sparrows and the lilies and now was so unwilling for them to go without a sword that He commanded them to buy one, even if they had to sell their coats, and preferred their going naked to not being armed with a sword. Just as He believes that everything pertaining to resistance to violence is inherent in the word "sword," so too He intends the word "bag" to include everything that pertains to the support of life. Thus this interpreter of the divine mind represents the Apostles as equipped with lances, crossbows, slings, and muskets in order to preach Christ crucified. He loads them with chests, boxes, and knapsacks, so that they would never have to leave an inn without having eaten. And the same man is not bothered by the fact that He rebukingly orders the sword to be sheathed which He has only a short while ago ordered to be bought at such a high price, nor by the fact that no one ever heard that the Apostles used swords and shields against the violence of the heathens, although they would have if Christ had meant what this interpreter claims. There is another man, who shall be nameless, though he has a name, and not the worst one in the world either; he would make of the tents mentioned by Habakkuk the skin of St. Bartholomew, who was flayed ("the skins of the land of Midian shall be shaken"). Recently I attended a theological discussion, as I often do. When someone demanded to know what authority there was in Holy Writ for demanding that heretics be destroyed by fire, instead of being vanquished by argument, a certain irritable old man, whose superciliousness proclaimed him to be a theologian, replied with considerable animus that the Apostle Paul had laid down that rule when he said, "After a first and second warning, get rid of a man that is a heretic." After he had repeated these words over and over again and people were beginning to wonder what was wrong with the man, he finally explained that the heretic was to be "gotten rid of" in the sense of Latin *devita* (shun) meaning *de vita* ("from life").[75] Some laughed, but there were also some present to whom this comment seemed theologically quite sound. When some continued to refute him, that Philadelphia lawyer ["Tenedian lawyer"] and irrepressible commentator said, "Consider this case: it is written that you shall not permit a witch (*maleficus*) to live.[76] Every heretic is a *maleficus* (evildoer), therefore, etc." All those present were amazed at the reasoning power of the man and dutifully agreed with his assertion. It did not even occur to anyone that the law pertained to soothsayers, enchanters, and sorcerers, whom the Hebrews call in their language *mekashephim,* which we render as *malefici.* Otherwise, according to the man's logic, whoring and drunkenness would also have to be punished by the death penalty.

It is really stupid of me to go into all these points, which are so innumerable that they could not be contained in the volumes of Chrysippus or Didymus. I merely wanted to have people bear this in mind: If such things are permitted those master of theology, I too, a theological nonentity, should be pardoned if I have not been meticulously exact in citing chapter and verse. Now I am finally getting back to Paul. He says, "Suffer fools gladly," [77] speaking of himself. Further, "Receive me as a fool," [78] and "I do not speak according to God, but as in foolishness." [79] Elsewhere he says, "We are fools for Christ's sake." [80] You have heard such great commendations of folly from so eminent an authority. For what he actually asserts publicly is that folly is a prime necessity and a salubrious thing for the community. "Let him that seems to be wise among you become a fool, that he may be wise." [81] And in Luke, the two disciples who joined Jesus on the road are called fools.[82] And I don't believe it should seem surprising that St. Paul attributes a certain amount of foolishness even to God, when he says, "The foolishness of God is wiser than men." [83] Of course, Origen objects, while interpreting this, that you cannot equate this foolishness with the ordinary conception of foolishness that men have, which is seen in this passage: "The preaching of the Cross is to them that perish foolishness." [84] But why should I continue with such painful care to present these things with so many attestations when Christ Himself in the mystical Psalms says so plainly to the Father, "Thou knowest my foolishness"? [85] It is not for nothing that God has been so fond of fools. I imagine that just as the princely heads of state are highly suspicious of overly sagacious men and look upon them with disfavor, as did Caesar regarding Brutus and Cassius, while having no fear at all of drunken Antony; or as Nero suspected Seneca, and Dionysius did Plato, whereas they were delighted by simpler and denser souls, similarly, Christ always detests and condemns those wise people who are much taken with their own brilliance. Paul attests this quite clearly when he says, "It has pleased God to save the world by foolishness,"[86] since it was not able to be put right by wisdom. But He points this out plainly enough when He proclaims through the mouth of the prophet Isaiah, "I will destroy the wisdom of the wise, and I will reject the prudence of the prudent,"[87] and again when He gives thanks that the mystery of salvation was hidden from the wise but revealed to the little ones, that is, fools. The Greek word for "little ones, babes" is *nepioi,* which He used as the opposite of *sophoi.* This is in keeping with the fact that in the Gospel He often attacks the scribes and Pharisees and doctors of the law, while staunchly defending the unlearned multitude. For what else is meant by "Woe unto you, scribes·and Pharisees" but "Woe unto you, wise men"? But He seems to have been especially fond of little children, women, and fishermen. And in the class of dumb animals He liked best those that were farthest removed from the cunning of the fox. Thus He preferred to ride on a donkey, even though He could have mounted the back of a lion without danger, had He wanted. And the Holy Spirit descended in the form of a dove, not an eagle or a falcon. There is also frequent mention of harts, fawns, and lambs in Holy Writ. Add to this the fact that He calls those chosen by Him for eternal life "sheep." There is no more foolish animal than these, as is attested by the Aristotelian expression "sheeplike nature." It derives from the innate stupidity of that animal and is customarily applied as an insult to stupid and foolish men. Yet Christ declared Himself to be the shepherd of that flock, and even took delight in being called the Lamb, as John called him, "Behold the Lamb of God." There is frequent mention of this name in Revelation, also. What does all this prove—if not that mortals are foolish, even the pious ones? Does it not also prove that Christ, though possessing the wisdom of the Father, nevertheless became foolish, in a sense, by assuming the nature and form of a man in order to free men from their foolishness? And in the same man He became sin, in order to cure man of sins, and He chose to do this by no other means than the foolishness of the Cross, as well as through simple and dull Apostles. To these He constantly recommended foolishness, discouraging them from seeking wisdom, as He called their attention to the examples of the lilies, the mustard seed, and the sparrows, simple things devoid of much sense, and living their lives as nature guided them, not by cunning or calculation. Furthermore, when He commanded them not to be worried when speaking before high officials and forbade them to search into time and the seasons, He did so in order that they should not only not rely on their own cleverness but that they should with all their souls rely only on Him. It is in that same sense that God, the creator of the world, warned against eating of the tree of knowledge, as if to say that knowledge is fatal to bliss. Paul plainly condemned knowledge as ruinous and leading to conceit. And I believe that St. Bernard followed him in interpreting that mountain on which Lucifer established his residence as the Mount of Knowledge. And there is this fact which should not perchance be overlooked as evidence that Folly is favored by those on high, that to her alone pardon for errors is granted, but a wise man is not forgiven. Therefore, when wise men have sinned and are begging forgiveness, they do it under the pretext and with the defense of foolishness. That is how Aaron prays for mercy for his sister in the Book of Numbers, if I remember correctly: "My Lord, I beseech thee, lay not the sin upon us, wherein we have done foolishly."[88] And thus did Saul excuse his blame to David, saying, "For it is apparent that I have done foolishly."[89] David himself, in turn, speaks to the Lord ingratiatingly, "I beseech thee, O Lord, take away the iniquity of thy servant, for I have done very foolishly,"[90] as if he would not obtain forgiveness except on the grounds of foolishness and ignorance. But a much stronger proof of this is seen in the fact that Christ on the Cross, while praying for His enemies, "Father, forgive them," offered no excuse for them but ignorance, saying, "They know not what they do." In the same way Paul writes to Timothy,[91] "But I obtained mercy, because I did it ignorantly and in unbelief." What does "I did it ignorantly" mean but I acted through folly and not malice? What is the meaning of "I obtained mercy," if not I would not have achieved this if I had not been supported by the defense of foolishness? And the mystical Psalmist (who should have come to my mind before this) says for us (Psalm 25:7), "Remember not the sins of my youth nor my ignorances." You notice the two things he offers as excuses, lack of maturity—to which I am always akin—and "ignorances," significantly in the plural, so that we may realize the vast scope of folly.

But in order to avoid going into endless details and to sum up briefly, the Christian religion, to all appearances, is closely associated with foolishness and practically not at all with wisdom. If you desire proof of this, first note that children, old folks, and women enjoy holy services and religious ceremonies more than other people and are therefore always near the altar, apparently moved only by an impulse of nature. Besides that, you note that the founders of religion, embracing simplicity with uncommon fervor, were the bitter enemies of learning and letters. Finally, there seem to be no more complete fools than those who are entirely gripped by the ardor of Christian piety. Therefore they squander their possessions, overlook injustices to themselves, allow themselves to be cheated, fail to distinguish friend from foe, abhor pleasure, are satiated by fasting, vigils, tears, troubles, and insults, despise life and wish only for death. In short, they seem to have become positively impervious to any common sense, as if their soul resided somewhere outside their body. Now what is that but madness? Therefore it should not be too surprising if the Apostles seemed to be drunk on new wine, just as Paul seemed to Festus the judge to be mad. But, since I have clad myself in that "lion's skin," let me also point out this, that the happiness which Christians seek with so many tribulations is nothing but a kind of madness and folly—let no offense be taken at these words; rather, consider the facts. First of all there is that view, in which Christians and Platonists virtually agree, that the soul is shackled and bound by the chains of the body, and because of its density is prevented from contemplating and enjoying the things that are real. Hence Plato defines philosophy as the contemplation of death, since it leads the mind away from visible and corporeal things—which is exactly what death does. Therefore, as long as the soul makes proper use of the organs of the body, it will be called sane, but when the chains are broken and it attempts to achieve freedom, as if intending a flight from that prison, it is called insane. If this happens to be the result of illness, practically all agree that it is insanity. Yet we see this class of people predict the future, speak in tongues, and display knowledge of subjects they have never studied, and, all in all, it can be said they have a certain air of the divine about them. There is no doubt that this occurs because the mind, when slightly freed from contamination of the body, begins to exercise its native power. And I believe that for the same reason people close to death are accustomed to experience the same sort of things, so that, for instance, they make marvelous predictions. Again, if this occurs as the result of religious zeal, it may not be exactly the same kind of madness, but it comes pretty close to it, so that a great number of people think it is sheer insanity, especially since only a very few people are so at odds with the whole way of life of the rest of the community of mankind. Therefore it usually happens to them, as in Plato's parable, I believe, it happened to those who, captive in the cave, marveled at the shadows of things. And then one escaped, and on returning to the mouth of the cave, claimed to have seen real things and told them they were badly deluded, since they thought there was nothing but those miserable shadows. For that knowing one pitied and deplored the madness of those caught up in such great error. But they, for their part, laughed at him as if he were mad and evicted him. The common run of mankind admires those things the most which are the most tangible and thinks these are the only real things. On the other hand, the pious ones ignore whatever is related to the body, and the closer it is, the more they ignore it, being entirely occupied with the contemplation of invisible things. The others esteem riches most highly, and next to that, the comforts of the body, and leave very little regard for the soul; most of them don't even believe it exists because it cannot be perceived with the eyes. By contrast, the pious all yearn for God as the most basic essence of all existence; next to Him comes the soul, because it is the closest thing to Him. They do not bother to care for the body and turn away from riches as so much junk. Or, if they are forced to deal with matters of that sort, they do so reluctantly and disdainfully; they have as if not having; and they possess as if not possessing. In individual matters of the senses they make far-reaching distinctions. First, although all senses are connected with the body, some are coarser, such as touch, hearing, sight, smell, and taste, while others are more remote from the body, such as memory, intellect, and will. Therefore, the soul strengthens whatever one it turns its attention to. Since every power of the soul of a pious one is directed to the things which are furthest removed from the coarser senses, these, as it were, grow dull and insensitive. The broad masses, on the other hand, are most involved with those coarse senses, and with the others as little as possible. Thus it is that it has happened to some holy men that they drank oil instead of wine. Among the passions of the mind, once more, there are some that are more closely connected to the outright physical body, such as lust, gluttony, and sloth, anger, pride, and envy. The pious are always implacably at war with these, whereas the masses cannot imagine life without them. Then there are certain middle-of-the-road emotions, natural ones, so to speak, such as love of one's father, of children, of relatives, of friends. Even the masses attach some worth to these. But the others, the pious people, endeavor to eradicate them from their minds, except insofar as they are exalted to the purely spiritual realm, so that they love a parent not as a parent—for what has he begotten but the body? Yet even that is due to God as our Parent. But they love him as a good man, and as one in whom the vision of that supreme mind shines forth which alone they call the "highest good" (*summum bonum*) and outside of whom they maintain nothing is to be loved or sought after. By the same standard they measure all other functions of life; and that which is visible, if it is not to be dismissed entirely, is nevertheless relegated to an area of much lower esteem than that accorded the things which cannot be seen. They say that even in the sacraments and acts of piety themselves, body and spirit can be distinguished. Thus, in fasting, they regard it as of no special value if someone merely abstains from meat or from supper, which the masses consider to be complete fasting, unless at the same time he gives up something of his emotions, so that he is less quick to anger than usual, less full of pride. Thus, the spirit, being less weighed down by corporeal burdens, rises to the enjoyment of heavenly goods. And they say it is similarly true that in the external process of the Eucharist, while it is not to be scorned, what is performed in the ceremonies is in and of itself of slight consequence, or even ruinous, unless the spiritual element is added to it, namely that which is represented by those visible signs. Moreover, the death of Christ is also represented, so that mortal men may experience it through taming, abolishing, and burying, so to speak, their physical passions, in order to be resurrected to a new life. These, then, are the things a pious man does and contemplates. But the masses, on the other hand, think that the sacrifice means merely being present at the altar, as close as possible, hearing the sound of the words and watching all the little ceremonies. But not only in these things—which we have mentioned merely by way of example—but simply everywhere in life the pious man flees the things of the body, to be caught up in eternal, invisible, spiritual things. Thus, since there is this complete disagreement on everything between the pious and the others, the result is that each seems mad to the other. Yet the term "mad" is more legitimately applied to the pious than to the masses, in my opinion. This will, in fact, become clearer if, as I have promised, I shall briefly prove that the highest ecstasy is nothing other than a kind of madness. Therefore consider first that Plato was imagining something of that sort when he wrote that the madness of lovers is the most delightful kind of all. For he who is madly in love no longer lives in himself but in the one he loves; and the farther away he gets from himself and merges with the other, the more he rejoices. When the soul contemplates leaving the body and does not properly make use of its own bodily organs, you would no doubt be justified in calling it madness. For what else is meant when they say (as they often do), "He's not himself," or "Come to yourself," or, "He's himself again"? The more complete the love, the greater the madness, and the happier. Now what will that heavenly life be like for which all pious souls so ardently strive? Why, the spirit will completely absorb the body, being the conqueror and the more potent. And it will do this all the more easily, partly because it will be in its own kingdom, but partly because it has already in this life cleansed the body and prepared it for the transformation. But then the spirit itself will be absorbed by that Supreme Spirit in wondrous fashion, for that is infinitely more powerful. Now, since the whole man will be outside himself he will experience some ineffable part of that supreme good, which draws everything to itself. This bliss, however, will be perfectly realized only when the souls, after receiving their former bodies again, are given immortality. Since, however, the life of the pious is nothing but the contemplation of that life and, as it were, a foreshadowing of it, they sometimes have a taste of the ardor to come. Although it is only the minutest drop compared to that fount of eternal bliss, it still exceeds by far all the pleasures of the body, even if all the delights of all humans are put together in one. So far do spiritual things surpass the corporeal, and the invisible the visible. And that is certainly what the prophet promises: "Eye has not seen, nor ear heard, neither have entered into the heart of man, the things which God hath prepared for them that love Him." And that is a part of Folly which will not be taken away with the transformation of life but which will be perfected.

Therefore, those who are permitted to feel this, although it happens to very few, undergo something very similar to madness; they speak incoherent things, not in the ordinary manner of human beings, but they utter sound without sense, and suddenly change their whole facial expression. Now they are excited, now dejected; now they cry, now they laugh, now they sigh—in short, they are totally beside themselves. When they come to—as they soon do—they have no knowledge of where they have been, whether in the body or outside of it, whether awake or asleep. They don't remember what they've seen, said, or done, recalling only as through a cloud or in a dream; they only know that they have been extremely happy as long as they have been out of their mind, and they regret having regained consciousness and would like best of all to be out of their mind forever in such a state of madness. Despite this, it is only a meager sample of bliss to come.

But, in my forgetfulness, I have wandered far beyond my original goal. If I have by any chance been too biting, or too loquacious in what I have said, bear in mind that I have addressed you as Folly, as a woman. But remember also the Greek proverb (I *think* it is Greek) to the effect that even a foolish man may very often speak a pertinent word; assuming you do not think that that excludes women.

I see you are expecting a peroration. You are not very bright if you think I can remember what I have said after dishing out this hodgepodge of words. An old proverb says, "I hate a drinking companion with a long memory." And a modern one says, "I hate a hearer with a long memory."

Good-bye, then. Clap your hands, keep on living and drinking, you most distinguished initiates of Folly!

Translated by Robert A. Fowkes

Notes

The text translated is that of the *Opera Omnia* edited by Joannes Clericus (Jean Leclerc), Leiden, 1703, as reprinted unaltered by Georg Olms Verlagsbuchhandel, Hildesheim, 1962. The translator has tried to work independently but has, of course, looked at the work of predecessors, notably, but not exclusively, Leonard F. Dean (New York: Farrar, Straus, 1946), Hoyt Hopewell Hudson (Princeton, N.J.: Princeton University Press, 1941), and Anton J. Gail (Stuttgart: Reclam, 1980).

Admiring the work of all these, and others, the present translator has produced yet another version. For Erasmus was a man for all seasons. May the Italian condemnation *traduttore traditore* not be found excessively applicable to this effort. If an occasional phrase sounds overly modern, it is probably no more so than the original, for Erasmus wrote such a fluent and lively Latin that it almost seems to be his mother tongue.

The copious notes of Gerardus Listrius included in the 1703 edition (some 840 in number) have been invaluable, though not infallible. They illumine with considerable brilliance the vast learning of Erasmus, the kind of learning at which he, through Folly, pretends to poke fun.

1. The "Battle of the Frogs and Mice" (*Batrachomyomachía*) is pseudo-Homeric. The references to Vergil and Ovid are wrongly ascribed. Busiris, a legendary Egyptian king, killed strangers and sacrificed them to Zeus. Thersites was the appallingly ugly man of insulting speech in Book II of the *Iliad*. Seneca's *Apokolokynthosis* ("Pumpkinification") satirized the apotheosis of Claudius. Gryllus, transformed into a pig by Circe, regretted being restored to the less enviable form of a man.

2. The date 1508 is perhaps two years too early.

3. Thales: the first of the "Seven Sages."

4. Hephaistos (= Vulcan) was born lame.

5. The Pythagoreans claimed their *tetraktýs* (the sum of $1 + 2 + 3 + 4$) to be the root of all creation. Their *tetrad* was a triangle in which the base had four units, or dots, the next higher level 3, etc.

6. Lucretius' *De Rerum Natura* begins with the famous apostrophe to Venus: "*Aeneadum genetrix . . .*" ("Through whom the earth is peopled and all creatures have their being").

7. On the wall of Troy, on beholding Helen.

8. "My Hollanders" obviously alludes to Erasmus' nationality.

9. Momus, god of mocking and censure (of the gods too).

10. Atellan farces (Oscan in origin), named for Atella, a town in Campania, were obscenely comical.

11. Symbol of Aesculapius.

12. Nereus was the handsomest of the Greeks at Troy, as Thersites (cf. n. 1) was the ugliest.

13. Euclid founded the philosophical school of the Megarians. The people of Megara were maligned as dull and narrow-minded.

14. When Amphion played his lyre, stones formed themselves into the walls of Thebes.

15. A fox covered with biting flies refused the help of a hedgehog to dispel them, reasoning that these flies had already had their fill and that they would only

be replaced by hungry ones. Sertorius pretended to consult a white hind on military moves and to predict the future. Lycurgus raised two puppies from the same litter, one to be a hunter, one to be a passive creature.

16. Ugly little clay statues of satyrs containing images of gods inside.

17. "Fat Minerva" meant bluntly, plainly.

18. Dama: apparently the name of a man of low rank and sordid occupation.

19. Marpesian rock: *Aeneid* VI:471.

20. Lynceus: the keen-sighted Argonaut who could see through earth, sea, and sky. Goethe called the tower watchman *Lynkeus* (*Faust II,* Acts III, V).

21. They all suddenly took their own lives.

22. Aristophanes, *Plutós,* Act V, 266–67.

23. Theuth, according to Socrates, was an old Egyptian god who invented arithmetic, calculus, geometry, astronomy, chess, etc.

24. Lucian, in his dialogue *The Dream or the Cock,* satirizes the Pythagorean doctrine of reincarnation.

25. Gryllus: cf. n. 1.

26. This is an allusion to the tale of the satyr invited to dine in a peasant's house. It is cold, and the peasant blows on his fingers. The satyr asks why he does so. The reply is, "To warm them." When soup is served, it is piping hot, and the peasant blows on it. When told that this is done to cool the soup, the annoyed satyr leaves.

27. In the *Symposium* Eros and Anteros (two aspects of Cupid-Eros) serve Venus Urania and Venus Vulgivaga ("wandering").

28. Argive = Greek.

29. An innocent youth whose death is unjustly caused.

30. A devil boasted to St. Bernard of knowing seven verses of the Psalms the daily recitation of which would guarantee salvation. When Bernard was unable to make the devil reveal which they were, he said that he would simply recite all the Psalms every day. The devil, reluctant to be the cause of so much pious activity, revealed which verses they were (allegedly banal ones, at that).

31. A parody of *Aeneid* VI:625–27.

32. Marcus Hermogenes Tigellus, a famous singer, mentioned in Horace.

33. That is, *Mōría* or *More* or *Morus.*

34. Veiovis: an old Roman (originally Etruscan?) god whose fearful thunderbolts caused deafness even before being hurled.

35. *Aeneid* VI:136–39.

36. Based on the start of the *Iliad* and partly depending on puns on *casus* "fall; grammatical case."

37. The tale of the ass in the tiger's skin possibly originated in Cumae, in Asia Minor.

38. Aldus: Erasmus' friend, the Venetian scholar and printer Aldo Manuzio.

39. Alcaeus: an Aeolian lyric poet. Callimachus: Alexandrian grammarian and poet.

40. Stentor (*Iliad* V:785) could shout as loud as fifty other men.

41. The ill-smelling Lake Camarina in Sicily. "Don't stir the Camarian Lake" = "Don't make waves."

42. Albertists: adherents of Albertus Magnus of Bavaria; Occamists: followers of William of Occam, English Scholastic; Scotists: followers of Duns Scotus (all of these being "Scholastic" philosophers or "Schoolmen").

43. Hebrews 11:1.

44. Chrysippus: a Stoic philosopher known for his keen dialectic.

45. This is thought to refer to the Oxford philosophers.

46. Coletes: named for the nun, St. Coleta/Coletta of northern France. Minorites: one of the three orders founded by St. Francis of Assisi. Minims: mendicant friars of an order founded by St. Francis of Paola. Button-wearers: probably the Observantines. Bridgetines: probably members of an order founded by St. Bridget of Ireland (rather than Brigitta of Sweden, as is sometimes asserted). Williamists: friars of an order founded by William of Aquitaine. Jacobines: Dominicans.

47. *Abraxas:* a secret gnostic word representing the Deity. Assigning Greek numerical values to the letters yields the sum 365, the number of days in the year and the number of heavens assumed by Basilides of Alexandria.

48. *Quorsum haec tam putida tendant? (putida* = stinking things).

49. Scottish must mean English here.

50. Priapus spied on the nightly ceremonies of the witches Canidia and Sagana. At the height of these goings-on, he broke wind.

51. *Speculum historiale* ("Mirror of History") by Vincent of Beauvais, part of his *Speculum maius,* purported to give the history of the world. It was often plundered by medieval preachers. The *Gesta Romanorum* ("Feats of the Romans") was the very popular collection of tales of miscellaneous origin (including oriental sources), mostly not Roman, compiled in England or Germany in the thirteenth or fourteenth century. Later writers (Chaucer, Shakespeare, Schiller, e.g.) made ample use of these tales.

52. Greek *epískopos* = "overseer, guardian."

53. Matt. 19:27, Mark 10:28, etc.

54. Athenian general famed for his extraordinary good fortune.

55. The flight of the owl was a good omen in Athens.

56. Seius' horse brought him and subsequent owners bad luck.

57. A consul who stole treasures from a temple in Toulouse reaped misfortune.

58. Erasmus' collection of proverbs (approximately eight thousand in number).

59. Horace called himself a hog from Epicurus' herd (*Epistles* I:4.15–16).

60. Ecclesiastes 1:15. Erasmus quotes the Latin Vulgate, which often differs from other versions of the Bible.

61. Jeremiah 10:14.

62. Jeremiah 9:23.

63. Ecclesiastes 1:2 and 12:8.

64. Ecclesiasticus (Apocrypha) 27:12 (27:11 in Authorized Version).

65. Proverbs 15:21.

66. Ecclesiastes 1:18.

67. Ecclesiastes 7:4.

68. Ecclesiastes 1:17.

69. Ecclesiasticus 20:33 (20:31 in some versions).

70. Ecclesiastes 10:3.

71. Proverbs 30:2.

72. 2 Cor. 11:21–23.

73. An allusion to Nicholas of Lyra.

74. Luke 22:36.

75. Titus 3:10.

76. Exodus 22:18.

77. 2 Cor. 11:19.

78. 2 Cor. 11:16.

79. 2 Cor. 11:17.

80. 1 Cor. 4:10.

81. 1 Cor. 3:18.

82. Luke 24:25.

83. 1 Cor. 1:25.
84. 1 Cor. 1:18.
85. Psalm 69:5 (Luther 69:6).
86. 1 Cor. 1:21.
87. Isaiah 29:14.
88. Numbers 12:11.
89. 1 Sam. 26:21.
90. 2 Sam. 24:10; 1 Chron. 21:8.
91. 1 Timothy 1:13.

CONRAD CELTIS

Conrad Celtis (1459–1508), besides being an important contribution to the proliferation of Humanism in Germany, was one of the few fine poets of this period. Born the son of peasants in a village near Würzburg, he was the first Humanist to receive his education in the North before going to Italy. He went to schools in Cologne, Heidelberg, Rostock, and Leipzig, and after he moved on to Italy, studied in Venice, Padua, Bologna, Florence, and Rome. After his return to the North, Celtis went to Cracow, Nuremberg, and Ingolstadt. In 1497 he received a call from Emperor Maximilian to the University of Vienna. Here he wrote and taught until his death in 1508.

His verse is in Latin, closely modeled on the great Latin poets, and yet imbued with the new spirit of this exciting time. His lyrics deal with the familiar topics of poetry; his best are love poems.

Ad Apollinem repertorem poetices ut ab Italis ad Germanos veniat

Phoebe qui blandae citharae repertor,
linque delectos Helicona, Pindum et,
ac veni in nostras vocitatus oras
    carmine grato.

cernis ut laetae properent Camenae,
et canunt dulces gelido sub axe.
tu veni incultam fidibus canoris
    visere terram.

barbarus quem olim genuit, vel acer
vel parens hirtus, Latii leporis
nescius, nunc sic duce te docendus
    dicere carmen

Orpheus qualis cecinit Pelasgis,
quem ferae atroces, agilesque cervi,
arboresque altae nemorum secutae
    plectra moventem.

tu celer vastum poteras per aequor
laetus a Graecis Latium videre,
invehens Musas, voluisti gratas
    pandere et artes.

Three Poems

Phoebus who invented the sweet-sounding lyre
leave your beloved home, Helicon and Pindus,
and come implored by a pleasing poem
    to our country.

Look our Muses joyfully hurry to you
singing sweetly under the icy skies
come and see with the sounds of your harp
    our barren land.

Teach the barbarian born from rough soldiers
or peasants oblivious of your arts
teach him under your skillful guidance
    to sing a song

just as once Orpheus sang to the Pagans
when animals wild and nimble stags
and even the tallest trees in the forests
    danced to his song.

For you swiftly sailed across the far sea
from Greece and gladly visited Rome
along with your Muses and there you taught gracefully
    all of your arts.

sic velis nostras rogitamus oras
Italas ceu quondam aditare terras;
barbarus sermo fugiatque, ut atrum
    subruat omne.

De nocte et osculo Hastilinae, erotice

Illa quam fueram beatus hora,
inter basia et osculationes,
contrectans teneras Hasae papillas,
et me nunc gremio inferens venusto,
nunc stringens teneris suum lacertis
pectus, languidulo gemens amore.
quod me in reciproco fovebat aestu,
cogens deinde suos meare in artus,
dum nostros animos per ora mixtos
cum vinclis adamantinis ligavit
Diva ex caeruleo creata ponto.

        o nox perpetuis decora stellis,
quae divum facies levas coruscas,
et fessis requiem refers salubrem.
nunc stes Herculeo velut sub ortu,
aut qualis Suetiis soles sub oris,
dum Phoebus pluvium revisit Austrum,
nullam per spatium bimestre lucem
fundit, perpetuas ferens tenebras,
sic fervens satiabitur voluptas.

Therefore come, we beg you, to our shores
as once you visited Italy, may the
barbarian tongue then be muted and all
    our darkness perish.

Night and Hasilina's Kiss

How happy I was in that hour
when we were kissing and kissing and kissing
when I squeezed Hasa's soft young breasts
and buried myself in her lap
when I gently embraced her bosom
and moaned exhausted with love.
How in return she kindled
fire in me which made
me entangle my limbs with hers
while our souls were mingling
in our mouths and we were bound
with diamond chains by the goddess
who rose from the green-blue sea.

O night forever sparkling with stars
you raise your radiant godhead
and offer soothing rest to the weary:
stand still—as you did at Hercules' birth
or on the darkened shores of the North
when Phoebus returns to the rain-filled South
and for months no day will dawn
but endless darkness reigns on earth—
only then can my burning lust be stilled.

Ad Sepulum disidaemonem

Miraris nullis templis mea labra moveri
    murmure dentifrago.
est ratio, taciti quia cernunt pectoris ora
    numina magna poli.
miraris videas raris me templa deorum
    passibus obterere.
est deus in nobis, non est quod numina pictis
    aedibus intuear.
miraris campos liquidos Phoebumque calentem
    me cupidum expetere.
hic mihi magna Iovis subit omnipotentis imago,
    templaque summa dei.
silva placet musis, urbs est inimica poetis
    et male sana cohors.
i nunc, et stolidis deride numina verbis
    nostra, procax Sepule.

To Sepulus, the Superstitious

You wonder why I don't murmur prayers
in church grinding my teeth.
This is the reason: the powers in heaven
hear also the silent prayers within me.
You wonder why but rarely you see me
shuffle my feet about in temples.
God lives in us, so I don't have to stare
at him in the pictures of painted idols.
You wonder why I prefer to go
into fields with running brooks and sunshine.
Here appears the Almighty to me in his splendor
and here his temples tower around me.
The Muses, too, love the woods, but hostile
to poets are cities and raging mobs.
So go and make fun of my faith with your stupid
prattle, Sepulus, fool that you are.

Translated by Reinhard P. Becker

MARTIN LUTHER

Martin Luther (1483–1546) became known far beyond the borders of his own country because of his confrontation with the most awesome power of his day: the Catholic Church. What is less known outside Germany is the fact that his German translation of the Bible was perhaps the single most formative influence upon the post-Medieval development of that language into a medium of poetic, philosophical, and religious expression. Maybe none of Luther's epoch-making activities had as benign, lasting, and admired an effect on his society as did his creation of the German Bible, which set a standard for poetic metaphors and literary tone, and which is a storehouse of sayings, maxims, and proverbial wisdom until today.

Of Luther's three famous treatises, *The Freedom of a Christian, The Babylonian Captivity of the Church,* and *To the Christian Nobility of the German Nation,* the last has been selected for inclusion here in its entirety because it articulates more concisely than the others the principal points of his attack on Rome and the Catholic Church.

Abbreviations

CIC —*Corpus Iuris Canonici*
CL —*Luthers Werke in Auswahl*
LW —American Edition of *Luther's Works*
MA³ —*Martin Luther. Ausgewählte Werke*
MPL —*Patrologia, Series Latina* (also as Migne)
PE —*Works of Martin Luther.* Philadelphia Edition
St. L.—D. *Martin Luthers sämmtliche Schriften*
WA —Weimar Edition of D. *Martin Luthers Werke*

To the Christian Nobility of the German Nation

JESUS

To the Esteemed and Reverend Master, Nicholas von Amsdorf, Licentiate of Holy Scripture, and Canon of Wittenberg, my special and kind friend, from Doctor Martin Luther.

The grace and peace of God be with you, esteemed, reverend, and dear sir and friend.

The time for silence is past, and the time to speak has come, as Ecclesiastes says [3:7]. I am carrying out our intention to put together a few points on the matter of the reform of the Christian estate, to be laid before the Christian nobility of the German nation, in the hope that God may help his Church through the laity, since the clergy, to whom this task more properly belongs, have grown quite indifferent. I am sending the whole thing to you, reverend sir, [that you may give] an opinion on it and, where necessary, improve it.

I know full well that I shall not escape the charge of presumption because I, a despised, inferior person, venture to address such high and great estates on such weighty matters, as if there were nobody else in the world except Doctor Luther to take up the cause of the Christian estate and give advice to such high-ranking people. I make no apologies no matter who demands them. Perhaps I owe my God and the world another work of folly. I intend to pay my debt honestly. And if I succeed, I shall for the time being become a court jester. And if I fail, I still have one advantage—no one need buy me a cap or put scissors to my head.[1] It is a question of who will put the bells on whom.[2] I must fulfill the proverb, "Whatever the world does, a monk must be in the picture, even if he has to be painted in."[3] More than once a fool has spoken wisely, and wise men have often been arrant fools. Paul says, "He who wishes to be wise must become a fool" [I Cor. 3:18]. Moreover, since I am not only a fool, but also a sworn doctor of Holy Scripture,[4] I am glad for the opportunity to fulfill my doctor's oath, even in the guise of a fool.

I beg you, give my apologies to those who are moderately intelligent, for I do not know how to earn the grace and favor of the superintelligent. I have often sought to do so with the greatest pains, but from now on I neither desire nor value their favor. God help us to seek not our own glory but his alone. Amen.

> At Wittenberg, in the monastery of the Augustinians,
> on the eve of St. John Baptist [June 23]
> in the year fifteen hundred and twenty.

To His Most Illustrious, Most Mighty, and Imperial Majesty, and to the Christian Nobility of the German Nation, from Doctor Martin Luther.

Grace and power from God, Most Illustrious Majesty, and most gracious and dear lords.

It is not from sheer impertinence or rashness that I, one poor man, have taken it upon myself to address your worships. All the estates of Christendom, particularly in Germany, are now oppressed by distress and affliction, and this has stirred not only me but everybody else to cry out time and time again and to pray for help. It has even compelled me now at this time to cry aloud that God may inspire someone with his Spirit to lend a helping hand to this distressed and wretched nation. Often the councils have made some pretense at reformation,[5] but their attempts have been cleverly frustrated by the guile of certain men, and things have gone from bad to worse. With God's help I intend to expose the wiles and wickedness of these men, so that they are shown up for what they are and may never again be so obstructive and destructive. God has given us a young man of noble birth as head of state,[6] and in him has awakened great hopes of good in many hearts. Presented with such an opportunity, we ought to apply ourselves and use this time of grace profitably.

The first and most important thing to do in this matter is to prepare ourselves in all seriousness. We must not start something by trusting in great power or human reason, even if all the power in the world were ours. For God cannot and will not suffer that a good work begin by relying upon one's own power and reason. He dashes such works to the ground, they do no good at all. As it says in Psalm 33 [:16], "No king is saved by his great might and no lord is saved by the greatness of his strength." I fear that this is why the good emperors Frederick I[7] and Frederick II[8] and many other German emperors were in former times shamefully oppressed and trodden underfoot by the popes, although all the world feared the emperors. It may be that they relied on their own might more than on God, and therefore had to fall. What was it in our own times that raised the bloodthirsty Julius II[9] to such heights? Nothing else, I fear, except that France, the Germans, and Venice relied upon themselves. The children of Benjamin slew forty-two thousand Israelites[10] because the latter relied on their own strength, Judges 30 [:21].

That it may not so fare with us and our noble Charles, we must realize that in this matter we are not dealing with men, but with the princes of hell. These princes could fill the world with war and bloodshed, but war and bloodshed do not overcome them. We must tackle this job by renouncing trust in physical force and trusting humbly in God. We must seek God's help through earnest prayer and fix our minds on nothing else than the misery and distress of suffering Christendom without regard to what evil men deserve. Otherwise, we may start the game with great prospects of success, but when we get into it the evil spirits will stir up such confusion that the whole world will swim in blood, and then nothing will come of it all. Let us act wisely, therefore, and in the fear of God. The more force we use, the greater our disaster if we do not act humbly and in the fear of God. If the popes and Romanists[11] have hitherto been able to set kings against each other by the Devil's help, they may well be able to do it again if we were to go ahead without the help of God on our own strength and by our own cunning.

The Romanists have very cleverly built three walls around themselves. Hitherto they have protected themselves by these walls in such a way that no one has been able to reform them. As a result, the whole of Christendom has fallen abominably.

In the first place, when pressed by the temporal power they have made decrees and declared that the temporal power had no jurisdiction over them, but that, on the contrary, the spiritual power is above the temporal. In the second place, when the attempt is made to reprove them with the Scriptures, they raise the objection that only the pope may interpret the Scriptures. In the third place, if threatened with a council, their story is that no one may summon a council but the pope.

In this way they have cunningly stolen our three rods from us, that they may go unpunished. They have ensconced themselves within the safe stronghold of these three walls so that they can practice all the knavery and wickedness which we see today. Even when they have been compelled to hold a council they have weakened its power in advance by putting the princes under oath to let them remain as they were.[12] In addition, they have given the pope full authority over all decisions of a council, so that it is all the same whether there are many councils or no councils. They only deceive us with puppet shows and sham fights. They fear terribly for their skin in a really free council! They have so intimidated kings and princes with this technique that they believe it would be an offense against God not to be obedient to the Romanists in all their knavish and ghoulish deceits.[13]

May God help us, and give us just one of those trumpets with which the walls of Jericho were overthrown[14] to blast down these walls of straw and paper in the same way and set free the Christian rods for the punishment of sin, [and] bring to light the craft and deceit of the devil, to the end that through punishment we may reform ourselves and once more attain God's favor.

Let us begin by attacking the first wall. It is pure invention that pope, bishop, priests, and monks are called the spiritual estate while princes, lords, artisans, and farmers are called the temporal estate. This is indeed a piece of deceit and hypocrisy. Yet no one need be intimidated by it, and for this reason: All Christians are truly of the spiritual estate, and there is no difference among them except that of office. Paul says in I Corinthians 12 [:12–13] that we are all one body, yet every member has its own work by which it serves the others. This is because we all have one baptism, one Gospel, one faith, and are all Christians alike; for baptism, Gospel, and faith alone make us spiritual and a Christian people.

The pope or bishop anoints, shaves heads,[15] ordains, consecrates, and prescribes garb different from that of the laity, but he can never make a man into a Christian or into a spiritual man by so doing. He might well make a man into a hypocrite or a humbug and blockhead,[16] but never a Christian or a spiritual man. As far as that goes, we are all consecrated priests through baptism, as St. Peter says in I Peter 2 [:9], "You are a royal priesthood and a priestly realm." The Apocalypse says, "Thou hast made us to be priests and kings by thy blood" [Rev. 5:9–10]. The consecration by pope or bishop would never make a priest, and if we had no higher consecration than that which pope or bishop gives, no one could say mass or preach a sermon or give absolution.

Therefore, when a bishop consecrates, it is nothing else than that in the place and stead of the whole community, all of whom have like power, he takes a person and charges him to exercise this power on behalf of the others. It is like ten brothers, all king's sons and equal heirs, choosing one of themselves to rule the inheritance in the interests of all. In one sense they are all kings and of equal power, and yet one of them is charged with the responsibility of ruling. To put it still more clearly: Suppose a group of earnest Christian laymen were taken prisoner and set down in a desert without an episcopally ordained priest among them. And suppose they were to come to a common mind there and then in the desert and elect one of their number, whether he were married[17] or not, and charge him to baptize, say mass, pronounce absolution, and preach the Gospel. Such a man would be as truly a priest as though he had been ordained by all the bishops and popes in the world. That is why in cases of necessity anyone can baptize and give absolution. This would be impossible if we were not all priests. Through canon law[18] the Romanists have almost destroyed and made unknown the wondrous grace and authority of baptism and justification. In times gone by, Christians used to choose their bishops and priests in this way from among their own number, and they were confirmed in their office by the other bishops without all the fuss that goes on nowadays. St. Augustine,[19] Ambrose,[20] and Cyprian[21] each became [a bishop in this way].

Since those who exercise secular authority have been baptized with the same baptism, and have the same faith and the same Gospel as the rest of us, we must admit that they are priests and bishops and we must regard their office as one which has a proper and useful place in the Christian community. For whoever comes out of the water of baptism can boast that he is already a consecrated priest, bishop, and pope, although of course it is not seemly that just anybody should exercise such office. Because we are all priests of equal standing, no one must push himself forward and take it upon himself, without our consent and election, to do that for which we all have equal authority. For no one dare take upon himself what is common to all without the authority and consent of the community. And should it happen that a person chosen for such office were deposed for abuse of trust, he would then be exactly what he was before. Therefore, a priest in Christendom is nothing else but an officeholder. As long as he holds office he takes precedence; where he is deposed, he is a peasant or a townsman like anybody else. Indeed, a priest is never a priest when he is deposed. But now the Romanists have invented *characteres indelebiles*[22] and say[23] that a deposed priest is nevertheless something different from a mere layman. They hold the illusion that a priest can never be anything other than a priest or ever become a layman. All this is just contrived talk, and human regulation.

It follows from this argument that there is no true, basic difference between laymen and priests, princes and bishops, between religious and secular, except for the sake of office and work, but not for the sake of status. They are all of the spiritual estate, all are truly priests, bishops, and popes. But they do not all have the same work to do. Just as all priests and monks do not have the same work. This is the teaching of St. Paul in Romans 12 [:4–5] and I Corinthians 12 [:12] and in I Peter 2 [:9], as I have said above, namely that we are all one body of Christ the Head, and all members one of another. Christ does not have two different bodies, one temporal, the other spiritual. There is but one Head and one body.

Therefore, just as those who are now called "spiritual," that is, priests, bishops, or popes, are neither different from other Christians nor superior to them, except that they are charged with the

administration of the word of God and the sacraments, which is
their work and office, so it is with the temporal authorities. They
bear the sword and rod in their hand to punish the wicked and
protect the good. A cobbler, a smith, a peasant—each has the work
and office of his trade, and yet they are all alike consecrated priests
and bishops. Further, everyone must benefit and serve every other
by means of his own work or office so that in this way many kinds
of work may be done for the bodily and spiritual welfare of the
community, just as all the members of the body serve one another
[I Cor. 12:14–26].

Consider for a moment how Christian is the decree which says
that the temporal power is not above the "spiritual estate" and
has no right to punish it.[24] That is as much as to say that the hand
shall not help the eye when it suffers pain. Is it not unnatural, not
to mention un-Christian, that one member does not help another
and prevent its destruction? In fact, the more honorable the member, the more the others ought to help. I say therefore that since
the temporal power is ordained of God to punish the wicked and
protect the good, it should be left free to perform its office in the
whole body of Christendom without restriction and without respect to persons, whether it affects pope, bishops, priests, monks,
nuns, or anyone else. If it were right to say that the temporal
power is inferior to all the spiritual estates (preacher, confessor,
or any spiritual office), and so prevent the temporal power from
doing its proper work, then the tailors, cobblers, stonemasons,
carpenters, cooks, innkeepers, farmers, and all the temporal crafts-
men should be prevented from providing pope, bishops, priests,
and monks with shoes, clothes, house, meat, and drink, as well as
from paying them any tribute. But if these laymen are allowed to
do their proper work without restriction, what then are the Romanist scribes doing with their own laws, which exempt them from
the jurisdiction of the temporal Christian authority? It is just so
that they can be free to do evil and fulfill what St. Peter said,
"False teachers will rise up among you who will deceive you, and
with their false and fanciful talk, they will take advantage of you"
[II Pet. 2:1–3].

For these reasons the temporal Christian authority ought to exercise its office without hindrance, regardless of whether it is pope,
bishop, or priest whom it affects. Whoever is guilty, let him suffer.
All that canon law has said to the contrary is the invention of

Romanist presumption. For thus St. Paul says to all Christians, "Let every soul (I take that to mean the pope's soul also) be subject to the temporal authority; for it does not bear the sword in vain, but serves God by punishing the wicked and benefiting the good" [Rom. 13:1, 4]. St. Peter, too, says, "Be subject to all human ordinances for the sake of the Lord, who so wills it" [I Pet. 2:13, 15]. He has also prophesied in II Peter 2 [:1] that such men would arise and despise the temporal authority. This is exactly what has happened through the canon law.

So, then, I think this first paper wall is overthrown. Inasmuch as the temporal power has become a member of the Christian body, it is a spiritual estate, even though its work is physical.[25] Therefore, its work should extend without hindrance to all the members of the whole body to punish and use force whenever guilt deserves or necessity demands, without regard to whether the culprit is pope, bishop, or priest. Let the Romanists hurl threats and bans about as they like. That is why guilty priests, when they are handed over to secular law, are first deprived of their priestly dignities.[26] This would not be right unless the secular sword previously had had authority over these priests by divine right. Moreover, it is intolerable that in canon law so much importance is attached to the freedom, life, and property of the clergy, as though the laity were not also as spiritual and as good Christians as they, or did not also belong to the Church. Why are your life and limb, your property and honor, so cheap and mine not, inasmuch as we are all Christians and have the same baptism, the same faith, the same Spirit, and all the rest? If a priest is murdered, the whole country is placed under interdict.[27] Why not when a peasant is murdered? How does this great difference come about between two men who are both Christians? It comes from the laws and fabrications of men.

Moreover, it can be no good spirit which has invented such exceptions and granted sin such license and impunity. For if it is our duty to strive against the words and works of the Devil and to drive him out in whatever way we can, as both Christ and His Apostles command us, how have we gotten into such a state that we have to do nothing and say nothing when the pope or his cohorts undertake devilish words and works? Ought we merely out of regard for these people allow the suppression of divine commandments and truth, which we have sworn in baptism to support with life and limb? Then we should have to answer for all the souls that would thereby be abandoned and led astray!

It must, therefore, have been the Chief Devil himself who said what is written in the canon law, that if the pope were so scandalously bad as to lead crowds of souls to the Devil, still he could not be deposed.[28] At Rome they build on this accursed and devilish foundation, and think that we should let all the world go to the Devil rather than resist their knavery. If the fact that one man is set over others were sufficient reason why he should not be punished, then no Christian could punish another, since Christ commanded that every man should esteem himself as the lowliest and the least [Matt. 18:4].

Where sin is, there is no longer any shielding from punishment. St. Gregory writes that we are indeed all equal, but guilt makes a man inferior to others.[29] Now we see how the Romanists treat Christendom. They take away its freedom without any proof from Scripture, at their own whim. But God, as well as the Apostles, made them subject to the temporal sword. It is to be feared that this is a game of the Antichrist,[30] or at any rate that his forerunner has appeared.

The second wall is still more loosely built and less substantial. The Romanists want to be the only masters of Holy Scripture, although they never learn a thing from the Bible all their life long. They assume the sole authority for themselves, and, quite unashamed, they play about with words before our very eyes, trying to persuade us that the pope cannot err in matters of faith,[31] regardless of whether he is righteous or wicked. Yet they cannot point to a single letter.[32] This is why so many heretical and unChristian, even unnatural, ordinances stand in the canon law. But there is no need to talk about these ordinances at present. Since these Romanists think the Holy Spirit never leaves them, no matter how ignorant and wicked they are, they become bold and decree only what they want. And if what they claim were true, why have Holy Scripture at all? Of what use is Scripture? Let us burn the Scripture and be satisfied with the unlearned gentlemen at Rome who possess the Holy Spirit! And yet the Holy Spirit can be possessed only by pious hearts. If I had not read the words with my own eyes,[33] I would not have believed it possible for the Devil to have made such stupid claims at Rome, and to have won supporters for them.

But so as not to fight them with mere words, we will quote the Scriptures. St. Paul says in I Corinthians 14 [:30], "If something better is revealed to anyone, though he is already sitting and listening to another in God's word, then the one who is speaking shall hold his peace and give place." What would be the point of this commandment if we were compelled to believe only the man who does the talking, or the man who is at the top? Even Christ said in John 6 [:45] that all Christians shall be taught by God. If it were to happen that the pope and his cohorts were wicked and not true Christians, were not taught by God and were without understanding, and at the same time some obscure person had a right understanding, why should the people not follow the obscure man? Has the pope not erred many times? Who would help Christendom when the pope erred if we did not have somebody we could trust more than him, somebody who had the Scriptures on his side?

Therefore, their claim that only the pope may interpret Scripture is an outrageous fancied fable. They cannot produce a single letter [of Scripture] to maintain that the interpretation of Scripture or the confirmation of its interpretation belongs to the pope alone. They themselves have usurped this power. And although they allege that this power was given to St. Peter when the keys were given him, it is clear enough that the keys were not given to Peter alone but to the whole community. Further, the keys were not ordained for doctrine or government, but only for the binding or loosing of sin.[34] Whatever else or whatever more they arrogate to themselves on the basis of the keys is a mere fabrication. But Christ's words to Peter, "I have prayed for you that your faith fail not" [Luke 22:32], cannot be applied to the pope, since the majority of the popes have been without faith, as they must themselves confess. Besides, it is not only for Peter that Christ prayed, but also for all Apostles and Christians, as He says in John 17 [:9, 20], "Father, I pray for those whom thou hast given me, and not for these only, but for all who believe on me through their word." Is that not clear enough?

Just think of it! The Romanists must admit that there are among us good Christians who have the true faith, spirit, understanding,

word, and mind of Christ. Why, then, should we reject the word
and understanding of good Christians and follow the pope, who
has neither faith nor the Spirit? To follow the pope would be to
deny the whole faith[35] as well as the Christian Church. Again, if
the article, "I believe in one holy Christian Church," is correct,
then the pope cannot be the only one who is right. Otherwise, we
would have to confess,[36] "I believe in the pope at Rome." This
would reduce the Christian Church to one man, and be nothing
else than a devilish and hellish error.

Besides, if we are all priests, as was said above, and all have one
faith, one Gospel, one sacrament,[37] why should we not also have
the power to test and judge what is right or wrong in matters of
faith? What becomes of Paul's words in I Corinthians 2 [:15]: "A
spiritual man judges all things, yet he is judged by no one"? And
II Corinthians 4 [:13]: "We all have one spirit of faith"? Why,
then, should not we perceive what is consistent with faith and
what is not, just as well as an unbelieving pope does?

We ought to become bold and free on the authority of all these
texts, and many others. We ought not to allow the Spirit of freedom (as Paul calls him [II Cor. 3:17]) to be frightened off by the
fabrications of the popes, but we ought to march boldly forward
and test all that they do, or leave undone, by our believing understanding of the Scriptures. We must compel the Romanists to
follow not their own interpretation but the better one. Long ago
Abraham had to listen to Sarah, although she was in more complete subjection to him than we are to anyone on earth [Gen.
21:12]. And Balaam's ass was wiser than the prophet himself
[Num. 22:21–35]. If God spoke then through an ass against a
prophet, why should he not be able even now to speak through a
righteous man against the pope? Similarly, St. Paul rebukes St.
Peter as a man in error in Galatians 2 [:11–12]. Therefore, it is
the duty of every Christian to espouse the cause of the faith, to
understand and defend it, and to denounce every error.

The third wall falls of itself when the first two are down. When
the pope acts contrary to the Scriptures, it is our duty to stand by
the Scriptures, to reprove him and to constrain him, according to
the word of Christ, Matthew 18[:15–17], "If your brother sins
against you, go and tell it to him, between you and him alone; if
he does not listen to you, then take one or two others with you;

if he does not listen to them, tell it to the church; if he does not listen to the church, consider him a heathen." Here every member is commanded to care for every other. How much more should we do this when the member that does evil is responsible for the government of the Church, and by his evildoing is the cause of much harm and offense to the rest! But if I am to accuse him before the Church, I must naturally call the Church together.

The Romanists have no basis in Scripture for their claim that the pope alone has the right to call or confirm a council.[38] This is just their own ruling, and it is only valid as long as it is not harmful to Christendom or contrary to the laws of God. Now when the pope deserves punishment, this ruling no longer obtains, for not to punish him by authority of a council is harmful to Christendom.

Thus we read in Acts 15 that it was not St. Peter who called the Apostolic Council but the Apostles and elders. If, then, that right had belonged to St. Peter alone, the council would not have been a Christian council, but a heretical *conciliabulum*.[39] Even the Council of Nicaea, the most famous of all councils, was neither called nor confirmed by the bishop of Rome, but by the emperor Constantine.[40] Many other emperors after him have done the same, and yet these councils were the most Christian of all.[41] But if the pope alone has the right to convene councils, then these councils would all have been heretical. Further, when I examine the councils the pope did summon, I find that they did nothing of special importance.

Therefore, when necessity demands it, and the pope is an offense to Christendom, the first man who is able should, as a true member of the whole body, do what he can to bring about a truly free council. No one can do this so well as the temporal authorities, especially since they are also fellow Christians, fellow priests, fellow members of the spiritual estate, fellow lords over all things. Whenever it is necessary or profitable they ought to exercise the office and work which they have received from God over everyone. Would it not be unnatural if a fire broke out in a city and everybody were to stand by and let it burn on and on and consume everything that could burn because nobody had the authority of the mayor, or because, perhaps, the fire broke out in the mayor's house? In such a situation is it not the duty of every citizen to arouse and summon the rest? How much more should be done in the spiritual city of Christ if a fire of offense breaks out, whether in the papal government, or anywhere else! The same argument holds if an enemy were to attack a city. The man who first roused the others deserves honor and gratitude. Why, then, should he not deserve honor who makes known the presence of the enemy from hell and rouses Christian people and calls them together?

But all their boasting about an authority which dare not be opposed amounts to nothing at all. Nobody in Christendom has authority to do injury or to forbid the resisting of injury. There is no authority in the Church except to promote good. Therefore, if the pope were to use his authority to prevent the calling of a free council, thereby preventing the improvement of the Church, we should have regard neither for him nor for his authority. And if he were to hurl his bans and thunderbolts, we should despise his conduct as that of a madman. On the contrary, we should excommunicate him and drive him out as best we could, relying completely upon God. This presumptuous authority of his is nothing. He does not even have such authority. He is quickly defeated by a single text of Scripture, where Paul says to the Corinthians, "God has given us authority not to ruin Christendom, but to build it up" [II Cor. 10:8]. Who wants to leap over the hurdle of this text? It is the power of the devil and of Antichrist which resists the things that serve to build up Christendom. Such power is not to be obeyed, but rather resisted with life, property, and with all our might and main.

Even though a miracle were to be done against the temporal authority on the pope's behalf, or if somebody were struck down by the plague—which they boast has sometimes happened—it should be considered as nothing but the work of the Devil designed to destroy our faith in God. Christ foretold this in Matthew 24 [:24], "False Christs and false prophets shall come in my name, who shall perform signs and wonders in order to deceive even the elect." And Paul says in II Thessalonians 2 [:9] that Antichrist shall, through the power of Satan, be mighty in false wonders.

Let us, therefore, hold fast to this: no Christian authority can do anything against Christ. As St. Paul says, "We can do nothing against Christ, only for Christ" [II Cor. 13:8]. But if an authority does anything against Christ, then that authority is the power of Antichrist and of the devil, even if it were to deluge us with wonders and plagues. Wonders and plagues prove nothing, especially in these evil latter days. The whole of Scripture foretells such false wonders. This is why we must hold fast to the word of God with firm faith, and then the Devil will soon drop his miracles!

With this I hope that all this wicked and lying terror with which the Romanists have long intimidated and dulled our conscience has been overcome, and that they, just like all of us, shall be made subject to the sword. They have no right to interpret Scripture merely by authority and without learning.[42] They have no authority to prevent a council, or even worse yet at their mere whim to pledge it, impose conditions on it, or deprive it of its freedom. When they do that they are truly in the fellowship of Antichrist and the Devil. They have nothing at all of Christ except the name.

We shall now look at the matters which ought to be properly dealt with in councils, matters with which popes, cardinals, bishops, and all scholars ought properly to be occupied day and night if they love Christ and His Church. But if this is not the case, let ordinary people[43] and the temporal authorities do it without regard to papal bans and fulminations, for an unjust ban is better than ten just and proper absolutions, and one unjust, improper absolution is worse than ten just bans.[44] Therefore, let us awake, dear Germans, and fear God more than man [Acts 5:29], lest we suffer the same fate of all the poor souls who are so lamentably lost through the shameless, devilish rule of the Romanists. The devil grows stronger[45] every day, if such a thing were possible, if such a hellish regime could grow any worse—a thing I can neither conceive nor believe.

1. It is horrible and shocking to see the head of Christendom, who boasts that he is the vicar of Christ and successor of St. Peter, going about in such a worldly and ostentatious style that neither king nor emperor can equal or approach him. He claims the title of "most holy" and "most spiritual," and yet he is more worldly than the world itself. He wears a triple crown,[46] whereas the highest monarchs wear but one. If that is like the poverty of Christ and of St. Peter, then it is a new and strange kind of likeness! When anybody says anything against it, the Romanists bleat, "Heresy!" They refuse to hear how un-Christian and ungodly all

this is. In my opinion, if the pope were to pray to God with tears, he would have to lay aside his triple crown, for the God we worship cannot put up with pride. In fact, the pope's office should be nothing else but to weep and pray for Christendom and to set an example of utter humility.

Be that as it may, this kind of splendor is offensive, and the pope is bound for the sake of his own salvation to set it aside. It was because of this kind of thing that St. Paul said, "Abstain from all practices which give offense" [I Thess. 5:22], and in Romans 12 [:17], "We should do good, not only in the sight of God, but also in the sight of all men." An ordinary bishop's miter ought to be good enough for the pope. It is in wisdom and holiness that he should be above his fellows. He ought to leave the crown of pride to Antichrist, as his predecessors did centuries ago. The Romanists say he is a lord of the earth. That is a lie! For Christ, whose vicar and vicegerent he claims to be, said to Pilate, "My kingdom is not of this world" [John 18:36]. No vicar's rule can go beyond that of his lord. Moreover, he is not the vicar of Christ glorified but of Christ crucified. As Paul says, "I was determined to know nothing among you save Christ, and him only as the crucified" [I Cor. 2:2], and in Philippians 2 [:5–7], "This is how you should regard yourselves, as you see in Christ, who emptied himself and took upon himself the form of a servant." Or again in I Corinthians 1 [:23], "We preach Christ, the crucified." Now the Romanists make the pope a vicar of the glorified Christ in heaven, and some of them have allowed the devil to rule them so completely that they have maintained that the pope is above the angels in heaven and has them at his command.[47] These are certainly the proper works of the real Antichrist.

2. Of what use to Christendom are those people called cardinals? I shall tell you. Italy and Germany have many rich monasteries, foundations,[48] benefices, and livings. No better way has been discovered of bringing all these to Rome than by creating cardinals and giving them bishoprics, monasteries, and prelacies for their own use[49] and so overthrowing the worship of God. You can see that Italy is now almost a wilderness: monasteries in ruins, bishoprics despoiled, the prelacies and the revenues of all the churches drawn to Rome, cities decayed, land and people ruined because services are no longer held and the word of God is not preached.

And why? Because the cardinals must have the income! No Turk could have devastated Italy and suppressed the worship of God so effectively!

Now that Italy is sucked dry, the Romanists are coming into Germany.[50] They have made a gentle beginning. But let us keep our eyes open! Germany shall soon be like Italy. We have a few cardinals already. The "drunken Germans" are not supposed to understand what the Romanists are up to until there is not a bishopric, a monastery, a living, a benefice, not a red cent left. Antichrist must seize the treasures of the earth, as it is prophesied [Dan. 11:39, 43]. It works like this: They skim the cream off the bishoprics, monasteries, and benefices, and because they do not yet venture to put them all to shameful use, as they have done in Italy, they in the meantime practice their holy cunning and couple together ten or twenty prelacies. They then tear off a little piece each year so as to make quite a tidy sum after all. The priory of Würzburg yields a thousand gulden; the priory of Bamberg also yields a sum; Mainz, Trier, and others. In this way one thousand or ten thousand gulden may be collected, so that a cardinal could live like a wealthy monarch at Rome.

When we have got that, we shall appoint thirty or forty cardinals in one day.[51] We shall give to one of them Mount St. Michael near Bamberg,[52] along with the bishopric of Würzburg, attach a few rich benefices to them until churches and cities are destitute, and then we will say, "We are Christ's vicars, and shepherds of Christ's sheep. The foolish, drunken Germans will just have to put up with it."

My advice is to make fewer cardinals, or to let the pope support them at his own expense. Twelve of them would be enough, and each of them might have an income of a thousand gulden.[53] How is it that we Germans must put up with such robbery and extortion of our goods at the hands of the pope? If the kingdom of France has prevented it,[54] why do we Germans let them make such fools and apes of us? We could put up with all this if they stole only our property, but they lay waste to the churches in so doing, rob Christ's sheep of their true shepherds, and debase the worship and word of God. If there were not a single cardinal, the Church would not perish. The cardinals do nothing to serve Christendom. They are only interested in the money side of bishoprics and prelacies, and they wrangle about them just as any thief might do.

3. If ninety-nine percent of the papal court[55] were abolished and only one percent kept, it would still be large enough to give answers in matters of faith. Today, however, there is such a swarm of parasites in that place called Rome, all of them boasting that they belong to the pope, that not even Babylon saw the likes of it. There are more than three thousand papal secretaries alone. Who could count the other officials? There are so many offices that one could scarcely count them. These are all the people lying in wait for the endowments and benefices of Germany as wolves lie in wait for the sheep. I believe that Germany now gives much more to the pope at Rome than it used to give to the emperors in ancient times. In fact, some have estimated that more than three hundred thousand gulden a year find their way from Germany to Rome. This money serves no use or purpose. We get nothing for it except scorn and contempt. And we still go on wondering why princes and nobles, cities and endowments, land and people, grow poor. We ought to marvel that we have anything left to eat!

Since we have now come to the heart of the matter, we will pause a little and let it be seen that the Germans are not quite such crass fools that they do not see or understand the sharp practices of the Romanists. I do not at the moment complain that God's command and Christian law are despised at Rome, for the state of Christendom is such—Rome in particular—that we may not complain of such exalted matters now. Nor am I complaining that natural law, or secular law, or even reason count for nothing. My complaint goes deeper than that. I complain that the Romanists do not keep their own self-devised canon law, though it is in fact just tyranny, avarice, and temporal splendor rather than law. That I shall now show you.

In former times German emperors and princes permitted the pope to receive annates from all the benefices of the German nation. This sum amounts to one half of the revenue of the first year from every single benefice.[56] This permission was given, however, so that by means of these large sums of money the pope might raise funds to fight against the Turks and infidels in defense of Christendom, and so that the burden of war might not rest too heavily upon the nobility, the clergy too should contribute something toward it. The popes have so far used the splendid and simple devotion of the German people—they have received this money for more than a hundred years and have now made it an obligatory tax and tribute, but they have not only accumulated no money, they have used it to endow many posts and positions at Rome and to provide salaries for these posts, as though the annates were a fixed rent.

When they pretend that they are about to fight the Turks, they send out emissaries to raise money. They often issue an indulgence[57] on the same pretext of fighting the Turks. They think that those half-witted Germans will always be gullible, stupid fools, and will just keep handing over money to them to satisfy their unspeakable greed. And they think this in spite of the fact that everybody knows that not a cent of the annates, or of the indulgence money, or of all the rest, is spent to fight the Turk. It all goes into their bottomless bag. They lie and deceive. They make laws and they make agreements with us, but they do not intend to keep a single letter of them. Yet all this is done in the holy names of Christ and St. Peter.

Now in this matter the German nation, bishops and princes, should consider that they, too, are Christians. They should rule the people entrusted to them in temporal and spiritual matters and protect them from these rapacious wolves in sheep's clothing who pretend to be their shepherds and rulers. And since the annates have been so shockingly abused, and not even kept for their original agreed purpose, [the bishops and princes] should not allow their land and people to be so pitilessly robbed and ruined contrary to all law. By decree either of the emperor or of the whole nation the annates should either be kept here at home or else abolished again. Since the Romanists do not keep to their agreement, they have no right to the annates. Therefore, the bishops and princes are responsible for punishing such thievery and robbery, or even preventing it, as the law requires.

In such a matter they ought to help the pope and strengthen his hand. Perhaps he is too weak to prevent such abuse single-handedly. Or, in those cases where he wants to defend and maintain his state of affairs, they ought to resist him and protect themselves from him as they would from a wolf or a tyrant, for he has no authority to do evil or fight on its behalf. Even if it were ever desirable to raise such funds for fighting the Turk, we ought to have enough sense at least to see that the German nation could be a better custodian of these funds than the pope. The German nation itself has enough people to wage the war if the money is available. It is the same with annates as it has been with many other Romanist pretenses.

Then, too, the year has been so divided between the pope and the ruling bishops and chapters that the pope has six months in the year (every other month) in which to bestow the benefices which become vacant in his months.[58] In this way almost all the best benefices have fallen into the hands of Rome, especially the very best livings and dignities.[59] And when they once fall into the hands of Rome, they never come out of them again, though a vacancy may never occur again in the pope's month. In this way the chapters are cheated. This is plain robbery, and the intention is to let nothing escape. Therefore it is high time to abolish the "papal months" altogether. Everything that has been taken to Rome in this way must be restored. The princes and nobles ought to take steps for the restitution of the stolen property, punish the thieves, and deprive of privilege those who have abused that privilege. If it is binding and valid for the pope, on the day after his election, to make regulations and laws in his chancery[60] by which our endowed chapters and livings are stolen from us—a thing he has absolutely no right to do—then it should be still more valid for Emperor Charles, on the day after his coronation,[61] to make rules and laws that not another benefice or living in all Germany should be allowed to pass into the hands of Rome by means of the "papal months." The livings which have already fallen into the hands of Rome should be restored and redeemed from these Romanist robbers. Charles V has the right to do this by virtue of his authority as ruler.

But now this Romanist See of avarice and robbery has not had the patience to wait for the time when all the benefices would fall to it one by one through this device of the "papal months." Rather, urged on by its insatiable appetite to get them all in its hands as speedily as possible, the Romanist See has devised a scheme whereby, in addition to the "annates" and "papal months," the benefices and livings should fall to Rome in three ways.

First, if anyone who holds a "free" living[62] should die in Rome or on a journey to Rome, his living becomes the property in perpetuity of the Romanist—I ought to say roguish—See.[63] But the Romanists do not want to be called robbers on this account, though they are guilty of robbery of a kind never heard of or read about before.

Second, if anyone belonging to the household of the pope or cardinals holds or takes over a benefice, or if anyone who had previously held a benefice subsequently enters the household of the pope or cardinals, [his living becomes the property in perpetuity of the Romanist See].[64] But who can count the household of the pope and cardinals? If he only goes on a pleasure ride, the pope takes with him three or four thousand on mules, all emperors and kings notwithstanding! Christ and St. Peter went on foot so that their successors might have all the more pomp and splendor. Now Avarice has cleverly thought out another scheme, and arranges it so that many even outside Rome have the name "member of the papal household" just as if they were in Rome. This is done for the sole purpose that, by the simple use of that pernicious phrase "member of the pope's household," all benefices may be brought to Rome and tied there for all time. Are not these vexatious and devilish little inventions? Let us beware! Soon Mainz, Magdeburg, and Halberstadt will quietly slip into the hands of Rome, and then the cardinalate will cost a pretty penny![65] After that they will make all the German bishops cardinals, and then there will be nothing left.

Third, when a dispute has started at Rome over a benefice.[66] In my opinion this is the commonest and widest road to bring livings into the hands of Rome. Even when there is no dispute here, countless knaves will be found at Rome who will unearth a dispute and snatch the benefices at will. Thus many a good priest must lose his living or pay a sum of money to avoid having his benefice disputed. Such a living, rightly or wrongly contested, becomes the property of the Roman See forever. It would be no wonder if God would rain fire and brimstone from heaven and sink Rome in the abyss, as he did Sodom and Gomorrah of old [Gen. 19:24]. Why should there be a pope in Christendom if his power is used for nothing else than for such gross wickedness and to protect and practice it? O noble princes and lords, how long will you leave your lands and your people naked and exposed to such ravening wolves?

Since even these practices were not enough, and Avarice grew impatient at the long time it took to get hold of all the bishoprics, my lord Avarice devised the fiction that the bishoprics should be nominally abroad but that their origin and foundation is at Rome. Furthermore, no bishop can be confirmed unless he pays a huge sum for his pallium[67] and binds himself with solemn oaths to the personal service of the pope. That explains why no bishop dares to act against the pope. That is what the Romanists were seeking when they imposed the oath. It also explains why all the richest bishoprics have fallen into debt and ruin. I am told that Mainz pays twenty thousand gulden.[68] That is the Romanists all over! To be sure, they decreed a long time ago in canon law that the pallium should be given without cost, that the number in the pope's household be reduced, disputes[69] lessened, and the chapters and bishops allowed their liberty. But this did not bring in money. So they have turned over a new leaf and taken all authority away from the bishops and chapters. These sit there like ciphers, and have neither office nor authority nor work. Everything is controlled by those arch-villains at Rome, almost right down to the office of sexton and bell ringer. Every dispute is called to Rome,[70] and everyone does just as he pleases, under cover of the pope's authority.

What has happened in this very year? The bishop of Strasbourg[71] wanted to govern his chapter properly and reform it in matters of worship. With this end in view he established certain godly and Christian regulations. But our dear friend the pope and the Holy Roman See wrecked and damned this holy and spiritual ordinance, all at the instigation of the priests. This is called feeding the sheep of Christ![72] That is how priests are strengthened against their own bishop, and how their disobedience to divine law is protected! Antichrist himself, I hope, will not dare to shame God so openly. There is your pope for you! Just as you have always wanted! Why did the pope do this? Ah! If one church were reformed, that would be a dangerous breakthrough. Rome might have to follow suit. Therefore, it is better that no priest be allowed to get along with another and, as we have grown accustomed to seeing right up to the present day, that kings and princes should be set at odds. It is better to flood the world with Christian blood, lest the unity of Christians compel the Holy Roman See to reform itself!

So far we have been getting an idea of how they deal with benefices which become vacant and free. But for tenderhearted Avarice, the free vacancies are too few. Therefore, he has kept a very close watch even on those benefices still occupied by their incumbents, so that these too can be made free, even though they are not now free. He does this in several ways.

First, Avarice lies in wait where fat prebends or bishoprics are held by an old and sick man, or even by one with an alleged disability. The Holy See gives a coadjutor, that is, an assistant, to an incumbent of this kind. This is done without the holder's consent or gratitude, and for the benefit of the coadjutor, because he is a member of the pope's "household," or because he has paid for it or has otherwise earned it by some sort of service to Rome. In this case the free rights of the chapter or the rights of the incumbent are disregarded, and the whole thing falls into the hands of Rome.

Second, there is the little word "commend." This means the pope puts a cardinal, or another of his underlings, in charge of a rich, prosperous monastery,[73] just as if I were to give you a hundred gulden to keep. This does not mean to give the monastery or bestow it. Nor does it mean abolishing it or the divine service. It means quite simply to give it into his keeping. Not that he to whom it is entrusted is to care for it or build it up, but he is to drive out the incumbent, receive the goods and revenues, and install some apostate, renegade monk[74] or another, who accepts five or six gulden a year and sits all day long in the church selling pictures and images to the pilgrims, so that neither prayers nor masses are said in that place anymore. If this were to be called destroying monasteries and abolishing the worship of God, then the pope would have to be called a destroyer of Christendom and an abolisher of divine worship. He certainly does well at it! But this would be harsh language for Rome, so they have to call it a "commend," or a command to take over the charge of the monastery. The pope can make "commends" of four or more of these monasteries in one year, any single one of which may have an income of more than six thousand gulden. This is how the Romanists increase the worship of God and maintain the monasteries! Even the Germans are beginning to find that out!

Third, there are some benefices they call *incompatabilia*,[75] which, according to the ordinances of canon law, cannot be held at the same time, such as two parishes, two bishoprics, and the like. In these cases the Holy Roman See of Avarice evades canon law by making glosses[76] to its own advantage, called *unio* and *incorporatio.* This means that the pope incorporates many *incompatabilia* into one single unity, so that each is a part of every other and all of them together are looked upon as one benefice. They are then no longer *incompatabilia,* and the holy canon law is satisfied because it is no longer binding, except upon those who do not buy these glosses from the pope or his *datarius.*[77] The *unio,* that is, the uniting, is very similar. The pope combines many such benefices like a bundle of sticks, and they are all regarded as one benefice. There is at present a certain court follower in Rome who alone holds twenty-two parishes, seven priories, as well as forty-four benefices. All these are held by the help of that masterly gloss, which declares that this is not against canon law. What the cardinals and other prelates get out of it is anybody's guess. And this is the way the Germans are to have their purses emptied and their itch scratched.[78]

Another of these glosses is the *administratio.* This means a man may hold, in addition to his bishopric, some abbacy or dignity and all its emoluments, without having the title attached to it. He is simply called the "administrator."[79] At Rome it is sufficient to change a word or two but leave the actuality what it was before. It is as if I were to teach that we were now to call the brothel-keeper the mayor's wife. She still remains what she was before. This kind of Romish regime Peter foretold in II Peter 2 [:1, 3]: "False teachers will come who will deal with you in greed and lying words for their gain."

Our worthy Roman Avarice has devised another technique. He sells or disposes of livings on the condition that the vendor or disposer retain reversionary rights to them. In that event, when the incumbent dies, the benefices automatically revert to him who had sold, disposed, or surrendered them in the first instance. In this way they have made hereditary property out of the benefices. Nobody else can come into possession of them except the man to whom the seller is willing to dispose of them, or to whom he bequeaths his rights at death. Besides, there are many who transfer to another the mere title to a benefice, but from which the title-holder does not draw a cent. Today, too, it has become an established custom to confer a benefice on a man while reserving a portion of the annual income for oneself.[80] This used to be called simony.[81] There are many more things of this sort than can be counted. They treat benefices more shamefully than the heathen soldiers treated Christ's clothes at the foot of the cross.[82]

But all that has been said up till now has been going on for so long that it has become established custom. Yet Avarice has devised one more thing, which I hope may be his last and choke him. The pope has a noble little device called *pectoralis reservatio*, meaning mental reservation, and *proprius motus*, meaning the arbitrary will of his authority.[83] It goes like this: A certain man goes to Rome and succeeds in procuring a benefice. It is duly signed and sealed in the customary manner. Then another candidate comes along, who brings money or else has rendered services to the pope, which we shall not mention here, and desires the same benefice of the pope. The pope then gives it to him and takes it away from the other.[84] If anybody complains that this is not right, then the Most Holy Father has to find some excuse lest he be accused of a flagrant violation of the [canon] law. He then says that he had mentally reserved that particular benefice to himself and had retained full rights of disposal over it, although he had neither given it a thought in his life nor even heard of it. In this way he has now found his usual little gloss. As pope he can tell lies, deceive, and make everybody look like a fool. And all this he does openly and unashamedly. And yet he still wants to be the head of Christendom, but lets himself be ruled by the evil spirit in obvious lies.

The arbitrary and deceptive reservation of the pope only creates a state of affairs in Rome that defies description. There is buying, selling, bartering, changing, trading, drunkenness, lying, deceiving, robbing, stealing, luxury, harlotry, knavery, and every sort of contempt of God. Even the rule of the Antichrist could not be more scandalous. Venice, Antwerp, and Cairo have nothing on this fair at Rome and all that goes on there.[85] In these places there is still some regard for right and reason, but in Rome the Devil himself is in charge. And out of this sea the same kind of morality flows into all the world. Is it any wonder that people like this are terrified of reformation and of a free council, and prefer rather to set all the kings and princes at enmity lest in their unity they should call a council? Who could bear to have such villainy brought to light?

Finally, the pope has built his own store for all this noble commerce, that is, the house of the *datarius* in Rome. All who deal in benefices and livings must go there. Here they have to buy their glosses, and transact their business, and get authority to practice such arch-knavery. There was a time when Rome was still gracious. In those days people had to buy justice or suppress it with money. But Rome has become so expensive today that it allows no one to practice knavery unless he has first bought the right to do so. If that is not a brothel, then I do not know what brothels are.

If you have money in this establishment, you can obtain all these things we have just discussed. Indeed, not just these! Here usury becomes honest money, the possession of property acquired by theft or robbery is legalized. Here vows are dissolved; monks are granted liberty to leave their orders. Here marriage is on sale to the clergy. Here bastards can be legitimized. Here all dishonor and shame can be made to look like honor and glory. Here every kind of iniquity and evil is knighted or raised to nobility. Here marriage is permitted which is within the prohibited relationships or otherwise forbidden. O what assessing and fleecing goes on there! It seems as though canon law were instituted solely for the purpose of making a great deal of money. Whoever would be a Christian has to buy his way out of its provisions.[86] In fact, here the Devil becomes a saint, and a god as well. What cannot be done anywhere else in heaven or on earth can be done in this place. They call these things *compositiones!* Compositions indeed! Better named confusions.[87] They put nothing together, but break everything all up! Compared with the exactions of this bureau, the Rhine toll[88] is but a drop in the bucket.

Let no one accuse me of exaggeration. It is all so open that even in Rome they have to admit that the state of affairs is more revolting and worse than anyone can say. I have not yet stirred the real hellish broth of their personal vices—nor do I want to. I speak only of general, current matters, and still words fail me. The bishops, priests, and above all the doctors in the universities ought to have done their duty and with common accord written against such goings-on and cried out against them. This is what they are paid to do! Just turn the page over, and then you'll find out.[89]

One final word remains, and I am bound to say it. Since this boundless Avarice is not satisfied with all this wealth, wealth with which three great kings would be content, he now begins to transfer this trade and sell it to the Fuggers of Augsburg.[90] The lending, trading, and buying of bishoprics and benefices, and the commerce in ecclesiastical holdings, have now come to the right place. Now spiritual and secular goods have become one. I would now like to hear of somebody clever enough to imagine what Roman Avarice could do more than what it has already done, unless perhaps Fugger were to transfer or sell this present combination of two lines of business to somebody else. I really think it has just reached the limit.

As for what they have stolen in all lands, and still steal and extort, through indulgences, bulls, letters of confession,[91] butter letters,[92] and other *confessionalia*[93]—all this is just patchwork. It is like casting one devil into hell. Not that these bring in little money, for a powerful king could well support himself on such proceeds, but it is not to be compared with the streams of treasure referred to above. I shall say nothing at present about where this indulgence money has gone. I shall have more to say about that later. The Campoflore[94] and the Belvindere[95] and certain other places probably know something about that.

Since, then, such devilish rule is not only barefaced robbery, deceit, and the tyranny of hell's portals, but ruinous to the body and soul of Christendom, it is our duty to exercise all diligence to protect Christendom from such misery and destruction. If we want to fight against the Turks, let us begin here where they are worst of all. If we are right in hanging thieves and beheading robbers, why should we let Roman Avarice go free? He is the worst thief and robber that has ever been or could ever come into the world, and all in the holy name of Christ and St. Peter! Who can put up with it a moment longer and say nothing? Almost everything Avarice possesses has been gotten by theft and robbery. It has never been otherwise, as all the history books prove. The pope never purchased such extensive holdings that the income from his *officia*[96] should amount to one million ducats, over and above the gold mines we have just been discussing and the income from his lands. Nor did Christ and St. Peter bequeath it to him. Neither has anyone given or lent it to him. Neither is it his by virtue of ancient rights or usage. Tell me, then, from what source he could have got it? Learn a lesson from this, and watch carefully what they are after and what they say when they send out their legates to collect money to fight the Turks.

Now, although I am too insignificant a man to make propositions for the improvement of this dreadful state of affairs, nevertheless I shall sing my fool's song through to the end and say, so far as I am able, what could and should be done, either by the temporal authority or by a general council.

1. Every prince, every noble, every city should henceforth forbid their subjects to pay annates to Rome and should abolish them entirely. The pope has broken the agreement and made the annates a robbery to the injury and shame of the whole German nation. He gives them to his friends, sells them for huge sums of money, and uses them to endow offices. In so doing, he has lost his right to them and deserves punishment. Consequently, the temporal authority is under obligation to protect the innocent and prevent injustice, as Paul teaches in Romans 13, and St. Peter in I Peter 2 [:14], and even the canon law in Case 16, Question 7, in the *de filiis* clause.[97] Thus it has come about that they say to the pope and his crowd, *"Tu ora,* thou shalt pray"; to the emperor and his servants, *"Tu protege,* thou shalt protect"; to the common man, *"Tu labora,* thou shalt work," not however as though everyone were not to pray, protect, and work. For the man who is diligent in his work prays, protects, and works in all that he does. But everyone should have his own special work assigned him.

2. Since the pope with his Romanist practices—his commends, coadjutors, reservations, *gratiae expectativae,*[98] papal months, incorporations, unions, pensions, pallia, chancery rules, and such knavery—usurps for himself all the German foundations without authority and right, and gives and sells them to foreigners at Rome who do nothing for Germany in return, and since he robs the local bishops of their rights and makes mere ciphers and dummies of them, and thereby acts contrary to his own canon law, common sense, and reason, it has finally reached the point where the livings and benefices are sold to coarse, unlettered asses and ignorant knaves at Rome out of sheer greed. Pious and learned people do

not benefit from the service or skill of these fellows. Consequently the poor German people must go without competent and learned prelates and go from bad to worse.

For this reason the Christian nobility should set itself against the pope as against a common enemy and destroyer of Christendom for the salvation of the poor souls who perish because of this tyranny. The Christian nobility should ordain, order, and decree that henceforth no further benefice shall be drawn into the hands of Rome, and that hereafter no appointment shall be obtained there in any manner whatsoever, but that the benefices should be dragged from this tyrannical authority and kept out of his reach. The nobility should restore to the local bishops their right and responsibility to administer the benefices in the German nation to the best of their ability. And when a lackey comes along from Rome he should be given a strict order to keep out, to jump into the Rhine or the nearest river, and give the Romish ban with all its seals and letters a nice, cool dip. If this happened, they would sit up and take notice in Rome. They would not think that the Germans are always dull and drunk, but have really become Christian again. They would realize that the Germans do not intend to permit the holy name of Christ, in whose name all this knavery and destruction of souls goes on, to be scoffed and scorned any longer, and that they have more regard for God's honor than for the authority of men.

3. An imperial law should be issued that no bishop's cloak and no confirmation of any dignity whatsoever shall henceforth be secured from Rome, but that the ordinance of the most holy and famous Council of Nicaea[99] be restored. This ordinance decreed that a bishop shall be confirmed by the two nearest bishops or by the archbishop. If the pope breaks the statutes of this and of all other councils, what is the use of holding councils? Who has given him the authority to despise the decisions of councils and tear them to shreds like this?

This is all the more reason for us to depose all bishops, archbishops, and primates and make ordinary parsons of them, with only the pope as their superior, as he now is. The pope allows no proper authority or responsibility to the bishops, archbishops, and primates. He usurps everything for himself and lets them keep only the name and the empty title. It has even gone so far that by papal exemption [100] the monasteries, abbots, and prelates as well are excepted from the regular authority of the bishops. Consequently there is no longer any order in Christendom. The inevitable result of all this is what has happened already: relaxation of punishment, and license to do evil all over the world. I certainly fear that the pope may properly be called "the man of sin" [II Thess. 2:3]. Who but the pope can be blamed for there being no discipline, no punishment, no rule, no order in Christendom? By his usurpation of power he ties the prelates' hands and takes away their rod of discipline. He opens his hands to all those set under him, and gives away or sells their release. [101]

Lest the pope complain that he is being robbed of his authority, it should be decreed that in those cases where the primates or the archbishops are unable to settle a case, or when a dispute arises between them, then the matter should be laid before the pope, but not every little thing. It was done this way in former times, and this was the way the famous Council of Nicaea [102] decreed. Whatever can be settled without the pope, then, should be so settled so that his holiness is not burdened with such minor matters, but gives himself to prayer, study, and the care of all Christendom. This is what he claims to do. This is what the Apostles did. They said in Acts 6 [:2–4], "It is not right that we should leave the word of God and serve tables, but we will hold to preaching and prayer, and set others over that work." But now Rome stands for nothing else than the despising of the Gospel and prayer, and for the serving of tables, that is, temporal things. The rule of the Apostles and of the pope have as much in common as Christ has with Lucifer, heaven with hell, night with day. Yet the pope is called "Vicar of Christ" and "Successor to the Apostles."

4. It should be decreed that no temporal matter is to be referred to Rome, but that all such cases shall be left to the temporal authority, as the Romanists themselves prescribe in that canon law of theirs, which they do not observe. It should be the pope's duty to be the most learned in the Scriptures and the holiest (not in the name only but in fact) and to regulate matters which concern the faith and holy life of Christians. He should hold the primates and archbishops to this task, and help them in dealing with these matters and taking care of these responsibilities. This is what St. Paul teaches in I Corinthians 6 [:7], and he takes the Corinthians se-

verely to task for their concern with worldly things. That such matters are dealt with in Rome causes unbearable grief in every land. It increases the costs, and, moreover, these judges do not know the usage, laws, and customs of these lands, so that they often do violence to the facts and base their decisions on their own laws and precedents. As a result the contesting parties often suffer injustice.

In addition, the horrible extortion practiced by the judges in the bishops' courts[103] must be forbidden in every diocese so that they no longer judge anything except matters of faith and morals, and leave matters of money and property, life and honor, to the temporal judges. The temporal authorities, therefore, should not permit sentences of excommunication and exile to be passed where faith and morality are not involved. Spiritual authorities should rule over matters which are spiritual; this is just a matter of common sense. But spiritual matters are not money or material things; they are faith and good works.

Nevertheless, it might be granted that cases concerning benefices or livings be tried before bishops, archbishops, and primates. Therefore, to settle disputes and disagreements, it might be possible for the primate of Germany to hold a general consistory court with its auditors and chancellors.[104] This court should have control of the *signaturae gratiae* and *signaturae justitiae*,[105] which are now controlled at Rome, and to this court of appeal the cases in Germany would normally be brought and tried. These courts ought not to be paid for by chance presents and gifts, as is the practice at Rome, by which they have grown accustomed to selling justice and injustice. They are forced to do this at Rome because the pope does not pay them a salary, but lets them grow fat from gifts. The fact is that at Rome no one bothers now about what is right or wrong, only about what is money and what is not. This court, however, might be paid from the annates, or in some other way devised by those who are more clever and more experienced in these things than I. All I seek to do is to arouse and set to thinking those who have the ability and inclination to help the German nation to be free and Christian again after the wretched, heathenish, and un-Christian rule of the pope.

5. Reservations should no longer be valid, and no more bene-

fices should be seized by Rome, even if the incumbent dies, or there is a dispute, or even if the incumbent is a member of the pope's household or on the staff of a cardinal. And it must be strictly forbidden and prevented for any member of the papal court to contest any benefice whatsoever, to summon pious priests to court, harass them, or force them into lawsuits. If, in consequence of this prohibition, any ban or ecclesiastical pressure should come from Rome, it should be disregarded, just as though a thief were to put a man under the ban because he would not let him steal. Indeed, they should be severely punished for blasphemous misuse of the ban and the divine name to strengthen their hand at robbery. They want to drive us with their threats, which are only lies and fabrications, to the point where we put up with, yes, even praise, such blasphemy of God's name and such abuse of spiritual authority. They want to force us to be partakers in their rascality in the sight of God. We are responsible before God to oppose them, as St. Paul in Romans 1 [:32] reproves as worthy of death not only those who do such things, but also those who approve and permit them to be done. Most unbearable of all is the lying *reservatio pectoralis,* [106] whereby Christendom is so scandalously and openly put to shame and scorn because its head deals with open lies and for filthy lucre unashamedly deceives and fools everybody.

6. The *casus reservati,* reserved cases,[107] should also be abolished. They are not only the means of extorting much money from the people, but by means of them the ruthless tyrants ensnare and confuse many tender consciences, intolerably injuring their faith in God. This is especially true of the ridiculous, childish cases they make such a fuss about in the bull *Coena domini,* [108] sins which should not even be called everyday sins, much less so great that the pope cannot remit them by indulgence. Examples of these sins are hindering a pilgrim on his way to Rome, supplying weapons to the Turk, or counterfeiting papal letters.[109] They make fools of us with such crude, silly, clumsy goings-on! Sodom and Gomorrah, and all those sins which are or may be committed against the commandments of God, are not reserved cases. But what God has never commanded, what they themselves have imagined—these must be reserved cases. The only reason for all this is to make sure that no one will be prevented from bringing money to Rome,

so that the Romanists may live in the lap of luxury, safe from the Turks, and by their wanton, worthless bulls and letters keep the world subjected to their tyranny.

Every priest simply ought to know, and a decree should publicly be made, that no secret, undenounced sin constitutes a reserved case; and that every priest has the power to remit every sin no matter what it is. Where sins are secret, neither abbot, bishop, nor pope has the power to reserve one to himself. If they did that, their action would be null and void. They ought even to be punished as men who without any right at all presume to make judgments in God's stead, and thereby ensnare and burden poor and ignorant consciences. In those cases, however, where open and notorious sins are committed, especially sins against God's commandment, then there are indeed grounds for reserved cases. But even then there should not be too many of them, and they should not be reserved arbitrarily and without cause. For Christ did not set tyrants in his church, but shepherds, as Peter said in the last chapter of his first epistle [I Pet. 5:2–3].

7. The Roman See should do away with the *officia,* and cut down the creeping, crawling swarm of vermin at Rome, so that the pope's household can be supported out of the pope's own pocket. The pope should not allow his court to surpass the courts of all kings in pomp and extravagance, because this kind of thing not only has never been of any use to the cause of the Christian faith, but has kept the courtesans from study and prayer until they are hardly able to speak about the faith at all. This they proved quite flagrantly at this last Roman council,[110] in which, among many other childish and frivolous things, they decreed that the soul of man is immortal and that every priest must say his prayers once a month unless he wants to lose his benefice. How can the affairs of Christendom and matters of faith be settled by men who are hardened and blinded by gross avarice, wealth, and worldly splendor, and who now for the first time decree that the soul is immortal? It is no small shame to the whole of Christendom that they deal so disgracefully with the faith at Rome. If they had less wealth and pomp, they could pray and study more diligently to be worthy and diligent in dealing with matters of faith, as was the case in ancient times when bishops did not presume to be the kings of kings.

8. The harsh and terrible oaths which the bishops are wrongfully compelled to swear should be abolished. These oaths bind the bishops like servants, and are decreed in that arbitrary, stupid, worthless, and unlearned chapter, *Significasti*.[111] Is it not enough that they burden us in body, soul, and property with their countless foolish laws by which they weaken faith and waste Christendom, without also making a prisoner of the bishop both as a person as well as in his office and function? In addition, they have also assumed the investiture,[112] which in ancient times was the right of the German emperor, and in France and other countries investiture still belongs to the king. They had great wars and disputes with the emperors about this matter until finally they had the brazen effrontery to take it over, and have held it until now; just as though the Germans more than all other Christians on earth had to be the country bumpkins of the pope and the Romanist See and do and put up with what no one else will either put up with or do. Since this is sheer robbery and violence, hinders the regular authority of the bishop, and injures poor souls, the emperor and his nobles are duty-bound to prevent and punish such tyranny.

9. The pope should have no authority over the emperor, except the right to anoint and crown him at the altar just as a bishop crowns a king.[113] We should never again yield to that devilish pride which requires the emperor to kiss the pope's feet, or sit at his feet, or, as they say, hold his stirrup or the bridle of his mule when he mounts to go riding. Still less should he do homage and swear faithful allegiance to the pope as the popes brazenly demand as though they had a right to it. The chapter *Solite*,[114] which sets papal authority above imperial authority, is not worth a cent, and the same goes for all those who base their authority on it or pay any deference to it. For it does nothing else than force the holy words of God, and wrest them out of their true meaning to conform to their own fond imaginations, as I have shown in a Latin treatise.[115]

This most extreme, arrogant, and wanton presumption of the pope has been devised by the Devil, who under cover of this intends to usher in the Antichrist and raise the pope above God, as many are now doing and even have already done. It is not proper for the pope to exalt himself above the temporal authorities, except in spiritual offices such as preaching and giving absolution.

In other matters the pope is subject to the crown, as Paul and Peter teach in Romans 13 [:1–7] and I Peter 2 [:13], and as I have explained above.[116]

The pope is not a vicar of Christ in heaven, but only of Christ as He walked the earth. Christ in heaven, in the form of a ruler, needs no vicar, but sits on His throne and sees everything, does everything, knows everything, and has all power. But Christ needs a vicar in the form of a servant, the form in which He went about on earth, working, preaching, suffering, and dying. Now the Romanists turn all that upside down. They take the heavenly and kingly form from Christ and give it to the pope, and leave the form of a servant to perish completely. He might almost be the Counter-Christ, whom the Scriptures call Antichrist, for all his nature, work, and pretensions run counter to Christ and only blot out Christ's nature and destroy His work.

It is also ridiculous and childish for the pope, on the basis of such perverted and deluded reasoning, to claim in his decretal *Pastoralis* [117] that he is rightful heir to the empire in the event of a vacancy. Who has given him this right? Was it Christ when He said, "The princes of the Gentiles are lords, but it shall not be so among you" [Luke 22:25–26]? Or did Peter bequeath it to him? It makes me angry that we have to read and learn such shameless, gross, and idiotic lies in the canon law, and must even hold them as Christian doctrine when they are devilish lies.

That impossible lie, the *Donation of Constantine,* [118] is the same sort of thing. It must have been some special plague from God that so many intelligent people have let themselves be talked into accepting such lies. They are so crude and clumsy that I should imagine any drunken peasant could lie more adroitly and skillfully. How can a man rule and at the same time preach, pray, study, and care for the poor? Yet these are the duties which most properly and peculiarly belong to the pope, and they were so earnestly imposed by Christ that He even forbade His disciples to take cloak or money with them [Matt. 10:9–10]. Christ commanded this because it is almost impossible for anybody to fulfill these duties if he has to look after one single household. Yet the pope would rule an empire and still remain pope. This is what those rogues have thought up who, under the cover of the pope's name, would like to be lords of the world and would gladly restore the Roman Empire to its former state through the pope and in the name of Christ.

10. The pope should restrain himself, take his fingers out of the pie, and claim no title to the kingdom of Naples and Sicily.[119] He has exactly as much right to that kingdom as I have, and yet he wants to be its overlord. It is property gotten by robbery and violence, like almost all his other possessions. The emperor, therefore, should not grant him this realm, and where it has been granted, he should no longer give his consent. Instead, he should draw the pope's attention to the Bible and the prayer book, that he preach and pray and leave the government of lands and people—especially those that no one has given to him—to the temporal lords.

The same goes for Bologna, Imola, Vicenza, Ravenna, and all the territories in the March of Ancona, Romagna, and other lands which the pope has seized by force and possesses without right.[120] Moreover, the pope has meddled in these things against every express command of Christ and St. Paul. For as St. Paul says, "No one should be entangled in worldly affairs who should tend to being a soldier of God." [121] Now the pope should be the head and chief of these soldiers, and yet he meddles in worldly affairs more than any emperor or king. We have to pull him out of these affairs and let him tend to being a soldier. Even Christ, whose vicar the pope boasts he is, was never willing to have anything to do with temporal rule. In fact, when somebody sought a judgment from Him in the matter of a brother's action, He said to that man, "Who made me a judge over you?" [Luke 12:14]. But the pope rushes in without invitation and boldly takes hold of everything as if he were a god, until he no longer knows who Christ is, whose vicar he pretends to be.

11. Further, the kissing of the pope's feet should cease. It is an un-Christian, indeed, an anti-Christian thing for a poor sinful man, to let his feet be kissed by one who is a hundred times better than himself. If it is done in honor of his authority, why does the pope not do the same to others in honor of their holiness? Compare them with each other—Christ and the pope. Christ washed His disciples' feet and dried them but the disciples never washed His feet [John 13:4–16]. The pope, as though he were higher than Christ, turns that about, and allows his feet to be kissed as a great

favor. Though properly, if anyone wanted to do so, the pope ought to use all his power to prevent it, as did St. Paul and Barnabas, who would not let the people of Lystra pay them divine honor, but said, "We are men like you" [Acts 14:15]. But our flatterers have gone so far as to make an idol [of the pope] for us, so that no one fears or honors God as much as he fears and honors the pope. They will stand for that, but not for diminishing the pope's majesty by so much as a hairbreadth. If they were only Christian and esteemed God's honor more than their own, the pope would never be happy to see God's honor despised and his own exalted. Nor would he let anyone honor him until he saw that God's honor was once more exalted and raised higher than his own.

Another example [122] of the same scandalous pride is that the pope is not satisfied to ride or be driven, but, although he is strong and in good health, he has himself borne by men like an idol and with unheard-of splendor. Dear readers, how does such satanic pride compare with Christ, who went on foot, as did all His disciples? Where has there ever been a worldly monarch who went about in such worldly pomp and glory as he who wants to be the head of all those who ought to despise and flee from the pomp and vanity of this world, that is, the Christians? Not that we should bother ourselves very much about him as a person, but we certainly ought to fear the wrath of God if we flatter this sort of pride and do not show our indignation. It is enough for the pope to rant and play the fool in this way. But it is more than enough for us to approve of it and let it go on.

What Christian heart can or ought to take pleasure in seeing that when the pope wishes to receive communion, he sits quietly like a gracious lord and has the sacrament brought to him on a golden rod by a bowing cardinal on bended knee? As though the holy sacrament were not worthy enough for the pope, a poor, stinking sinner, to rise and show respect to his God, when all other Christians, who are much holier than the Most Holy Father the pope, receive it with all due reverence! Would it be a wonder if God sent down a plague upon us all because we tolerate such dishonor of God by our prelates and praise them for doing it, and because we share in this damnable pride by our silence or by our flattery?

It is the same when the pope carries the sacrament in procession. He must be carried, but the sacrament is set before him like a flagon of wine on a table. At Rome Christ counts for nothing, but the pope counts for everything. And yet the Romanists want to compel us—and even use threats—to approve, praise, and honor these sins of the Antichrist, even though they are against God and all Christian doctrine. Help us, O God, to get a free, general council which will teach the pope that he, too, is a man, and not more than God, as he sets himself up to be!

12. Pilgrimages to Rome should either be abolished or else no one should be allowed to make such a pilgrimage for reasons of curiosity or his own pious devotion, unless it is first acknowledged by his parish priest, his town authorities, or his overlord that he has a good and sufficient reason for doing so. I say this not because pilgrimages are bad, but because they are ill-advised at this time. At Rome men do not find a good example, but, on the contrary, pure scandal. The Romanists themselves devised the saying, "The nearer Rome, the worse Christians." After a pilgrimage to Rome men bring back with them contempt for God and his commandments. They say the first time a man goes to Rome he seeks a rascal; the second time he finds one; the third time he brings him back home with him.[123] Now, however, the Romanists have grown so clever that they can make three pilgrimages in one! The pilgrims have brought back such a pretty mess of experiences from Rome that it would be better never to have seen Rome or known anything about it.

Even if this were not the case there is still another and a better reason: simple people [124] are led into error and misunderstanding of the divine command. Such people think that going on a pilgrimage is a precious good work. This is not true. It is a very small good work—frequently it is evil and misleading, for God has not commanded it. But God has commanded that a man should care for his wife and children, perform the duties of a husband, and serve and help his neighbor. Today a man makes a pilgrimage to Rome and spends fifty, maybe a hundred, gulden, something nobody commanded him to do. He permits his wife and child, or his neighbor at any rate, to suffer want back home. And yet the silly fellow thinks he can gloss over such disobedience and contempt of the divine commandment with his self-assigned pilgrimage, which is really nothing but impertinence or a delusion of the Devil.

The popes have encouraged this sort of thing with their false, feigned, foolish "golden years," [125] by which the people are excited, torn away from God's commandments, and enticed to follow the popes' own erroneous undertakings. The popes have done the very thing they ought to have prevented. But it has brought in money and fortified their illegitimate authority. That is why it has to go on, even if it is contrary to God and the salvation of souls.

To eradicate such false, seductive faith from the minds of simple Christian people and to restore a right understanding of good works, all pilgrimages should be dropped. There is no good in them: no commandment enjoins them, no obedience attaches to them. Rather do these pilgrimages give countless occasions to commit sin and to despise God's commandments. This is why there are so many beggars who commit all kinds of mischief by going on these pilgrimages. These people learn to beg when there is no need to beg, and they make a habit of begging. This accounts for vagabondage and many ills about which I shall not speak here.

If any man wants to go on a pilgrimage today or vow to make a pilgrimage, he should first show his reasons for doing so to his priest or his master. If it turns out that he wants to do it for the sake of a good work, then let the priest or master put his foot down firmly and put an end to the vow and the good work as a devilish delusion. Let priest and master show him how to use the money and effort for the pilgrimage for God's commandments and for works a thousand times better by spending it on his own family or on his poor neighbors. But if he wishes to make the pilgrimage out of curiosity, to see other lands and cities, he may be allowed to do so. But if he made the vow during an illness, then that vow must be annulled and canceled. God's commandment should be emphasized so that henceforth he will be content to keep the vow made in baptism and the commandments of God. Nevertheless, he may be allowed to perform his foolish vow just once to quiet his conscience. Nobody wants to walk in the straight path of God's commandments common to all of us. Everybody invents new ways and vows for himself as if he had already fulfilled all of God's commandments.

13. Next we come to the masses who make many vows but keep few. Do not be angry, my noble lords! I really mean it for the best. It is the bittersweet truth that the further building of

mendicant houses should not be permitted. God help us, there are already too many of them. Would to God they were all dissolved, or at least combined into two or three orders! Their running about the country has never done any good and never will do any good. My advice is to join together ten of these houses, or as many as need be, and make them a single institution for which adequate provision is made so that begging will not be necessary. It is far more important to consider what the common people need for their salvation than what St. Francis, St. Dominic, and St. Augustine,[126] or anyone else has established as a rule, especially because things have not turned out as they planned.

The mendicants should also be relieved of preaching and hearing confession, unless they are called to do this by the bishops, parishes, congregations, or the civil authorities. Nothing but hatred and envy between priests and monks has come out of this kind of preaching and shriving, and this has become a source of great offense and hindrance to the common people. It ought to stop because it can well be dispensed with. It looks suspiciously as though the Holy Roman See has purposely increased this army lest the priests and bishops, unable to stand the pope's tyranny any longer, someday become too powerful for him and start a reformation. That would be unbearable to His Holiness.

At the same time the manifold divisions and differences[127] within one and the same order should be abolished. These divisions have arisen from time to time for very trivial reasons; they have been maintained for even more trivial reasons, and they quarrel with each other with unspeakable hatred and envy. Nevertheless, the Christian faith, which can well exist without any of these distinctions, comes to grief because of both parties, and a good Christian life is valued and sought after only according to the standards of outward laws, works, and methods. Nothing comes of this but hypocrisy and the ruination of souls, as all can plainly see.

The pope must also be forbidden to found or endorse any more of these orders; in fact he must be ordered to abolish some and reduce the numbers of others. Inasmuch as faith in Christ,[128] which alone is the chief possession, exists without any kind of orders, there is no little danger that men will be easily led astray to live according to many and varied works and ways rather than to pay heed to faith. And unless there are wise superiors in the monaster-

188 · *German Humanism and Reformation*

ies who preach and stress faith more than the rule of the order, it is impossible for that order not to harm and mislead the simple souls who have regard only for works.

But in our day the superiors who did have faith and who founded the orders have passed away almost everywhere. It is just as it was centuries ago among the children of Israel. When the fathers who had known the wonders and the works of God had passed on, their children, ignorant of God's works and of faith, immediately elevated idolatry and their own human works. In our day, unfortunately, these orders have no understanding of God's works or of faith, but make wretched martyrs of themselves by striving and working to keep their own rules, laws, and ways of life. Yet they never come to a right understanding of a spiritually good life. It is just as II Timothy 3 [:5, 7]declares, "They have the appearance of a spiritual life, but there is nothing behind it: they are constantly learning, but they never come to a knowledge of what true spiritual life is." If the ruling superior has no understanding of Christian faith, it would be better to have no monastery at all; for such a superior cannot govern an order without doing hurt and harm, and the holier and better the superior appears to be in his external works, the more injury and ruin he causes.

To my way of thinking it would be a necessary measure, especially in our perilous times, to regulate convents and monasteries in the same way they were regulated in the beginning, in the days of the Apostles, and for a long time afterward.[129] In those days convents and monasteries were all open to everyone to stay in them as long as he pleased. What else were the convents and monasteries but Christian schools where Scripture and the Christian life were taught, and where people were trained to rule and to preach? Thus we read that St. Agnes[130] went to school, and we still see the same practice in some of the convents, like that at Quedlinburg[131] and elsewhere. And in truth all monasteries and convents ought to be so free that God is served freely and not under compulsion. Later on, however, they became tied up with the vows and became an eternal prison. Consequently, these monastic vows are more highly regarded than the vows of baptism. We see, hear, read, and learn more and more about the fruit of all this every day.

I can well suppose that this advice of mine will be regarded as the height of foolishness, but I am not concerned about that at the moment. I advise what seems good to me, let him reject it who will. I see for myself how the vows are kept, especially the vow of chastity. This vow has become universal in these monasteries, and yet it was never commanded by Christ. On the contrary, chastity is given to very few, as He Himself says [Matt. 19:11–12], as well as St. Paul [I Cor. 7:7]. It is my heartfelt wish for everybody to be helped. I do not want to let Christian souls get entangled in the self-contrived traditions and laws of men.[132]

14. We also see how the priesthood has fallen, and how many a poor priest is overburdened with wife and child, his conscience troubled. Yet no one does anything to help him, though he could easily be helped. Though pope and bishops may let things go on as they are, and allow what is heading for ruin to go to ruin, yet I will redeem my conscience and open my mouth freely, whether it vexes pope, bishop, or anybody else. And this is what I say: according to the institution of Christ and the Apostles, every city should have a priest or bishop, as St. Paul clearly says in Titus 1 [:5]. And this priest should not be compelled to live without a wedded wife, but should be permitted to have one, as St. Paul writes in I Timothy 3 [:2, 4] and Titus 1 [:6–7],saying, "A bishop shall be a man who is blameless, and the husband of but one wife, whose children are obedient and well behaved," etc. According to St. Paul, and also St. Jerome,[133] a bishop and a priest are one and the same thing. But of bishops as they now are, the Scriptures know nothing. Bishops have been appointed by ordinance of the Christian Church, so that one of them may have authority over several priests.

So then, we clearly learn from the Apostle that it should be the custom for every town to choose from among the congregation a learned and pious citizen, entrust to him the office of the ministry, and support him at the expense of the congregation. He should be free to marry or not. He should have several priests or deacons, also free to marry or not as they choose, to help him minister to the congregation and the community with word and sacrament, as is still the practice in the Greek Church. Because there was sometimes so much persecution and controversy with heretics after the Apostolic Age, there were many holy fathers who voluntarily abstained from matrimony that they might better devote themselves to study and be prepared at any moment for death or battle.

But the Roman See has interfered and out of its own wanton wickedness made a universal commandment forbidding priests to marry.[134] This was done at the bidding of the devil, as St. Paul declares in I Timothy 4 [:1, 3], "There shall come teachers who bring the Devil's teaching and forbid marriage." Unfortunately so much misery has arisen from this that tongue could never tell it. Moreover, this caused the Greek Church to separate,[135] and discord, sin, shame, and scandal were increased no end. But this always happens when the devil starts and carries on. What, then, shall we do about it?

My advice is, restore freedom to everybody and leave every man free to marry or not to marry. But then there would have to be a very different kind of government and administration of church property; the whole canon law would have to be demolished; and few benefices would be allowed to get into Roman hands. I fear that greed is a cause of this wretched, unchaste celibacy. As a result, everyone has wanted to become a priest and everyone wants his son to study for the priesthood, not with the idea of living in chastity, for that could be done outside the priesthood. [Their idea is to] be supported in temporal things without work or worry, contrary to God's command in Genesis 3 [:19] that "in the sweat of your face you shall eat your bread." The Romanists have colored this to mean that their labor is to pray and say mass.

I am not referring here to popes, bishops, canons, and monks. God has not instituted these offices. They have taken these burdens upon themselves, so they will have to bear them themselves. I want to speak only of the ministry which God has instituted, the responsibility of which is to minister word and sacrament to a congregation, among whom they reside. Such ministers should be given liberty by a Christian council to marry to avoid temptation and sin. For since God has not bound them, no one else ought to bind them or can bind them, even if he were an angel from heaven, let alone a pope. Everything that canon law decrees to the contrary is mere fable and idle talk.

Furthermore, I advise anyone henceforth being ordained a priest or anything else that he in no wise vow to the bishop that he will remain celibate. On the contrary, he should tell the bishop that he has no right whatsoever to require such a vow, and that it is a devilish tyranny to make such a demand. But if anyone is compelled to say, or even wants to say, "so far as human frailty permits," as indeed many do, let him frankly interpret these same words in a negative manner to mean "I do not promise chastity." For human frailty does not permit a man to live chastely, but only the strength of angels and the power of heaven. In this way he should keep his conscience free of all vows.

I will advise neither for nor against marrying or remaining single. I leave that to common Christian order and to everyone's better judgment. I will not conceal my real opinion or withhold comfort from that pitiful band who with wives and children have fallen into disgrace and whose consciences are burdened because people call them priests' whores and their children priests' children. As the court jester [136] I say this openly.

You will find many a pious priest against whom nobody has anything to say except that he is weak and has come to shame with a woman. From the bottom of their hearts both are of a mind to live together in lawful wedded love, if only they could do it with a clear conscience. But even though they both have to bear public shame, the two are certainly married in the sight of God. And I say that where they are so minded and live together, they should appeal anew to their conscience. Let the priest take and keep her as his lawful wedded wife, and live honestly with her as her husband, whether the pope likes it or not, whether it be against canon or human law. The salvation of your soul is more important than the observance of tyrannical, arbitrary, and wanton laws which are not necessary to salvation or commanded by God. You should do as the children of Israel did who stole from the Egyptians the wages they had earned;[137] or as a servant who steals from his wicked master the wages he has earned: steal from the pope your wedded wife and child! Let the man who has faith enough to venture this boldly follow me. I shall not lead him astray. Though I do not have the authority of a pope, I do have the authority of a Christian to advise and help my neighbor against sins and temptations. And that not without cause or reason!

First, not every priest can do without a woman, not only on account of human frailty, but much more on account of keeping house. If he then may keep a woman, and the pope allows that, and yet may not have her in marriage, what is that but leaving a man and a woman alone together and yet forbidding them to fall? It is just like putting straw and fire together and forbidding them to smoke or burn!

Second, the pope has as little power to command this as he has to forbid eating, drinking, the natural movement of the bowels, or growing fat. Therefore, no one is bound to keep it, but the pope is responsible for all the sins which are committed against this ordinance, for all the souls which are lost, and for all the consciences which are confused and tortured because of this ordinance. He has strangled so many wretched souls with this devilish rope that he has long deserved to be driven out of this world. Yet it is my firm belief that God has been more gracious to many souls at their last hour than the pope was to them in their whole lifetime. No good has ever come nor will come out of the papacy and its laws.

Third, although the law of the pope is against it, nevertheless, when the estate of matrimony has been entered against the pope's law, then his law is already at an end and is no longer valid. For God's commandment, which enjoins that no man shall put husband and wife asunder [Matt. 19:6], is above the pope's law. And the commandments of God must not be broken or neglected because of the pope's commandment. Nevertheless, many foolish jurists, along with the pope, have devised impediments and thereby prevented, broken, and brought confusion to the estate of matrimony so that God's commandment concerning it has altogether disappeared.[138] Need I say more? In the entire canon law of the pope there are not even two lines which could instruct a devout Christian, and, unfortunately, there are so many mistaken and dangerous laws that nothing would be better than to make a bonfire of it.[139]

But if you say that marriage of the clergy would give offense, and that the pope must first grant dispensation, I reply that whatever offense there is in it is the fault of the Roman See which has established such laws with no right and against God. Before God and the Holy Scriptures marriage of the clergy is no offense. Moreover, if the pope can grant dispensations from his greedy and tyrannical laws for money, then every Christian can grant dispensations from these very same laws for God's sake and for the salvation of souls. For Christ has set us free from all manmade laws, especially when they are opposed to God and the salvation of souls, as St. Paul teaches in Galatians 5 [:1] and I Corinthians 10 [:23].

15. Nor must I forget the poor monasteries. The evil spirit, who has now confused all the estates of life and made them unbearable through man-made laws, has taken possession of some abbots, abbesses, and prelates. As a result they govern their brothers and sisters in such a way that they quickly go to hell and lead a wretched existence here and now, as do the Devil's martyrs. That is to say, these superiors have reserved to themselves in confession, all, or at least some, of the mortal sins which are secret, so that no brother can absolve another on pain of excommunication and under the vow of obedience. Now nobody finds angels all the time in all places; but we do find flesh and blood which would rather undergo all excommunications and threats rather than confess secret sins to prelates and appointed confessors. Thus these people go to the sacrament with such consciences that they become irregulars [140] and even worse. O blind shepherds! O mad prelates! O ravenous wolves!

To this I say: If a sin is public or notorious, then it is proper for the prelate alone to punish it, and it is only these sins and no others that he may reserve and select for himself. He has no authority over secret sins, even if they were the worst sins that ever are or can be found. If the prelate makes exceptions of these secret sins, then he is a tyrant. He has no such right and is trespassing upon the prerogative of God's judgment.

And so I advise these children, brothers and sisters: If your superiors are unwilling to permit you to confess your secret sins to whom you choose, then take them to your brother or sister, whomever you like, and be absolved and comforted. Then go and do what you want and ought to do. Only believe firmly that you are absolved, and nothing more is needed. And do not be distressed or driven mad by threats of excommunication, becoming irregulars, or whatever else they threaten. These disciplines are valid only in the case of public or notorious sins which none will confess. They do not apply to you. What are you trying to do, you blind prelates, prevent secret sins by threats? Relinquish what you obviously cannot hold on to so that God's judgment and grace may work in the people under your care! He has not given them so entirely into your hands as to let them go entirely out of His own! In fact, you have the smaller part under you. Let your statutes be merely statutes. Do not exalt them to heaven or give them the weight of divine judgments!

16. It is also necessary to abolish all endowed masses for the dead,[141] or at least to reduce their number, since we plainly see that they have become nothing but a mockery. God is deeply angered by these, and their only purpose is money grubbing, gluttony, and drunkenness. What pleasure can God take in wretched vigils[142] and masses which are so miserably rattled off, not read or prayed. And if they were prayed, it would not be for God's sake and out of love, but for the sake of money and of getting a job finished. Now it is impossible for a work which is not done out of unconstrained love to please or suffice God. So it is altogether Christian to abolish, or at least diminish, everything we see which is growing into an abuse and which angers God rather than reconciles Him. I would rather—in fact, it would be more pleasing to God and much better—that a chapter, church, or monastery combine all its anniversary masses and vigils and on one day, with sincerity of heart, reverence, and faith, hold one true vigil and mass on behalf of all its benefactors, than hold thousands every year for each individual benefactor without reverence and faith. O dear Christians, God does not care for much praying but for true praying. In fact, He condemns long and repetitious prayers, and says in Matthew 6 [:7; 23:14], "They will only earn the more punishment thereby." But greed, which cannot put its trust in God, brings such things to pass. Avarice is anxious lest it starve to death.

17. Certain penalties or punishments of canon law should be abolished, too, especially the interdict,[143] which without any doubt was invented by the evil spirit. Is it not a devilish work to correct one sin through many and great sins? It is actually a greater sin to silence or suppress the word and worship of God than if one had strangled twenty popes at one time, to say nothing of a priest, or had misused Church holdings. This is another of the tender virtues taught in canon law. One of the reasons this law is called "spiritual"[144] is that it comes from spirit: not from the Holy Spirit but from the evil spirit.

Excommunication must never be used except where the Scriptures prescribe its use, that is, against those who do not hold the true faith or who live in open sin, not for material advantage. But today it is the other way around. Everybody believes and lives as he pleases, especially those who use excommunication to fleece and defame other people. All the excommunications are for material advantage, for which we have nobody to thank but the holy canon law of unrighteousness. I have said more about this in an earlier discourse.[145]

The other punishments and penalties—suspension, irregularity, aggravation, reaggravation, deposition, lightning, thundering, cursings, damnings, and the rest of these devices[146]—should be buried ten fathoms deep in the earth so that their name and memory not be left on earth. The evil spirit unleashed by canon law has brought such a terrible plague and misery into the heavenly kingdom of holy Christendom, having done nothing but destroy and hinder souls by canon law, that the words of Christ in Matthew 23 [:13] may well be understood as applying to them:[147] "Woe to you scribes! You have taken upon yourselves the authority to teach, and closed up the kingdom of heaven to men. You do not go in and you stand in the way of those who enter."

18. All festivals should be abolished, and Sunday alone retained.[148] If it is desired, however, to retain the festivals of Our Lady and of the major saints, they should be transferred to Sunday, or observed only by a morning mass, after which all the rest of the day should be a working day. Here is the reason: Since the feast days are abused by drinking, gambling, loafing, and all manner of sin, we anger God more on holy days than we do on other days. Things are so topsy-turvy that holy days are not holy, but working days are. Nor is any service rendered God and His saints by so many saints' days. On the contrary, they are dishonored; although some foolish prelates think that they have done a good work if each, following the promptings of his own blind devotion, celebrates a festival in honor of St. Otilie[149] or St. Barbara. But they would be doing something far better if they honored the saint by turning the saint's day into a working day.

Over and above the spiritual injury, the average man incurs two material disadvantages from this practice. First, he neglects his work and spends more money than he would otherwise spend. Second, he weakens his body and makes it less fit. We see this every day, yet nobody thinks of correcting the situation. In such cases we ought not to consider whether or not the pope has instituted the feasts, or whether we must have a dispensation or permission [to omit them]. Every town, council, or governing authority not only has the right, without the knowledge and consent of the pope or bishop, to abolish what is opposed to God and injurious to men's bodies and souls, but indeed is bound at the risk of the salvation of its souls to fight it, even though popes and bishops, who ought to be the first to do so, do not consent.

Above all, we ought to abolish church anniversary celebrations [150] outright, since they have become nothing but taverns, fairs, and gambling places, and only increase the dishonoring of God and foster the soul's damnation. It does not help matters to boast that festivals had a good beginning and are a good work. Did not God set aside his own law, which he had given from heaven, when it was perverted and abused? And does he not daily overturn what he has set up and destroy what he has made because of the same perversion and abuse? As it is written of him in Psalm 18 [:26], "You show yourself perverse with the perverted."

19. The grades or degrees within which marriage is forbidden, such as those affecting godparents or the third and fourth degree of kinship, should be changed. If the pope in Rome can grant dispensations and scandalously sell them for money, then every priest may give the same dispensations without price and for the salvation of souls. Would to God that every priest were able to do and remit without payment all those things we have to pay for at Rome, such as indulgences, letters of indulgence, butter letters, mass letters, and all the rest of the *confessionalia* and skullduggery [151] at Rome and free us from that golden noose the canon law, by which the poor people are deceived and cheated of their money! If the pope has the right to sell his noose of gold and his spiritual snares (I ought to say "law") [152] for money, then a priest certainly has more right to tear these nooses and snares apart, and for God's sake tread them underfoot. But if the priest does not have this right, neither has the pope the right to sell them at his disgraceful fair.

Furthermore, fasts should be left to individuals and every kind of food left optional, as the Gospel makes them. [153] Even those gentlemen at Rome scoff at the fasts, and leave us commoners to eat the fat they would not deign to use to grease their shoes, and then afterward they sell us the liberty to eat butter and all sorts of other things. The holy Apostle says that we already have freedom in all these things through the Gospel.[154] But they have bound us with their canon law and robbed us of our rights so that we have to buy them back again with money. In so doing, they have made our consciences so timid and fearful that it is no longer easy to preach about liberty of this kind because the common people take offense at it and think that eating butter is a greater sin than lying, swearing, or even living unchastely. It is still a human work decreed by men. You may do with it what you will, yet nothing good will ever come of it.

20. The chapels in forests and the churches in fields,[155] such as Wilsnack,[156] Sternberg,[157] Trier,[158] the Grimmenthal,[159] and now Regensburg[160] and a goodly number of others which recently have become the goal of pilgrimages, must be leveled. Oh, what a terrible and heavy reckoning those bishops will have to give who permit this devilish deceit and profit by it.[161] They should be the first to prevent it and yet they regard it all as a godly and holy thing. They do not see that the Devil is behind it all, to strengthen greed, to create a false and fictitious faith, to weaken the parish churches, to multiply taverns and harlotry, to lose money and working time to no purpose, and to lead ordinary people by the nose. If they had read Scripture as well as the damnable canon law, they would know how to deal with this matter!

The miracles that happen in these places prove nothing, for the evil spirit can also work miracles, as Christ has told us in Matthew 24 [:24]. If they took the matter seriously and forbade this sort of thing the miracles would quickly come to an end. But if the thing were of God, their prohibition would not hinder it.[162] And if there were no other evidence that it is not of God, the fact that men come running to them like herds of cattle, as if they had lost all reason, would be proof enough. This could not be possible if it were of God. Further, God never gave any command about all this. There is neither obedience nor merit in doing it. The thing to do is to step in boldly and protect the people. For whatever has not been commanded and is done beyond what God commands is certainly the Devil's doing. To their disadvantage, the parish churches are held in less respect. In short, these things are signs of great unbelief among the people, for if they really had faith, they would find all they need in their own parish churches, to which they are commanded to go.

But what shall I say now? Every bishop thinks only of how he can set up and maintain such a place of pilgrimage in his diocese. He is not at all concerned that the people believe and live aright. The rulers are just like the people. The blind lead the blind [Luke 6:39]. In fact, where pilgrimages do not catch on, they set to work to canonize saints,[163] not to honor the saints, who would be honored enough without being canonized, but to draw the crowds and bring in the money. At this point pope and bishops lend their aid. There is a deluge of indulgences. There is always money enough for these. But nobody worries about what God has commanded. Nobody runs after these things; nobody has money for them. How blind we are! We not only give the devil free rein for his mischief, but we even strengthen and multiply his mischief. I would rather the dear saints were left in peace and the simple people not led astray! What spirit gave the pope authority to canonize saints? Who tells him whether they are saints or not? Are there not enough sins on earth already without tempting God, without interfering in his judgment and setting up the dear saints as decoys to get money?

My advice is to let the saints canonize themselves. Indeed, it is God alone who should canonize them. And let every man stay in his own parish; there he will find more than in all the shrines even if they were all rolled into one. In your own parish you find baptism, the sacrament, preaching, and your neighbor, and these things are greater than all the saints in heaven, for all of them were made saints by God's word and sacrament. As long as we esteem such wonderful things so little, God is just in his wrathful condemnation in allowing the devil to lead us where he likes, to conduct pilgrimages, found churches and chapels, canonize saints, and do other such fool's works so that we depart from true faith into a novel and wrong kind of belief. This is what the Devil did in ancient times to the people of Israel, when he led them away from the temple at Jerusalem to countless other places. Yet he did it all in the name of God and under the pretense of holiness. All the prophets preached against it, and they were martyred for doing so. But today nobody preaches against it. If somebody were to preach against it all, perhaps bishop, pope, priest, and monk would martyr him, too. St. Antoninus of Florence[164] and certain others must now be made saints and canonized in this way, so that their holiness, which would otherwise have served only for the glory of God and set a good example, may be used to bring fame and money.

Although the canonization of saints may have been a good thing in former days, it is certainly never good practice now. Like many other things that were good in former times, feast days, church holdings, and ornaments now are scandalous and offensive. For it is evident that through the canonization of saints neither God's glory nor the improvement of Christians is sought, but only money and reputation. One church wants to have the advantage over the other and would not like to see another church enjoy that advantage in common. Spiritual treasures have even been misused to gain temporal goods in these last evil days so that everything, even God Himself, has been forced into the service of Avarice. Such advantage only promotes schisms, sects, and pride. A church that has advantages over others looks down on them and exalts itself. Yet all divine treasures are common to all and serve all and ought to further the cause of unity. But the pope likes things as they are. He would not like it if all Christians were equal and one with each other.

It is fitting to say here that all church licenses, bulls, and whatever else the pope sells in that skinning house[165] of his in Rome should be abolished, disregarded, or extended to all. But if he sells or gives special licenses,[166] privileges, indulgences, graces, advantages, and faculties[167] to Wittenberg, Halle, Venice, and above all to his own city of Rome, why does he not give these things to all churches in general? Is it not his duty to do everything in his power for all Christians, freely and for God's sake, even shed his blood for them? Tell me, then, why does he give or sell to one church and not to another? Or must the accursed money make so great a difference in the eyes of His Holiness among Christians, who all have the same baptism, word, faith, Christ, God, and all else? Do the Romanists want us to be so blind to all these things, though we have eyes to see, and be such fools, though we have a perfectly good faculty of reason, that we worship such greed, skullduggery, and pretense? The pope is a shepherd, but only so long as you have money, and no longer. And still the Romanists are not ashamed of his rascality of leading us hither and thither with their bulls. They are concerned only about the accursed money and nothing else!

My advice is this: If such fool's work cannot be abolished, then every decent Christian should open his eyes and not permit himself to be led astray by the Romanist bulls and seals and all their glittering show. Let him stay at home in his own parish church and be content with the best; his baptism, the Gospel, his faith, his Christ, and his God, who is the same God everywhere. Let the pope remain a blind leader of the blind. Neither an angel nor a pope can give you as much as God gives you in your parish church. The fact is, the pope leads you away from the gifts of God, which are yours without cost, to his gifts, for which you have to pay. He gives you lead for gold, hide for meat, the string for the purse, wax for honey, words for goods, the letter for the spirit.[168] You see all this before your very eyes, but you refuse to take notice. If you intend to ride to heaven on his wax and parchment, this chariot will soon break down and you will fall into hell, and not in God's name!

Let this be your one sure guide: Whatever you have to buy from the pope is neither good nor from God. For what God gives is not only given without charge, but the whole world is punished and damned for not being willing to receive it as a free gift. I mean the Gospel and God's work. We have deserved God's letting us be so led astray because we have despised His holy word and the grace of baptism. It is as St. Paul says, "God shall send a strong delusion upon all those who have not received the truth to their salvation, so that they believe and follow lies and knavery" [II Thess. 2:11]. This serves them right.

21. One of the greatest necessities is the abolition of all begging throughout Christendom. Nobody ought to go begging among Christians. It would even be a very simple matter to make a law to the effect that every city should look after its own poor, if only we had the courage and the intention to do so. No beggar from outside should be allowed into the city whether he might call himself pilgrim or mendicant monk. Every city should support its own poor, and if it is too small, the people in the surrounding villages should also be urged to contribute, since in any case they had to

feed so many vagabonds and evil rogues who call themselves mendicants. In this way, too, it could be known who was really poor, and who was not.

There would have to be an overseer or warden who knows all the poor and informs the city council or the clergy what they need. Or some other better arrangement might be made. As I see it, there is no other business in which so much skullduggery and deceit are practiced as in begging, and yet it could all be easily abolished. Moreover, this unrestricted universal begging is harmful to the common people. I have figured out that each of the five or six mendicant orders[169] visits the same place more than six or seven times every year. In addition to these there are the usual beggars, the "ambassador" beggars,[170] and the panhandlers.[171] This adds up to sixty times a year that a town is laid under tribute! This is over and above what the secular authorities demand in the way of taxes and assessments. All this the Romanist See steals in return for its wars and consumes for no purpose. To me, it is one of God's greatest miracles that we can still go on existing and find the wherewithal to support ourselves!

To be sure, some think that if these proposals were adopted, the poor would not be so well provided for, that fewer great stone houses and monasteries would be built, and fewer so well furnished. I can well believe all this. But none of it is necessary. He who has chosen poverty ought not to be rich. If he wants to be rich, let him put his hand to the plow and seek his fortune from the land. It is enough if the poor are decently cared for so that they do not die of hunger or cold. It is not fitting that one man should live in idleness on another's labor, or be rich and live comfortably at the cost of another's hardship, as it is according to the present perverted custom. St. Paul says, "Whoever will not work shall not eat" [II Thess. 3:10]. God has not decreed that any man shall live off another man's property, save only the clergy who preach and have a parish to care for, and these should, as St. Paul says in I Corinthians 9 [:14], on account of their spiritual labor. And also as Christ says to the Apostles, "Every laborer is worthy of his wage" [Luke 10:7].

22. It is also to be feared that the many masses which were endowed in ecclesiastical foundations and monasteries are not only of little use, but arouse the great wrath of God. It would therefore

be profitable not to endow any more of these masses, but rather to abolish many that are already endowed. It is obvious that these masses are regarded only as sacrifices and good works, even though they are sacraments just like baptism and penance, which profit only those who receive them and no one else. But now the custom of saying masses for the living and the dead has crept in, and all hopes are built upon them. This is why so many masses are endowed, and why the state of affairs we see around us has developed out of it.

My proposal is perhaps too bold and an unheard-of thing, especially for those who are concerned that they would lose their job and means of livelihood if such masses were discontinued. I must refrain from saying more about it until we arrive again at a proper understanding of what the mass is and what it is for. Unfortunately, for many years now it has been a job, a way to earn a living. Therefore, from now on I will advise a man to become a shepherd or some sort of workman rather than a priest or a monk, unless he knows well in advance what his celebrating of masses is all about.

I am not speaking, however, of the old foundations and cathedrals, which were doubtless established for the sake of the children and the nobility. According to German custom not every one of a nobleman's children can become a landowner or a ruler. It was intended that these children should be looked after in such foundations, and there be free to serve God, to study, to become educated people, and to educate others.[172] I am speaking now of the new foundations which have been established just for the saying of prayers and masses, and because of their example the older foundations are being burdened with the same sort of praying and mass celebrating so that even these old foundations serve little or no purpose. And it is by the grace of God that they finally hit the bottom, as they deserve. That is to say, they have been reduced to anthem singers, organ wheezers, and reciters of decadent, indifferent masses to get and consume the income from the endowments. Pope, bishops, and university scholars ought to be looking into these things and writing about them, and yet it is precisely they who do the most to promote them. Whatever brings in money they let go on and on. The blind lead the blind [Luke 6:39]. This is what greed and canon law accomplish.

It should no longer be permissible for one person to hold more than one canonry or benefice. Each must be content with a modest position so that someone else may also have something. This would do away with the excuses of those who say that they must hold more than one such office to maintain their proper station. A proper station could be interpreted in such broad terms that an entire country would not be enough to maintain it. But greed and a secret lack of trust in God go hand in hand in this matter, so that what is alleged to be the needs of a proper station is nothing but greed and unbelief.

23. The brotherhoods,[173] and for that matter, indulgences, letters of indulgence, butter letters, mass letters, dispensations, and everything of that kind should be snuffed out and brought to an end. There is nothing good about them. If the pope has the authority to grant you a dispensation to eat butter, to absent yourself from mass, and the like, then he ought also to be able to delegate this authority to the priests, from whom he had no right to take it in the first place. I am speaking especially of those brotherhoods in which indulgences, masses, and good works are apportioned. My dear friend, in your baptism you have entered into a brotherhood with Christ, with all the angels, with the saints, and with all Christians on earth. Hold fast to this and live up to its demands, and you have all the brotherhoods you want. Let the others glitter as they will. Compared with the true brotherhood in Christ, those brotherhoods are like a penny compared with a gulden. But if there were a brotherhood which raised money to feed the poor or to help the needy, that would be a good idea. It would find its indulgences and its merits in heaven. But today nothing comes of these groups except gluttony and drunkenness.

Above all, we should drive out of German territory the papal legates with their faculties, which they sell to us for large sums of money. This traffic is nothing but skullduggery. For example, for payment of money they make unrighteousness into righteousness, and they dissolve oaths, vows, and agreements, thereby destroying and teaching us to destroy the faith and fealty which have been pledged. They assert that the pope has authority to do this. It is the Devil who tells them to say these things. They sell us doctrine so satanic, and take money for it, that they are teaching us sin and leading us to hell.

If there were no other base trickery to prove that the pope is the true Antichrist, this one would be enough to prove it. Hear this, O pope, not of all men the holiest but of all men the most sinful! O that God from heaven would soon destroy your throne and sink it in the abyss of hell! Who has given you authority to exalt yourself above your God, to break and loose his commandments, and teach Christians, especially the German nation, praised throughout history for its nobility, its constancy and fidelity, to be inconstant, perjurers, traitors, profligates, and faithless? God has commanded us to keep word and faith even with an enemy, but you have taken it upon yourself to loose His commandment and have ordained in your heretical, anti-Christian decretals that you have His power. Thus through your voice and pen the wicked Satan lies as he has never lied before. You force and twist the Scriptures to suit your fancy. O Christ, my Lord, look down; let the day of judgment break down and destroy this nest of devils at Rome. There sits the man of whom St. Paul said, "He shall exalt himself above you, sit in your church, and set himself up as God, that man of sin, the son of perdition" [II Thess. 2:3–5]. What else is papal power but simply the teaching and increasing of sin and wickedness? Papal power serves only to lead souls into damnation in your name and, to all outward appearances, with your approval!

In ancient times the children of Israel had to keep the oath which they had unwittingly been deceived into giving to their enemies, the Gibeonites [Josh. 9:3–21]. And King Zedekiah was miserably lost along with all his people because he broke his oath to the king of Babylon [II Kings 24:20—25:7]. In our own history, a hundred years ago, that fine king of Hungary and Poland, Ladislaus, was tragically slain by the Turk along with so many of his people because he allowed himself to be led astray by the papal legate and cardinal and broke the good and advantageous treaty and solemn agreement he had made with the Turk.[174] The pious Emperor Sigismund had no more success after the Council of Constance when he allowed those scoundrels to break the oath that had been given to John Huss and Jerome.[175] All the trouble between the Bohemians and ourselves stems from this. Even in our own times—God help us!—how much Christian blood has been shed because of the oath and the alliance which Pope Julius made between Emperor Maximilian and King Louis of France, and afterward broke![176] How could I tell all the trouble the popes have stirred up by their devilish presumption with which they annul oaths and vows made between powerful princes, making a mockery of these things, and taking money for it? I hope that the day of judgment is at hand. Things could not possibly be worse than the state of affairs the Romanist See is promoting. The pope suppresses God's commandment and exalts his own. If he is not the Antichrist, then somebody tell me who is! But more of this another time.

24. It is high time we took up the Bohemian question and dealt seriously and honestly with it. We should come to an understanding with them so that the terrible slander, hatred, and envy on both sides comes to an end. As befits my folly, I shall be the first to submit an opinion on this subject, with due deference to everyone who may understand the case better than I.

First, we must honestly confess the truth and stop justifying ourselves. We must admit to the Bohemians that John Huss and Jerome of Prague were burned at Constance against the papal, Christian, imperial oath and the promise of safe-conduct. This happened contrary to God's commandment and gave the Bohemians ample cause for bitterness. And although they should have acted as perfect Christians and suffered this grave injustice and disobedience to God by these people, nevertheless they were not obliged to condone such conduct and acknowledge it as just. To this day they would rather give up life and limb than admit that it is right to break and deal contrarily with an imperial, papal, and Christian oath. So then, although it is the impatience of the Bohemians that is at fault, yet the pope and his crowd are still more to blame for all the misery, error, and the loss of souls which have followed that council.

I will not pass judgment here on the articles of John Huss, or defend his errors, although I have not yet found any errors in his writings according to my way of thinking. I firmly believe that those who violated a Christian safe-conduct and a commandment of God with their faithless betrayal gave neither a fair judgment nor an honest condemnation. Without doubt they were possessed more by the evil spirit than by the Holy Spirit. Nobody will doubt that the Holy Spirit does not act contrary to the commandment of

God, and nobody is so ignorant as not to know that the violation of good faith and of a promise of safe-conduct is contrary to the commandment of God, even though they had been promised to the Devil himself, to say nothing of a mere heretic. It is also quite evident that such a promise was made to John Huss and the Bohemians and was not kept, and that he was burned at the stake as a result. I do not wish, however, to make John Huss a saint or a martyr, as some of the Bohemians do. But at the same time I do acknowledge that an injustice was done to him, and that his books and doctrines were unjustly condemned. For the judgments of God are secret and terrible, and no one save God alone should undertake to reveal or utter them.

I only want to say this: John Huss may have been as bad a heretic as it is possible to be; nevertheless he was burned unjustly and in violation of the commandment of God. Further, the Bohemians should not be forced to approve of such conduct, or else we shall never achieve any unity. Not obstinacy, but the open admission of the truth must make us one. It is useless to pretend, as was done at the time, that the oath of safe-conduct given to a heretic need not be kept. That is as much as to say that God's commandments need not be kept so that God's commandments may be kept. The Devil made the Romanists mad and foolish so that they did not know what they had said and done. God has commanded that a promise of safe-conduct shall be kept. We should keep such a commandment though the whole world collapses. How much more, then, when it is only a question of freeing a heretic! We should overcome heretics with books, not with fire, as the ancient fathers did. If it were wisdom to vanquish heretics with fire, then the public hangmen would be the most learned scholars on earth. We would no longer need to study books, for he who overcomes another by force would have the right to burn him at the stake.

Second, the emperor and princes should send a few really godly and sensible bishops and scholars over to the Bohemians. On no account should they send a cardinal or a papal legate or an inquisitor, for officials like these are most unversed in Christian things. They do not seek to save souls, but, like all the pope's henchmen, only their own power, profit, and prestige. In fact, these very people were the chief actors in this miserable business at

Constance. The men sent into Bohemia should find out from the Bohemians how things stand in regard to their faith, and whether it is possible to unite all their sects.[177] In this case the pope ought to use his authority awhile for the sake of saving souls and, in accordance with the decree of the truly Christian Council of Nicaea, allow the Bohemians to choose an archbishop of Prague from among their number and let him be confirmed by the bishop of Olmütz in Moravia, or the bishop of Gran in Hungary, or the bishop of Gnesen in Poland, or the bishop of Magdeburg in Germany. It will be enough if he is confirmed by one or two of these, as was the custom in the time of St. Cyprian.[178] The pope has no right to oppose such an arrangement, and if he does oppose it, he will be acting like a wolf and a tyrant; no one ought to obey him and his ban should be met with a counterban.

If, however, in deference to the Chair of Peter, it was desired to do this with the pope's consent, then let it be done that way, provided it does not cost the Bohemians anything and provided the pope does not put them under the slightest obligation or bind them with his tyrannical oaths and vows as he does all other bishops, contrary to God and right. If he is not satisfied with the honor of having his consent asked, then let them not bother anymore about the pope or his vows and his rights, his laws and his tyrannies. Let the election suffice, and let the blood of all the souls endangered by this state of affairs cry out against him. No one ought to consent to what is wrong. It is enough to have shown courtesy to tyranny. If it cannot be otherwise, then an election and the approval of the common people can even now be quite as valid as confirmation by a tyrant, though I hope this will not be necessary. Someday some of the Romanists or some of the good bishops and scholars will take notice of the pope's tyranny and repudiate it.

I would also advise against compelling the Bohemians to abolish both kinds in the sacrament[179] since that practice is neither unChristian nor heretical. If they want to, I would let them go on in the way they have been doing. Yet the new bishop should be careful that no discord arises because of such a practice. He should kindly instruct them that neither practice is wrong,[180] just as it ought not to cause dissension that the clergy differ from the laity in manner of life and dress. By the same token, if they are unwilling to receive Roman canon law, they should not be forced to so do, but rather the prime concern should be that they live sincerely in faith and in accordance with Holy Scripture. For Christian faith and life can well exist without the intolerable laws of the pope. In fact, faith cannot properly exist unless there are fewer of these Romanist laws or unless they are even abolished altogether. In baptism we have become free and have been made subject only to God's word. Why should we become bound by the word of any man? As St. Paul says, "You have become free; do not become a bondservant of men,"[181] that is, of those men who rule by man-made laws.

If I knew that the Pickards[182] held no other error regarding the sacrament of the altar except believing that the bread and wine are present in their true nature, but that the body and blood of Christ are truly present under them, then I would not condemn them but would let them come under the bishop of Prague. For it is not an article of faith that bread and wine are not present in the sacrament in their own essence and nature, but this is an opinion of St. Thomas[183] and the pope. On the other hand, it is an article of faith that the true natural body and blood of Christ are present in the natural bread and wine. So then, we should tolerate the opinions of both sides until they come to an agreement because there is no danger in believing that the bread is there or that it is not. We have to endure all sorts of practices and ordinances which are not harmful to faith. On the other hand, if they believed otherwise, I would rather think of them as outside,[184] though I would teach them the truth.

Whatever other errors and schisms are discovered in Bohemia should be tolerated until the archbishop has been restored and has gradually brought all the people together again on one common doctrine. They will certainly never be united by force, defiance, or by haste. Patience and gentleness are needed here. Did not even Christ have to tarry with His disciples and bear with their unbelief for a long time until they believed His resurrection? If only the Bohemians had a regular bishop and church administration again, without Romanist tyranny, I am sure that things would soon be better.

The restoration of the temporal goods which formerly belonged to the Church should not be too strictly demanded, but since we are Christians and each is bound to help the rest, we have full power to give them these things for the sake of unity and allow them to retain them in the sight of God and before the eyes of the world. For Christ says, "Where two are in agreement with one another on earth, there am I in the midst of them" [Matt. 18:19–20]. Would to God that on both sides we were working toward this unity, extending to each other the hand of brotherhood and humility. Love is greater and is more needed than the papacy at Rome, which is without love. Love can exist apart from the papacy.

With this counsel I shall have done what I could. If the pope or his supporters hinder it, they shall have to render an account for having sought their own advantage rather than their neighbor's, contrary to the love of God. The pope ought to give up his papacy and all his possessions and honors, if thereby he could save one soul. But today he would rather let the whole world perish than yield one hairsbreadth of his presumptuous authority. And yet he wants to be the holiest! With that my responsibility comes to an end.

25. The universities, too, need a good, thorough reformation. I must say that, no matter whom it annoys. Everything the papacy has instituted and ordered serves only to increase sin and error. What else are the universities, unless they are utterly changed from what they have been hitherto, than what the book of Maccabees calls *gymnasia epheborum et graecae gloriae?* [185] What are they but places where loose living is practiced, where little is taught of the Holy Scriptures and Christian faith, and where only the blind, heathen teacher Aristotle rules [186] far more than Christ? In this regard my advice would be that Aristotle's *Physics, Metaphysics, Concerning the Soul,* and *Ethics,* which hitherto have been thought to be his best books, should be completely discarded along with all the rest of his books that boast about nature, although nothing can be learned from them either about nature or the Spirit. Moreover, nobody has yet understood him, and many souls have been burdened with fruitless labor and study, at the cost of much precious time. I dare say that any potter has more knowledge of nature than is written in these books. It grieves me to the quick that this damned, conceited, rascally heathen has deluded and made

fools of so many of the best Christians with his misleading writings. God has sent him as a plague upon us on account of our sins.

Why, this wretched fellow in his best book, *Concerning the Soul,* teaches that the soul dies with the body, although many have tried without success to save his reputation. As though we did not have the Holy Scriptures, in which we are fully instructed about all things, things about which Aristotle has not the faintest clue! And yet this dead heathen has conquered, obstructed, and almost succeeded in suppressing the books of the living God. When I think of this miserable business I can only believe that the devil has introduced this study.

For the same reasons his book on ethics is the worst of all books. It flatly opposes divine grace and all Christian virtues, and yet it is considered one of his best works. Away with such books! Keep them away from Christians. No one can accuse me of overstating the case, or of condemning what I do not understand. Dear friend, I know what I am talking about. I know my Aristotle as well as you or the likes of you. I have lectured on him and been read without commentaries and notes, so Aristotle's *Logic* lectured on him,[187] and I understand him better than St. Thomas or Duns Scotus[188] did. I can boast about this without pride and, if necessary, I can prove it. It makes no difference to me that so many great minds have devoted their labor to him for so many centuries. Such objections do not disturb me as once they did, for it is plain as day that other errors have remained for even more centuries in the world and in the universities.

I would gladly agree to keeping Aristotle's books, *Logic, Rhetoric,* and *Poetics,* or at least keeping and using them in an abridged form, as useful in training young people to speak and to preach properly. But the commentaries and notes must be abolished and, as Cicero's *Rhetoric* is, they should be read as they are without all these commentaries. But today nobody learns how to speak or how to preach from them. The whole thing has become nothing but a matter for disputation and a weariness to the flesh.

In addition to all this there are, of course, the Latin, Greek, and Hebrew languages, as well as the mathematical disciplines and history. But all this I commend to the experts. In fact, reform would come of itself if only we gave ourselves seriously to it. Actually a great deal depends on it, for it is here in the universities that the Christian youth and our nobility, with whom the future of Christendom lies, will be educated and trained. Therefore, I believe that there is no work more worthy of pope or emperor than a thorough reform of the universities. And on the other hand, nothing could be more devilish or disastrous than unreformed universities.

I leave the medical men to reform their own faculties; I take the jurists and theologians as my own responsibility. The first thing I would say is that it would be a good thing if canon law were completely blotted out, from the first letter to the last, especially the decretals.[189] More than enough is written in the Bible about how we should behave in all circumstances. The study of canon law only hinders the study of the Holy Scriptures. Moreover, the greater part smacks of nothing but greed and pride. Even if there were much in it that was good, it should still be destroyed, for the pope has the whole canon law imprisoned in the "chamber of his heart,"[190] so that henceforth any study of it is just a waste of time and a farce. These days canon law is not what is written in the books of law, but whatever the pope and his flatterers want. Your cause may be thoroughly established in canon law, but the pope always has his chamber of the heart in the matter, and all law, and with it the whole world, has to be guided by that. Now it is often a villain, and even the devil himself, who rules the *scrinium*—and they proudly boast that it is the Holy Spirit who rules it! Thus they deal with Christ's poor people. They impose many laws upon them but obey none themselves. They compel others to obey these laws, or buy their way out with money.

Since, then, the pope and his followers have suspended the whole canon law as far as they themselves are concerned, and since they pay it no heed but give thought only to their own wanton will, we should do as they do and discard these volumes. Why should we waste our time studying them? We could never fathom the arbitrary will of the pope, which is all that canon law has become. Let canon law perish in God's name for it arose in the Devil's name. Let there be no more "doctors of decrees"[191] in the world, but only "doctors of the papal chamber of the heart,"[192] that is, popish hypocrites! It is said that there is no better temporal rule anywhere than among the Turks, who have neither spiritual nor temporal law, but only their Koran. But we must admit that there is no more shameful rule than ours with its spiritual and temporal law, which has resulted in nobody living according to common sense, much less according to Holy Scripture anymore.

The secular law [193]—God help us—has become a wilderness! Though it is much better, wiser, and more honest than the spiritual law, which has nothing good about it except its name, nevertheless, there is far too much of it. Surely, wise rulers, side by side with Holy Scripture, would be law enough. As St. Paul says in I Corinthians 6 [:5–6], "Is there no one among you who can judge his neighbor's cause, that you must go to law before heathen courts?" It seems just to me that territorial laws and customs should take precedence over general imperial laws, and that the imperial laws be used only in case of necessity. Would to God that every land were ruled by its own brief laws suitable to its gifts and peculiar character. This is how these lands were ruled before these imperial laws were designed, and as many lands are still ruled without them! Rambling and farfetched laws are only a burden to the people, and they hinder cases more than they help them. But I hope that others have already given more thought and attention to this matter than I am able to do.

Our dear theologians have saved themselves worry and work. They just let the Bible alone and lecture on the sentences.[194] I should have thought that the sentences ought to be the first study for young students of theology, and the Bible left to the doctors. But today it is the other way around. The Bible comes first and is then put aside when the bachelor's degree is received. The sentences come last, and they occupy a doctor as long as he lives. There is such a solemn obligation attached to these sentences that a man who is not a priest may well lecture on the Bible, but the sentences must be lectured on by a man who is a priest. As I see it, a married man may well be a Doctor of the Bible, but under no circumstances could he be a Doctor of the Sentences. How can we prosper when we behave so wrongly and give the Bible, the holy word of God, a back seat? To make things worse, the pope commands in the strongest language that his words are to be studied in the schools and used in the courts, but very little is thought of the Gospel. Consequently, the Gospel lies neglected in the schools and in the courts. It is pushed aside under the bench and gathers dust so that the scandalous laws of the pope alone may have full sway.

If we bear the name and title of teachers of Holy Scripture, then by this criterion we ought to be compelled to teach the Holy Scripture and nothing else, although we all know that this high and mighty title is much too exalted for a man to take pride in it and let himself be designated a Doctor of Holy Scripture. Yet that title might be permitted if the work justified the name. But nowadays, the sentences alone dominate the situation in such a way that we find among the theologians more heathenish and humanistic [195] darkness than we find the holy and certain doctrine of Scripture. What are we to do about it? I know of nothing else to do than to pray humbly to God to give us such real Doctors of Theology as we have in mind. Pope, emperor, and universities may make Doctors of Arts, of Medicine, of Laws, of the Sentences; but be assured that no man can make a Doctor of Holy Scripture except the Holy Spirit from heaven. As Christ says in John 6 [:45], "They must all be taught by God Himself." Now the Holy Spirit does not ask for red or brown birettas [196] or other decorations. Nor does He ask whether a person is young or old, lay or cleric, monk or secular, unmarried or married. In fact, in ancient times He actually spoke through an ass against the prophet who was riding it [Num. 22:28]. Would to God that we were worthy to have such doctors given to us, regardless of whether they were lay or cleric, married or single! They now try to force the Holy Spirit into pope, bishops, and doctors, although there is not the slightest sign or indication whatever that He is in them.

The number of books on theology must be reduced and only the best ones published. It is not many books that make men learned, nor even reading. But it is a good book frequently read, no matter how small it is, that makes a man learned in the Scriptures and godly. Indeed, the writings of all the holy fathers should be read only for a time so that through them we may be led into the Scriptures. As it is, however, we only read them these days to avoid going any further and getting into the Bible. We are like men who read the sign posts and never travel the road they indicate. Our dear fathers wanted to lead us to the Scriptures by their writings, but we use their works to get away from the Scriptures. Nevertheless, the Scripture alone is our vineyard in which we must all labor and toil.

Above all, the foremost reading for everybody, both in the universities and in the schools, should be Holy Scripture—and for the younger boys, the gospels. And would to God that every town had a girls' school as well, where the girls would be taught the Gospel for an hour every day either in German or in Latin. Schools indeed! Monasteries and nunneries began long ago with that end in view, and it was a praiseworthy and Christian purpose, as we learn from the story of St. Agnes[197] and of other saints. Those were the days of holy virgins and martyrs when all was well with Christendom. But today these monasteries have come to nothing but praying and singing. Is it not only right that every Christian man know the entire Holy Gospel by the age of nine or ten? Does he not derive his name and his life from the Gospel? A spinner or a seamstress teaches her daughter her craft in her early years. But today even the great, learned prelates and the very bishops do not know the Gospel.

Oh, we handle these poor young people who are committed to us for training and instruction in the wrong way! We shall have to render a solemn account of our neglect to set the word of God before them. Their lot is as described by Jeremiah in Lamentations 2 [:11–12]: "My eyes are grown weary with weeping, my bowels are terrified, my heart is poured out upon the ground because of the destruction of the daughter of my people for the youth and the children perish in all the streets of the entire city. They said to their mothers, 'Where is bread and wine?' as they fainted like wounded men in the streets of the city and gave up the ghost on their mothers' bosom." We do not see this pitiful evil, how today the young people of Christendom languish and perish miserably in our midst for want of the Gospel, in which we ought to be giving them constant instruction and training.

Moreover, even if the universities were diligent in Holy Scripture, we need not send everybody there as we do now, where their only concern is numbers and where everybody wants a doctor's degree. We should send only the most highly qualified students who have been well trained in the lower schools. A prince or city council ought to see to this, and permit only the well qualified to be sent. I would advise no one to send his child where the Holy Scriptures are not supreme. Every institution that does not unceasingly pursue the study of God's word becomes corrupt. Because of this we can see what kind of people they become in the universities and what they are like now. Nobody is to blame for this except the pope, the bishops, and the prelates, who are all charged with training young people. The universities only ought to turn out men who are experts in the Holy Scriptures, men who can become bishops and priests, and stand in the front line against heretics, the Devil, and all the world. But where do you find that? I greatly fear that the universities, unless they teach the Holy Scriptures diligently and impress them on the young students, are wide gates to hell.

26.[198] I know full well that the pope and his gang will pretend and boast about how the pope took the Holy Roman Empire from the Greek emperor and bestowed it upon the Germans, for which honor and benevolence he is said to have justly deserved and obtained submission, thanks, and all good things from the Germans.[199] For this reason they will, perhaps, undertake to throw all attempts to reform themselves to the four winds, and will not allow us to think about anything but the bestowal of the Roman Empire. For this cause they have persecuted and oppressed many a worthy emperor so willfully and arrogantly that it is a shame even to mention it. And with the same adroitness they have made themselves overlords of every secular power and authority, contrary to the Holy Gospel. I must therefore speak of this, too.

There is no doubt that the true Roman Empire, which the writings of the prophets foretold in Numbers 24 [:17–19] and Daniel 2 [:44], has long since been overthrown and come to an end, as Balaam clearly prophesied in Numbers 24 [:24] when he said, "The Romans shall come and overthrow the Jews, and afterward they also shall be destroyed." That happened under the Goths,[200] but more particularly when the Muslim empire arose almost a thousand years ago. Then eventually Asia and Africa fell away, and in time France and Spain. Finally Venice arose, and nothing was left to Rome of its former power.

Now when the pope could not subdue to his arrogant will the Greeks and the emperor at Constantinople, who was the hereditary Roman emperor, he invented a little device to rob this emperor of his empire and his title and to turn it over to the Germans, who at that time were warlike and of good repute. In so doing, the Romanists brought the power of the Roman Empire under their control so they could parcel it out themselves. And this is just what happened. The empire was taken away from the emperor at Constantinople, and its very name and title given to us Germans. Through this we became servants of the pope. There is now a second Roman Empire, built by the pope upon the Germans. The former Roman Empire, the first one, has long since fallen, as I said earlier.

So, then, the Roman See now gets its own way. It has taken possession of Rome, driven out the German emperor, and bound him by oaths not to dwell at Rome. He is supposed to be Roman emperor, and yet he is not to have possession of Rome; and besides, he is to be dependent on and move within the limits of the good pleasure of the pope and his supporters. We have the title, but they have the land and the city. They have always abused our simplicity to serve their own arrogant and tyrannical designs. They call us crazy Germans for letting them make fools and monkeys of us as they please.

All right! It is a small thing for God to throw empires and principalities about. He is so gentle with them that once in a while He gives a kingdom to a scoundrel and takes one from a good man, sometimes by the treachery of wicked, faithless men, and sometimes by inheritance. This is what we read about the kingdoms of Persia and Greece, and about almost all kingdoms. It says in Daniel 2 [:21] and 4 [:34–35], "He who rules over all things dwells in heaven, and it is he alone who overthrows kingdoms, tosses them to and fro, and establishes them." Since no one, particularly a Christian, can think it a very great thing to have a kingdom given him, we Germans, too, need not lose our heads because a new Roman Empire is bestowed on us. For in God's eyes it is but a trifling gift, one which He often gives to the most unworthy, as it says in Daniel 4 [:35]: "All who dwell on earth are as nothing in his eyes, and he has the power in all the kingdoms of men to give them to whom he will."

But although the pope used violence and unjust means to rob the true emperor of his Roman Empire, or of the title of his Roman Empire, and gave it to us Germans, yet it is nevertheless certain that God has used the pope's wickedness to give such an empire to the German nation, and after the fall of the first Roman Empire, to set up another, the one which now exists. And although we had nothing to do with this wickedness of the popes, and although we did not understand their false aims and purposes, nevertheless we have paid tragically and far too dearly for such an empire with incalculable bloodshed, with the suppression of our liberty, the hazarding and theft of all our possessions, especially of our churches and benefices, and with the suffering of unspeakable deception and insult. We carry the title of empire, but it is the pope who has our wealth, honor, body, life, soul, and all that we possess. This is how they deceive the Germans and cheat us with tricks.[201] What the popes have gladly sought was to be emperors, and when they could not achieve this, they at least succeeded in setting themselves over the emperors.

Since the empire has been given us by the providence of God as well as by the plotting of evil men, without any guilt on our part, I would not advise that we give it up, but rather that we rule it wisely and in the fear of God, as long as it pleases Him for us to rule it. For, as has been said already, it does not matter to Him where an empire comes from; His will is that it be governed. Though the popes were wrong in taking it from others, we were not wrong in receiving it. It has been given us through evil men by the will of God: it is the will of God we have regard for rather than the wicked intentions of the popes. Their intention when they gave it to us was to be emperors, indeed, more than emperors, and only to fool and mock us with the title. The king of Babylon also seized his kingdom by robbery and violence. Yet it was God's will that that kingdom be ruled by the holy princes Daniel, Hananiah, Azariah, and Michael.[202] Much more, then, is it God's will that this empire should be ruled by the Christian princes of Germany, no matter whether the pope stole it, got it by force, or established it fresh. It is all God's ordering, which came about before we knew about it.

Therefore, the pope and his followers have no right to boast that they have done the German nation a great favor by giving us the Roman Empire. In the first place, they did not mean it for our good. Rather, they took advantage of our simplicity when they did it in order to strengthen their proud designs against the real

Roman emperor at Constantinople. The pope took this empire against God and right, which he had no right to do. In the second place, the pope's intention was not to give us the empire, but to get it for himself that he might bring all our power, our freedom, our wealth, our souls and bodies into subjection to himself, and through us (had God not prevented it) to subdue all the world. He clearly says so himself in his decretals, and has attempted to do so by means of many wicked wiles with a number of the German emperors. Thus have we Germans been taught our German. While we supposed we were going to be masters, we became in fact slaves of the most deceitful tyrants of all time. We have the name, the title, and the insignia of empire, but the pope has its treasures, authority, rights, and liberties. The pope gobbles the kernel while we are left playing with the husk!

Now may God, who, as we have said, tossed this empire into our lap by the wiles of tyrants and has charged us with its rule, help us to live up to the name, title, and insignia, and to retrieve our liberty. Let the Romanists see once and for all what it is that we have received from God through them! If they boast that they have bestowed an empire on us, let them! If that is true, then let the pope give us back Rome and all that he has gotten from the empire; let him free our land from his intolerable taxing and fleecing; let him give us back our liberty, our rights, our honor, our body and soul; and let the empire be what an empire should be, so that the pope's words and pretensions might be fulfilled.

If he will not do that, then what is he playing at with his false and lying words and his juggler's tricks? Has there not been enough of constantly and rudely leading this noble nation by the nose for these many centuries? It does not follow that the pope must be above the emperor because he crowns him or appoints him. The prophet St. Samuel anointed and crowned the kings Saul and David[203] at God's command, and yet he was their subject. The prophet Nathan anointed King Solomon,[204] but he was not set over the king on that account. Similarly, St. Elisha had one of his servants anoint Jehu[205] king of Israel, but they still remained obedient and subject to the king. It has never happened in all the history of the world that he who consecrated or crowned the king was over the king, except in this single instance of the pope.

If the pope lets himself be crowned by three cardinals who are beneath him, he is nonetheless their superior. Why should he then go against his own example, against universal practice, and against the teaching of Scripture by exalting himself above temporal authority or imperial majesty simply because he crowns or consecrates the emperor? It is quite enough that he is the emperor's superior in the things of God, that is, in preaching, teaching, and the administration of the sacraments. In these respects any bishop and any priest is over everybody else, just as St. Ambrose in his see was over the emperor Theodosius,[206] the prophet Nathan over David, and Samuel over Saul. Therefore, let the German emperor be really and truly emperor. Let neither his authority nor his power be suppressed by such sham pretensions of these papist deceivers as though they were to be excepted from his authority and were themselves to rule in all things.

27.[207] Enough has now been said about the failings of the clergy, though you may find more, and will find more if you look in the right place. We shall now devote a section to the failings of the temporal estate.

In the first place, there is a great need for a general law and decree in the German nation against extravagant and costly dress, because of which so many nobles and rich men are impoverished.[208] God has certainly given us, as He has to other countries, enough wool, hair, flax, and everything else necessary for the seemly and honorable dress of every class. We do not need to waste fantastic sums for silk, velvet, golden ornaments, and foreign wares. I believe that even if the pope had not robbed us with his intolerable fleecing, we would still have more than enough of these domestic robbers, the silk and velvet merchants. We see that now everybody wants to be like everybody else, and pride and envy are thereby aroused and increased among us, as we deserve. All this misery and much more besides would be happily left behind if only our desire to be noticed would let us be thankful and satisfied with the good things God has already given us.

It is also necessary to restrict the spice traffic, which is another of the great ships in which money is carried out of German lands. By the grace of God more things to eat and drink grow in our own land than in any other, and they are just as nourishing and good. Perhaps my proposals seem foolish, impractical, and give the impression that I want to ruin the greatest of all trades, that of commerce. But I am doing my best, and if there is no improvement in these matters, then let him who will try his hand at improving them. I do not see that many good customs have ever come to a land through commerce, and in ancient times God made His people Israel dwell away from the sea on this account, and did not let them engage in much commerce.

But the greatest misfortune of the German nation is certainly the *zynskauf*.[209] If that did not exist, many a man would have to leave his silks, velvets, golden ornaments, spices, and display of every kind unbought. This traffic has not existed much longer than a hundred years, and it has already brought almost all princes, endowed institutions, cities, nobles, and their heirs to poverty, misery, and ruin. If it goes on for another hundred years, Germany will not have a penny left, and the chances are we shall have to eat one another. The Devil invented the practice, and by confirming it,[210] the pope has brought woe upon the whole world.

Therefore, I beg and pray at this point that everyone open his eyes and see the ruin of his children and heirs. Ruin is not just at the door, it is already in the house. I pray and beseech emperor, princes, lords, and city councilors to condemn this trade as speedily as possible and prevent it from now on, regardless of whether the pope with all his law—"unlaw" rather—objects or whether benefices or monasteries are based upon it. It is better for a city to have one benefice supported by honest legacies or revenue than to have a hundred benefices supported by *zynskauf*. Indeed, a benefice supported by a *zynskauf* is more grievous and oppressive than twenty supported by legacies. In fact, the *zynskauf* must be a sign and proof that the world has been sold to the devil because of its grievous sins, and that at the same time we are losing both temporal and spiritual possessions. And yet we do not even notice it.

In this connection, we must put a bit in the mouth of the Fuggers and similar companies. How is it possible in the lifetime of one man to accumulate such great possessions, worthy of a king, legally and according to God's will? I don't know. But what I really cannot understand is how a man with one hundred gulden can make a profit of twenty in one year. Nor, for that matter, can I understand how a man with one gulden can make another—and all this not from tilling the soil or raising cattle, where the increase of wealth depends not on human wit but on God's blessing. I leave this to men who understand the ways of the world. As a theologian I have no further reproof to make on this subject except that it has an evil and offending appearance, about which St. Paul says, "Avoid every appearance or show of evil" [I Thess. 5:22]. I know full well that it would be a far more godly thing to increase agriculture and decrease commerce. I also know that those who work on the land and seek their livelihood from it according to the Scriptures do far better. All this was said to us and to everybody else in the story of Adam: "Cursed be the ground when you work it; it shall bear you thistles and thorns, and in the sweat of your face you shall eat your bread" [Gen. 3:17–19]. There is still a lot of land lying unworked and neglected.

Next comes the abuse of eating and drinking,[211] which gives us Germans a bad reputation in foreign lands, as though it were a special vice of ours. Preaching cannot stop it, so deeply is it rooted and so firmly has it got the upper hand. The waste of money would be its least evil, were it not followed by all the vices that accompany it—murder, adultery, stealing, blasphemy, and every other form of immorality. Government can do something to prevent it; otherwise, what Christ says will come to pass, that the last day shall come like a secret snare, when they shall be eating and drinking, marrying and wooing, building and planting, buying and selling.[212] It is so much like what is now going on that I sincerely hope the day of judgment is at hand, although very few people give it any thought.

Finally, is it not lamentable that we Christians tolerate open and common brothels in our midst, when all of us are baptized unto chastity? I know perfectly well what some say to this, that is, that it is not a custom peculiar to one nation, that it would be difficult to put a stop to it, and, moreover, that it is better to keep such a house than that married women, or girls, or others of still more honorable estate should be outraged. Nevertheless, should not the government, which is temporal and also Christian, realize that such evil cannot be prevented by that kind of heathenish practice? If the children of Israel could exist without such an abomination, why cannot Christians do as much? In fact, how do so many cities, country towns, market towns, and villages do without such houses? Why can't large cities do without them as well?

In this matter of brothels, and in other matters previously mentioned, I have tried to point out how many good works the temporal government could do, and what the duty of every government should be, so that everyone may learn what an awful responsibility it is to rule and sit in high places. What use would it be if an overlord were as holy in his own life as St. Peter, if he did not diligently try to help his subjects in these matters? His very authority will condemn him. It is the duty of authorities to seek the best for those they govern. But if the authorities were to give some thought to how young people might be brought together in marriage, the hope of marriage would greatly help every one of them to endure and resist temptation.

But today everybody is attracted to the priesthood or the monastic life, and among them, I am sorry to say, there is not one in a hundred who has any other reason than that he seeks a living and doubts that he will ever be able to support himself and a family. Therefore, they live wildly enough beforehand, and wish, as they say, to get it out of their system, but experience shows that it is only more deeply embedded in them. I find the proverb true, "Despair makes most monks and priests." [213] That is what happens and that is how it is, as we see.

I will, however, sincerely advise that to avoid the many sins which entice so shamelessly, neither youth nor maid should be bound by the vow of chastity or a vow to adopt the religious life before the age of thirty. [214] Chastity, as St. Paul says, is a special gift [I Cor. 7:7]. Therefore, I would advise those upon whom God has not conferred his special gift not to enter religious orders or take the vows. Furthermore, I say that if you trust God so little that you cannot support yourself as a married man and wish to become a religious only because of this distrust, then I beg you for your own soul's sake not to become a religious at all, but rather a farmer or anything you like. For where a single measure of faith in God is needed to earn your daily bread, there must be ten times that amount of faith to remain a religious. If you do not trust God to support you in temporal things, how will you trust Him to support you in spiritual things? Alas, unbelief and distrust spoil everything and lead us into all kinds of misery, as we see in all walks of life.

Much more could be said of this pitiable state of affairs. The young people have nobody to look after them. They all do as they please, and the government is as much use to them as if it never existed. And yet the care of young people ought to be the chief concern of the pope, bishops, the ruling classes, and of the councils. They want to exercise authority far and wide, and yet they help nobody. For just this reason a lord and ruler will be a rare sight in heaven, even though he build a hundred churches for God and raise up all the dead!

That is enough for the moment. [I think I have said enough in my little book *Treatise on Good Works* about what the secular authorities and the nobility ought to do. There is certainly room for improvement in their lives and in their rule, yet the abuses of the temporal power are not to be compared with those of the spiritual power, as I have shown in that book.] [215]

I know full well that I have been very outspoken. I have made many suggestions that will be considered impractical. I have attacked many things too severely. But how else ought I to do it? I am duty-bound to speak. If I had the power, these are the things I would do. I would rather have the wrath of the world upon me than the wrath of God. The world can do no more to me than take my life. In the past I have made frequent overtures of peace to my enemies, but as I see it, God has compelled me through them to keep on opening my mouth wider and wider and to give them enough to say, bark, shout, and write because they have nothing else to do. Well, I know another little song about Rome and the Romanists. [216] If their ears are itching to hear it, I will sing that one to them, too—and pitch it in the highest key! You understand what I mean, dear Rome.

Moreover, many times have I offered my writings for investigation and hearing, but to no avail. Nevertheless, I know full well that if my cause is just, it must be condemned on earth and be justified only by Christ in heaven, for all the Scriptures show that the cause of Christians and of Christendom must be judged by God alone. Moreover, no cause has ever yet been justified on earth by men because the opposition has always been too great and too strong. It is still my greatest concern and anxiety that my cause may not be condemned, by which I would know for certain that it is not yet pleasing to God.

Therefore, just let them go hard at it, pope, bishop, priest, monk, or scholar. They are just the ones to persecute the truth, as they have always done.

God give us all a Christian mind, and grant to the Christian nobility of the German nation in particular true spiritual courage to do the best they can for the poor Church. Amen.

Wittenberg, in the year 1520

Translated by C. M. Jacobs
and revised by James Atkinson

Notes

1. A jocular comparison of the monk's cowl and tonsure to the jester's cap and bells.
2. I.e., who is the bigger fool.
3. *Monachus semper praesens.*
4. Luther often stressed that he had acquired his doctorate and its obligation to teach the gospel not out of his own desire but out of obedience to his superiors.
5. See *LW* 44, 91, n. 52.
6. Charles V, who had been elected emperor in 1519 when only twenty years of age, and before whom Luther appeared at the Diet of Worms in 1521.
7. Emperor Frederick Barbarossa (1152–1190).
8. Frederick II (1212–1250), grandson of Barbarossa and last of the great Hohenstaufen emperors, died under excommunication.
9. Pope Julius II (1503–1513) was notorious for his unscrupulous use of political power. Continually involved in war, he led his armies in person and was "the scourge of Italy."
10. Luther's memory is not accurate here. Judges speaks of twenty-two thousand.
11. Advocates of papal supremacy.
12. Luther alludes to the failure of the conciliar movement to reform the church. It failed chiefly because the papacy refused to submit to the authority of the council. Moreover, the papacy refused to cooperate in convening a council unless the secular powers first swore not to deprive the pope of his authority.
13. *Spugnissen*, literally, "ghosts." The sense of the passage is that the Romanists have frightened the world with threats of purgatory and hell.
14. Cf. Josh. 6:20.
15. I.e., confers tonsure.
16. *Olgotzen*, literally, wood images of saints; figuratively, any dull person.
17. *Ehelich*. *PE* and other English translations also render this word as "married." It can, however, also mean "legitimately born." Karl Benrath notes that according to canon law only one born in wedlock may receive ordination as a priest. Cf. *LW* 44, 128, n. 17.
18. Canon law, which Luther throughout this treatise and elsewhere calls the "spiritual law," is a general name for the decrees of councils and the decisions of

popes collected in the *Corpus Iuris Canonici*. It comprised the whole body of Church law and embodied the medieval theory of papal absolutism, which accounts for the bitterness with which Luther speaks of it, especially in this treatise.

19. Augustine, bishop of Hippo (395–430).

20. Ambrose, bishop of Milan (374–397), was elected to the office by the people of Milan, even though he was not yet baptized.

21. Cyprian, bishop of Carthage (247–258), was also elected by the laity.

22. The so-called *character indelibilis*, peculiar gift of ordination, meant "once a priest, always a priest." This "indelible mark" received authoritative statement in the bull *Exultate Deo* (1439). Eugene IV, summing up the decrees of the council of Florence, says, "Among these sacraments there are three—baptism, confirmation, and orders—which indelibly impress upon the soul a character, i.e., a certain spiritual mark which distinguishes them from the rest." The Council of Trent (1563) further defined the correct Roman teachings as follows: "The Holy Synod justly condemns the opinion of those who assert that the priests of the New Testament have only temporary power, and that those once rightly ordained can again be made laymen, if they do not exercise the ministry of the Word of God." *PE* 2, 68, n. 5.

23. *Schwetzen;* literally, "to chatter nonsense."

24. The sharp distinction drawn by the Roman Church between clergy and laity made possible the contention that the clergy was exempt from the jurisdiction of the civil courts.

25. I.e., temporal.

26. Church authorities insisted that clergy charged with infractions of laws of the state first be tried in ecclesiastical courts. Priests found guilty were deprived of their priesthood and surrendered to the temporal authorities.

27. The interdict prohibits the administration of the sacraments and other rites of the Church within a given territory. At the height of papal power it was an effective means of bringing rulers to terms. Interdicts of local extent were quite frequent. Their use for trifling infractions of Church law was protested at diets in 1521 and 1524.

28. The statement is found in the *Decreti Prima Pars,* dist. XL, C. VI, *Si papa.* CIC I, 146. In his *Epitome* Prierias had quoted this canon against Luther: "A *Pontifex indibitatus* [i.e., a pope not accused of heresy or schism] cannot lawfully be disposed or judged either by a council or by the whole world, even if he is so scandalous as to lead people with him by crowds into the possession of hell." Luther's comment is, "Be astonished, O heaven; shudder, O earth! Behold, O Christians, what Rome is!" *WA* 6,336.

39. Gregory the Great (590–604), in *Regula pastoralis,* II, 6. MPL 77, 34.

30. Antichrist is the incarnation of all that is hostile to Christ and his kingdom and whose appearance is prophesied in II Thess. 2:3–10; I John 2:18, 22; 4:3; and revelation 13.

31. The doctrine of papal infallibility was never officially sanctioned in the Middle Ages, but the claim was repeatedly made by the champions of papal power. In his attack on the *Ninety-five Theses* (*Dialogus de potestate papae,* 1517) Prierias had asserted, "The supreme pontiff cannot err when giving a decision as pontiff, i.e., when speaking officially [*ex officio*]"; and also, "Whoever does not rest upon the teaching of the Roman church and the supreme pontiff as an infallible rule of faith, from which even Holy Scripture draws its vigor and authority, is a heretic." In the *Epitome* Prierias had said, "Even though the pope as an individual [*singularis persona*] can do wrong and hold a wrong faith, nevertheless as pope he cannot give a wrong decision" (*WA* 6, 337). Cf. *LW* 44, 133, n. 31.

32. I.e., a single letter of Scripture to support their claim.

33. In the *Epitome* of Prierias.

34. Matt. 16:19, 18:18, and John 20:23. Throughout his career Luther dealt with the office of the keys. He first mentioned it in 1517 in his *Ninety-five Theses* (*LW* 31, 27, 31) and devoted a substantial portion of his last treatise, *Against the Roman Papacy, An Institution of the Devil* (1545), to a discussion of the keys (*LW* 41, 315–20 *passim*). His clearest and most extensive treatment was set forth in his 1530 treatise, *The Keys* (*LW* 40, 321–77).

35. Literally, "the creed," referring to the Apostles' Creed.

36. *Beten;* literally, "To pray."

37. Luther means baptism.

38. On November 28, 1518, Luther appealed his cause from the decision of the pope, which he could foresee to be adverse, to the decision of a council to be held at some future time. In the *Epitome* Prierias discusses this appeal, asserting that "when there is one undisputed pontiff, it belongs to him alone to call a council," and that "the decrees of councils neither bind nor hold unless they are confirmed by authority of the Roman pontiff." *WA* 6, 335.

39. A mere gathering of people as opposed to a *concilium*, i.e., a valid council.

40. In 325. Luther's contention is historically correct.

41. Luther is referring to the first four ecumenical councils: Nicaea, Constantinople (381), Ephesus (431), and Chalcedon (451).

42. *Kunst;* literally, "skill."

43. *Der Hauff;* literally, rank and file Christians without authority in the Church.

44. That is, if the ecclesiastical hierarchy will not do its duty and convene a council, then the secular authorities and ordinary Christians must take the matter in hand despite ecclesiastical sanctions. To come under one such sanction for the sake of this good cause is better than to receive ten absolutions.

45. *Zunympt;* literally, "grows larger" or "increases."

46. The papal crown dates from the eleventh century; the triple crown or tiara, from the fourteenth. It signified the superiority of the pope over temporal rulers.

47. Cf. also *LW* 44, 140, n. 48. In the jubilee year of 1500, as thousands of pilgrims died of the plague on their way through war-ravaged Lombardy toward Rome, a spurious bull of Pope Clement VI from the year 1350 was widely promulgated, in which were the words: "We command the angels of paradise that their souls [the souls of the pilgrims who died en route] be taken directly to the bliss of paradise, as being fully redeemed from purgatory." *WA* 30^{11}, 282; Buchwald, *Luthers Werke für das christliche Haus* (Braunschweig, 1890) II, 457 n. 1. In *Defense and Explanation of All the Articles* (1521), Luther writes: "This is what happened in the days of John Huss. In those days the pope commanded the angels in heaven to lead to heaven the souls of those pilgrims who died on the way to Rome. John Huss objected to this horrible blasphemy and more than diabolic presumption. This protest cost him his life, but at least caused the pope to change his tune and, embarrassed by this sacrilege, to refrain from such proclamation." *LW* 32, 74–75.

48. *Stifft;* i.e., endowed institutions.

49. For example, Pope Julius II, when a cardinal, held the revenues of the archbishopric of Avignon, the bishoprics of Bologna, Lausanne, Coutances, Viviers, Mende, Ostia, and Velletri, and the abbacies of Nonantola and Grottaferrata.

50. The complaint that the cardinals were provided with incomes by appointment to German benefices goes back to the Council of Constance (1414–1418). Cf. Luther's complaint in *Treatise on Good Works. LW* 44, 89. Cf below, n. 56.

51. Luther puts these words into the mouths of the Romanists, hence the change

from "they" to "we." The creation of cardinals was a lucrative matter for the popes. On July 31, 1517, Pope Leo X created thirty-one cardinals. He is reported to have received 300,000 ducats from the appointees. WA 6, 417, n. 1.

52. A Benedictine monastery on Mount St. Michael [*Mönchberg*].

53. The Council of Constance had suggested a yearly salary of three to four thousand gulden for cardinals.

54. In the fourteenth century England and France enacted laws protecting themselves against these practices. Cf. *LW* 44, 142, n. 56.

55. According to a document printed in Rome in 1545 and found among the belongings of John Eck, there were 949 curial positions obtained by paying a fee. This figure does not include officials who administered the city of Rome and the papal states, or members of the "papal household." The Diet of Worms in 1521 complained that the increase of these offices had added greatly to the financial burdens of the German Church, Cf. *LW* 44, 142, n. 57.

56. The annates were originally the various incomes a bishop received from vacant benefices in his diocese. The term was extended to include payments made to the Curia by bishops and abbots at the time of their accession. These charges soon became a fixed tax on all Church offices that became vacant, and claims against overassessment and extortion were frequent. The Council of Constance (1415) restricted annates, and the Council of Basel resolved to abolish them (1439), but could not enforce the decision. They were protested at the Diet of Worms in 1521. Cf. *LW* 44, 144, n. 58.

57. The Crusades indulgence was established by Urban II (1088–1099) and granted to those who went to Palestine. In 1198 Innocent III extended it to include those who supported the Crusades in other than military ways.

58. This whole section deals with the "right of reservation," i.e., the alleged right of the pope to fill vacant Church positions by appointment. The papal theory held that the right of appointment belonged to the pope, who in some cases yielded the right to others. The rule of the "papal months" provided that livings (except those of cathedrals and the chief posts in monasteries) that became vacant in February, April, June, August, October, and December should be filled by the ordinary methods—election, presentation, and appointment by the bishop, etc. Vacancies occuring in the other months were to be filled by the pope.

59. A dignity or prelacy was originally an ecclesiastical office in which jurisdiction was exercised in the name of the incumbent. Cf. *LW* 44, 146, n. 62.

60. Luther refers to policies governing the conferring of reserved benefices, etc. The pope usually established these policies just after his ascension to the papal throne. The Germans had protested the arbitrariness of these regulations and insisted that they be fixed by legislation. Cf. *LW* 44, 146, n. 63.

61. Charles V had not yet been crowned emperor when this treatise was written.

62. A living not hitherto filled by papal appointment.

63. A rule found in the Concordat of Vienna. Cf. *WA* 6, 420, n. 3.

64. Every one to whom the name "papal servant" could be made to apply. Luther later refers to them as "courtesans."

65. In 1513 Prince Albert of Brandenburg was made archbishop of Magdeburg. Later that same year he became administrator of Halberstadt. The next year he became archbishop of Mainz as well and in 1518 was made a cardinal. The expenses attending this pluralism were defrayed by the sale of indulgences.

66. This rule is also mentioned in the Concordat of Vienna.

67. A wool shoulder cape, the emblem of the archbishop's office. Luther's contentions are correct. Cf. *LW* 44, 148, n. 71.

68. Cf. n. 65.

69. I.e., the contesting of benefices.
70. For adjudication.
71. Wilhelm III, count of Honstein, was bishop from 1506 to 1541.
72. Cf. John 21:15–17.
73. The recipient was not obligated to exercise the duties attached to the benefice. Even Duke George of Saxony, an opponent of the Reformation, complained in 1521 about such commendations. Cf. *LW* 44, 150, n. 78.
74. Apostate monks were those who left their monasteries without permission and functioned as secular priests (*MA*[3] 2, 395). They wandered from place to place, often wearing the garb and exercising the rights and privileges of their order. They were a nuisance because they often disrupted parish life.
75. Offices that cannot be united in the hand of one man.
76. Glosses are more or less authoritative comments on canon law. Their chief aim is to show how the law applies to practical cases. Cf. *LW* 44, 151, n. 82.
77. The bureau that granted dispensations and was responsible for the issuing, registration, and dating of papal appointments. A fee had to be paid for its services.
78. I.e., have their pride deflated. Court follower Johannes Zink received 56 appointments between 1513 and 1521; Johannes Ingenwinkel received 106 appointments between 1496 and 1521.
79. Cardinal Albrecht of Mainz had the title Administrator of Halberstadt.
80. The complaint was made at Worms in 1521 that it was impossible for a German to secure a clear title to a benefice from Rome unless he applied for it in the name of an Italian, who demanded a lump sum, a yearly pension, or a percentage of the income in return for the use of his name.
81. Simony (Acts 8:18–20) is the ecclesiastical name for buying or procuring an office in the Church for money, favor, or any consideration or reward.
82. Cf. Matt. 27:35.
83. Since the pope ultimately held all rights of appointment, any case could be made an exception to the usual regulations, if the canonists' theory is supported, and in these cases the matter was "reserved in the heart of the pope," and the appointment then made "on his own motion."
84. An instance of giving and taking back was cited at Worms in 1521.
85. These three great centers of foreign trade were notorious.
86. I.e., buy exemptions from canon law in the form of dispensations.
87. Fees paid for dispensations were called *compositiones*. Luther makes a pun on *compositiones* and *confusiones*. Cf. *WA* 6, 426, n. 1.
88. Levied by the Rhine castle "robber barons" on passing merchants.
89. Cf. *CL* 1, 383, which interprets this obscure expression to mean "the opposite case."
90. The greatest international bankers of the sixteenth century and bankers to the Curia. They were zealous Romanists and supported Eck against Luther. They made the financial arrangements between the pope and Albrecht of Mainz that occasioned the indulgence controversy of 1517.
91. Certificates that entitled the holder to choose his own confessor and authorized the confessor to absolve him from certain "reserved" sins.
92. *Butterbriefe* were dispensations permitting Catholics to eat eggs and milk products during periods of fasting. Cf. *LW* 44, 155, n. 102.
93. *Confessionalia* is used here in the broad sense, and means dispensations of all sorts, including those relating to penance.
94. The Campo di Fiore, a Roman marketplace, was restored and adorned at great expense by Eugene IV (1431–1447) and his successors.

95. A part of the Vatican palace notorious as the banquet hall of Alexander VI (1492–1503). Julius II (1503–1513) turned it into a museum to house his collection of ancient works of art.

96. The host of positions for sale having substantial incomes.

97. Not *de filiis,* but *Filiis vel nepotibus.* The clause provides that in case the income from endowments bequeathed to the Church is misused, and appeals to the bishop and archbishop fail to correct the misuse, the heirs may appeal to the royal courts. Luther wants to apply this principle to the annates.

98. Promises to bestow livings not yet vacant. Complaints of the evils arising out of the practice were heard continually after 1416.

99. Luther refers to Canon 4 of this council.

100. "Exemption" was a constant subject of complaint by the bishops, and the Fifth Lateran Council passed a decree (1516) abolishing all monastic exemptions. This decree seems not to have been effective.

101. I.e., release from their lawful superiors.

102. A reference to Canon 5 of the Council of Sardica (343), which was later incorporated into canon law as a canon of Nicaea.

103. The complaint was that these judges assumed jurisdiction over cases belonging in the secular courts and enforced their decisions through ecclesiastical censure. The *Gravamina* of 1521 specify these charges.

104. This idea is not original with Luther. Jacob Wimpheling, the Alsatian-born humanist and German patriot, had made just such a suggestion to the emperor in 1510. Its effect would have been substantial independence of the German church from Roman control.

105. Bureaus through which the pope regulated matters of administration belonging to his own special prerogative.

106. Cf. n. 83.

107. Specifically those cases in which only the pope could absolve.

108. *Coena domini* was a papal bull published annually against heretics since 1364 in the Lateran Church at Rome on Holy Thursday. But to the condemnation of their heresies were added those offenses, absolvable only by the pope or by his authorization, which might conceivably endanger or impair the papal state. Luther was named in the bull for the first time on March 28, 1521, along with Wycliffe and Huss. In 1522 Luther translated this bull into German as a New Year's present for the pope. *WA* 8, 691.

109. A papal decree of equal authority with the bull, but differing from it in form and usually dealing with matters of lesser importance.

110. The Fifth Lateran Council (1512–1517), convened by Pope Julius II. The main item on the agenda was the reformation of the Church.

111. *Decretalium D. Gregorii Papae IX,* lib. i,tit. VI, C, IV (*CIC* 2, cols. 49–50). This chapter forbids the bestowing of the pallium on an archbishop-elect until he first shall have sworn allegiance to the Holy See.

112. The ceremony inducting Church officials into offices to which revenues and certain temporal powers are attached. Cf. *LW* 44, 164, n. 125.

113. Since the coronation of Charlemagne in 800, the German Empire had been regarded as the continuation of the Roman Empire, a fiction fostered by the pope, who had the right to crown an emperor. Perhaps, though, Luther is referring to the election of the half-German Charles V, despite papal agitation in favor of a French king. *Luthers Werke für das christliche Haus,* ed. Buchwald, *et al.* (Braunschweig, 1890) [hereinafter cited as Buchwald], II, 386 n. 1.

114. *Decretalium D. Gregorii Papae IX,* lib. i., tit. XXXIII, C. VI. *CIC* 2, col. 196.

115. *On the Power of the Pope (De potestate papae)* (1520). WA 2, 217.

116. Cf. pp. 153–156.

117. A decree of Pope Clement V issued in 1313 and later incorporated into canon law in *Clementinarum,* lib. ii, tit. XI, C. II. *CIC* 2, cols. 1151–1153.

118. This document purported to be the testament of Emperor Constantine (306–337). It conveyed to the pope title to the city of Rome, certain lands in Italy, and "the islands of the sea." Medieval pontiffs used the document to support their claims to temporal power. Cf. *LW* 44, 166, n. 133.

119. The papal claim to sovereignty over this little kingdom went back to the eleventh century. At the time Luther wrote this treatise, sovereignty was claimed by the royal houses of France and Spain, of which latter house Charles V was head.

120. Behind this papal claim lay a thousand years of history. When the western half of the Roman Empire collapsed in the fifth century, the sole surviving authority was the papacy. By the end of the sixth century the Roman See held large areas of Italy and Sicily. Responsibility for these territories sometimes involved war. Cf. *LW* 44, 167, n. 135.

121. A free rendering of the Vulgate version of II Tim. 2:4.

122. The rest of section II was not part of the first edition. Cf. *LW* 44, 168, n. 138.

123. Cf. Ulrich von Hutten's remark, "Three things there are which those who go to Rome usually bring back with them: a bad conscience, a ruined stomach, and an empty purse." Erasmus also criticized pilgrimages. Cf. *LW* 44, 170, n. 140.

124. *Die einfeltigen menschen,* the simple, or those of untrained mind.

125. The "golden" or "jubilee" years were started by Boniface VIII in 1300. Originally every hundredth year was to be a jubilee, but by 1473 every twenty-fifth year was. During these years indulgences were granted to those who visited Rome. These indulgences were extended on a limited scale by Clement VI in 1350 to those who could not make the pilgrimage. Still later Boniface IX sent commissioners throughout Europe to dispense the indulgences for the cost of a journey to Rome and back. Many times these indulgences were represented as offering pardon without penitential or sacramental formality. For this representation as well as for irregularity of their financial accounts, a great many commissioners were punished by the pope. Cf. *LW* 44, 171, n. 142.

126. Luther alludes here to the three leading mendicant orders. The Augustinian Hermits originated during the thirteenth century when several small hermit societies were united under the so-called Augustinian Rule. Luther was an Augustinian.

127. Divisions resulting from disputes over the interpretation of their "rules" were common among and within the religious orders. In the case of the Franciscans, for example, there were the fractions known as the *zelanti* and the *relaxti* in earlier times, and later on the division between the "Strict Observance" and the "Conventuals."

128. *Der glaub Christi;* literally, "the faith of Christ."

129. Luther knew perfectly well that convents and monasteries did not exist in apostolic times. He is arguing for a monastic system based on the apostolic teaching of the New Testament. Cf. *LW* 44, 312.

130. St. Agnes, a martyr of the early fourth century, was a popular medieval saint associated with youthful chastity and innocence. Cf. *LW* 44, 174, n. 147.

131. One of the most famous German convents, founded in 936.

132. Cf. Col. 2:20.

133. Cf. Luther's understanding of Cor. 4:1 in *Concerning the Ministry* (*LW* 40, 35). Cf. Jerome, *Commentary on Titus.* MPL 26, 562; cf. also 22, 656.

134. The first definitive and documented canon to prescribe and enforce clerical celibacy was that of Pope Siricius in 385. Cf. *LW* 44, 176, n. 151.

135. The controversy over celibacy was involved in the schism.

136. Luther had cast himself in this role in the Introduction. Cf. pp. 149–150.

137. Cf. Exod. 12:35–36.

138. The laws governing marriage were entirely ecclesiastical and prohibited the marriage of blood relatives as far as the seventh degree of consanguinity. In 1204 the prohibition was restricted by a council to the first four degrees; lawful marriage within these degrees was possible only by dispensation, which was not difficult to secure by those willing to pay for it. The relation of godparents to godchildren was looked upon as "spiritual consanguinity."

139. This is exactly what Luther did. A copy of the canon law was burned with the papal bull of excommunication on December 10, 1520.

140. Monks who have violated the rules of their order and been deprived of the benefits enjoyed by those living within the rule. Cf. *LW* 44, 180, n. 157.

141. *Jartag, begencknis, seelmessen,* translated here as "endowed masses for the dead" were celebrated at various times: *jartag,* on the annual anniversary of the beneficiary's death; *begencknis,* on the appointed day of the year when all the benefactors of a religious order were commemorated; and *seelmessen,* the masses regularly offered in behalf of souls in purgatory. Cf. *LW* 44, 180, n. 158.

142. I.e., liturgical offices connected with the festivals.

143. Cf. n. 27.

144. Luther's term for canon law is *geystlich recht,* i.e., "spiritual law."

145. *A Sermon on the Ban. LW* 39, 3–22.

146. Penalties imposed by the Church upon priests. Aggravation is the threat of excommunication; reaggravation is excommunication itself. Deposition is a permanent expulsion from clerical office. Cf. *MA*³ 2, 399.

147. I.e., those who teach and enforce canon law.

148. Luther refers here to the numerous saints' days and minor religious holidays which fell on weekdays. Cf. *Treatise on Good Works. LW* 44, 55.

149. An obscure saint honored in the territory of Strasbourg. Cf. *LW* 44, 183, n. 166.

150. *Kirchweye,* the anniversary celebration of the consecration of a church.

151. On butter letters, see n. 92; on *confessionalia,* see n. 93. Mass letters were certificates entitling the holder to the benefits of masses celebrated by sodalities.

152. A pun on *geistliche netz,* spiritual snares, and *geystlich gesetz,* spiritual or canon law.

153. Cf. Matt. 15:11.

154. I Cor. 10:23; Col. 2:16.

155. Chapels built in the country for pilgrims.

156. Wilsnack, a town northwest of Berlin, was a much frequented place of pilgrimage after 1383, when three hosts, singed only about the edges, survived a fire which destroyed a church. In the middle of each host was what appeared to be a drop of blood, taken to be the blood of Christ. When these hosts were taken to a neighboring church they were said to become fiery and luminous without burning. Large numbers of pilgrims were drawn to Wilsnack, where the bishop erected a new and impressive edifice. Opposition to the pilgrimages was soon voiced by many people, including John Huss. Despite protests from several universities, the shrine continued to be popular for some years after 1548, when a Protestant pastor burned the hosts. Cf. *LW* 44, 185, n. 176.

157. A monastery that also displayed a bleeding host after 1491.

158. A garment alleged to be the seamless garment of Christ for which the executioners cast lots beneath the cross (John 19:23–24) was first exhibited in Trier in 1512.

159. Grimmenthal had attracted pilgrimages since 1499. An image of the Virgin, said to have been miraculously created, was displayed there.

160. A shrine of the "Fair Virgin of Regensburg," an image similar to that at Grimmenthal, was opened March 25, 1519, and within a month fifty thousand pilgrims are said to have worshipped there.

161. Pilgrimages provided a large revenue from the sale of medals to be worn as amulets, fees for masses at the shrines, and free-will offerings of pilgrims. The popes did not overlook opportunities for selling indulgences at these shrines. The *Gravamina* of 1521 state that the bishops of the dioceses demanded at least 25–33 per cent of the offerings made at the shrines.

162. Cf. Acts 5:39.

163. Because of the income to be had from pilgrimages, church authorities were willing to pay large sums for the canonization of deceased clergy and dignitaries. Canonization is the definitive sentence by which the pope declares a soul to have entered into eternal glory.

164. Antoninus (1389–1459) had been archbishop of his native city of Florence and won renown as reformer of the Dominican Order. When Luther wrote this treatise the canonization of Antoninus was already under way.

165. *Schindleich,* i.e., a place where the carrion of skinned animals is piled.

166. *Indulta,* i.e., special papal dispensations.

167. Extraordinary powers to grant indulgences and absolution in reserved cases. They were usually held by legates or commissioners sent from Rome. Complaints were made at Diets in 1521 and 1523 that the papal representatives interfered with normal ecclesiastical jurisdiction and appointment.

168. Luther alludes to the exchange of a papal bull for money. Lead was the lead seal attached to the bull; hide, the parchment on which it was written; the string was the cord from which the seal hung; wax, the seal that held the cord to the parchment.

169. Franciscans, Dominicans, Augustinians, Carmelites, and Servites.

170. I.e., wandering beggars who enrolled their benefactors on the list of beneficiaries of the saint they claimed to represent. This enrollment, they claimed, provided immunity from peculiar diseases, accidents, and misfortunes. Protests were raised against this practice at diets in 1521 and 1523. Cf. *LW* 44, 190, n. 191.

171. I.e., men who spent their lives wandering from one place of pilgrimage to another subsisting on the alms of the faithful.

172. Bertram Lee Woolf notes that in this passage Luther touches upon an important matter in the history of social structure, namely the appointment of the younger sons of the upper classes to ecclesiastical positions. These younger sons were embittered because the more substantial benefices were given to papal favorites. Luther's hope was that if these sons were given the opportunity to study the Bible and sound teaching, they would infuse an evangelical spirit into the priests and the hierarchy. Cf. Woolf's *Reformation Writings of Martin Luther* (London: Lutterworth Press), I (1952), 175, n. I.

173. The brotherhoods flourished in the sixteenth century. Members were obligated to recite certain prayers and attend certain masses. Each member participated in the benefits accruing from the good works of all and usually enjoyed certain indulgences. In 1520 Wittenberg boasted of twenty such fraternities; Cologne, eighty; Hamburg, more than one hundred. In 1519 one Wittenberger was a member of eight brotherhoods in his hometown and of twenty-seven in other places. Luther

had expressed his views on these groups more fully in his *The Blessed Sacrament of the Holy and True Body of Christ, and the Brotherhoods* (1519). *LW* 35, 47–73.

174. Ladislaus III, king of Poland (1424–1444), and as Uladislaus I, king of Hungary (1440–1444), forced the sultan to sue for peace in 1443. The papal legate, Cardinal Caesarini, absolved the king from fulfilling the treaty's conditions. Ladislaus renewed the war, and at the Battle of Varna in 1444, the Hungarians were decisively defeated and Ladislaus and Caesarini both killed.

175. Huss had a safe-conduct granted by the emperor. Luther errs when he assumes that Jerome of Prage also had one. In 1415 the council decreed that "neither by natural, divine, nor human law was any promise to be observed to the prejudice of the Catholic faith." Both Huss and Jerome of Prage were executed.

176. In 1508 Pope Julius II, Louis XII of France, Emperor Maximilian I, and Ferdinand the Catholic of Spain entered into an alliance against Venice. When Venice capitulated to the pope in 1510, he broke the alliance and waged war on France.

177. After the death of Huss a number of movements holding in varying degrees to his teachings developed in Bohemia and caused political and ecclesiastical turmoil for well over a century. Many Hussites looked favorably upon Luther. Cf. *LW* 44, 197, n. 201.

178. Bishop of Carthage (249–258).

179. A chief point of controversy between the Roman Church and the Hussites.

180. Luther had not yet reached the conviction that the administration of the cup to the laity was a necessity.

181. Cf. I Cor. 7:23; Gal. 5:1.

182. The term Pickard, a corruption of Beghards, was a derisive name for the Bohemian Brethren, a Hussite sect.

183. "Accidents" were the qualities that, in medieval thought, were held to adhere to the invisible "substance" and, together with it, form the object. In Transubstantiation the "substance" of the bread and wine was changed into the "substance" of Christ's body and blood, while only the "accidents" or "form" of the bread and wine (such as shape, color, and taste) remained. The name refers to Thomas Aquinas (1225–1274), a Dominican, greatest of the Scholastic theologians, still regarded as the foremost doctrinal authority in the Roman Catholic Church. He taught Transubstantiation.

184. I.e., outside the Church.

185. I.e., places for training youth in the Greek way of life.

186. Aristotle taught that a man becomes good by doing good and ultimately led theologians to a belief in man's power to save himself. Luther taught that it was only when a man lost all belief in himself that he ever knew what it was to have faith in Christ. Luther objected to Aristotle's displacing Christ, who alone could save a man and give him true knowledge of natural and spiritual things. Roger Bacon and Erasmus were also against the Aristotelian domination in medieval universities.

187. Luther lectured on Aristotle's *Nicomachean Ethics* four times a week during his first year in Wittenberg (1508–1509).

188. Duns Scotus (d. 1308) was highly regarded in the fifteenth and sixteenth centuries as a rival to Thomas Aquinas for first place among theologians.

189. Papal decrees.

190. *Scrinium pectoris.* In the Roman Empire official documents were stored in a chest called the *scrinium.* This term was carried over into the Middle Ages and designated the chest in which the instruments of a monastery were stored. Boniface

VIII (1294–1303), who added his own book to the five books of the decretals of Gregory IX, said, "The Roman pontiff has all laws in the chamber [*scrinium*] of his heart." This statement was incorporated within canon law and meant that the pope claimed authority over canon law. Cf. *Decretalium D. Gregorii Papae IX*, lib. vi, tit. II, C. I. *CIC* 2, 937. Cf. *CIC* 2, 929.

191. *Doctores decretorum*.

192. *Doctores scrinii papalis*.

193. Roman law had been introduced into Germany in the twelfth century and by the fifteenth century it was the accepted legal system. There was a continual conflict between Roman law and the feudal customs and remnants of Germanic legal ideas, which justified Luther's description.

194. Famous medieval textbook of theology, compiled ca. 1150 by Peter Lombard (d. 1160) and containing brief statements or "sentences" of the main arguments pro and con with respect to the principal themes in Christian doctrine.

195. "Heathenish" and "humanistic" are not abusive epithets. The first refers to the dominance of the heathen Aristotle in schools; the second, to the dominance of canon law and other humanly devised doctrines over the gospel.

196. A square cap worn by a teacher. Red is the academic color of theology; brown, of liberal arts.

197. See n. 130.

198. This section did not appear in the first edition. Cf. *LW* 44, 207, n. 224.

199. See n. 113.

200. Rome was sacked by the Visigoths in A.D. 410.

201. *Szo sol man die Deutschen teuschen und mit teuschen teuschenn*, an untranslatable pun on *Deutschen* ("German") and *teuschenn* ("to deceive").

202. Dan. 1:6–7; 2:48; 5:29.

203. Cf. I Sam. 10:1; I Sam. 16:13.

204. Cf. I Kings 1:39. Luther errs; Zadok the priest did the anointing.

205. Cf. II Kings 9:6.

206. On a possible historical allusion, cf. *LW* 44, 211, n. 233.

207. This section followed immediately after Section 25 in the first edition and was numbered 26. Cf. *WA* 6, 465, n. 2.

208. Such a law was proposed to the Diet of Worms in 1521.

209. A technically nonusurious way to lend money profitably. Cf. *LW* 44, 96, n. 61.

210. The *zynskauf* was legalized by the Fifth Lateran Council in 1512.

211. The diets of Augsburg (1500) and Cologne (1512) passed edicts against drunkenness. The Diet of Worms (1521) adjourned before a recommendation that these earlier edicts be reaffirmed was acted upon.

212. Cf. Luke 21:34, 12:45, and Matt. 24:36–44.

213. *Desperatio facit monachum*.

214. In *Discussion on How Confession Should Be Made* (1520) Luther sets the minimum age for men at eighteen or twenty and for women at fifteen or sixteen (*LW* 39, 44). In *The Judgment of Martin Luther on Monastic Vows* (1521) he sets the minimum age at sixty (*LW* 44, 387–88).

215. Cf. *LW* 44, 15–114. The bracketed material did not appear in the first edition.

216. This "little song" is *The Babylonian Captivity of the Church*, written shortly after the present treatise was published.

ULRICH VON HUTTEN

Ulrich von Hutten (1488–1523) was one of the most flamboyant figures of the early sixteenth century. He received his early education at the monastery school in Fulda, whence his close friend Crotus Rubianus persuaded him to flee in 1505. He arrived in Erfurt in 1506, where he joined the circle of scholars and poets around Mutianus Rufus for a while. In 1509 he began his wanderings through Germany and Italy, seeking and finding knowledge and adventure. In 1513 he enlisted as a lansquenet at Padua, and in 1517 he was crowned poet laureate at the Imperial Diet in Augsburg.

A nobleman with a militant mind, an intellectual with an excellent education, Hutten joined the Humanists of his generation and became for a while one of their most eloquent spokesmen. The following dialogue clearly shows his fearless participation in political and religious controversies. He was a very articulate critic of the power brokers in Rome and at the Imperial Court, but at the same time his writings have an unmistakable tone of passionate patriotism that is unique for this time in Germany. It is this tone that accounts for his lasting popularity and glamorous image in the eyes of his countrymen.

Book of Dialogues

Fever the First

Speakers: HUTTEN, FEVER

HUTTEN: I'd like you to leave now. You've been a great nuisance as a guest, and I really ought to have chased you away the first day. Don't you hear? Get going at once, beat it!

FEVER: Well, from what I know of your kindness and the traditional hospitality of the Germans, even though you are sending me away, I'd expect you to direct me to other lodgings before you do so. But I beg you not to throw me out this winter, for I wouldn't know where to turn.

HUTTEN: First of all, I'm telling you to go. Then, since you ask about other lodgings, look at those gates. Do you see them? The road for you to take leads right through them.

FEVER: I hope for my sake they may lead to someone fond of luxurious living, a man of wealth and power, with horses, servants galore, hangers-on, a huge retinue, fine clothes, nice gardens, and baths.

HUTTEN: The one I am sending you to is a guest here himself, but he has no lack of the things you mention and makes good use of them. Do you see that house over there? That's where Cardinal St. Sixtus is staying, together with a tremendous courtly retinue. He's come up from Rome to raise money from us Germans so that the Romans will have enough to eat, I suppose, while arming against the Turks. They are planning another campaign against them, for the Turks are very experienced and capable warriors.

Incidentally, they are a people generally devoted to you. Take my advice and go to him. You'll find him comfortably ensconced in a scarlet robe, behind plenty of drapes. He eats only off silver dishes and drinks from golden vessels, but he's such a gourmet that he won't admit that people in Germany have any taste at all. He despises our local wild fowl and field fare and says they can't compare with the Italian kinds in flavor or in any other way. He finds our game repulsive, says the bread has no taste, and when he drinks our wine he bursts into tears and cries, "O, Italia, O, Italia," and calls for good Corsican wine [*Cursz*]. And, chiefly for the reasons mentioned, he calls us uncouth beasts and drunken louts. He also says he hasn't enjoyed his meals once in four months because he hasn't been able to find tasty dishes or decent cuisine.

FEVER: You're wasting your breath with that story.

HUTTEN: How so? Doesn't he strike your fancy as a host? Why, where could you find a greater prince in this place, or one who is more honored, venerated, and kowtowed to? Or do you think he is undeserving of fever?

FEVER: Not at all. He deserves the gout too.

HUTTEN: Well, what have you got against him?

FEVER: He's lean and scrawny, thin as a reed, and has no life in him. He goes around moping and hanging his head. He used to be a monk, a cheese-begging Dominican; now he's a new cardinal, but everything else about him is old. He spends a few pennies for lunch, and his cook often brings home half an ounce of meat from the market.

HUTTEN: Ah, you've got it all wrong. I tell you, he's most respected and revered. He's addressed even at the Lateran as Your Excellence, Your Grace, Your Princely Beneficence—how can you believe that he doesn't live well and sumptuously simply because he regards the Germans as lacking in understanding of elegance and fine living?

FEVER: I'm not disputing the way he lives himself. But how would he treat me when he feeds and clothes his own people so shabbily? You see, I did knock at his door not long ago to ask for a day or two's lodging, and his doorman positively screamed at me, "Can't you hear that noise?" I answered, "Yes, I certainly can." I heard a thumping, as if people were demanding something. The doorman said, "That's the household asking for bread; yet they have just been fed!" "What?" I asked. "Bread? Are the meals so stingy that they don't even serve enough bread here?" "Yes," he replied, "they're that stingy. And there are also no cushions or down-filled pillows, or comfortable bedclothes—except those used by the cardinal himself for his own comfort. But he is armed against the likes of you with the Church's curse, and he would put a ban on you as soon as you set foot inside this house. He's Pope Leo's legate and has the power to aid or to damn anybody according to his deserts, or according to the cardinal's own whim." That was all I needed to hear. I left, and by doing so, found a better host.

HUTTEN: I realize now that I should have been stingier with the food than I have been, if I wanted to get rid of you. Well, from now on—unless I forget myself—you will never see me taking lavish meals at the homes of lords and nobles. But I imagine that workmen and common folk are not what you're looking for either.

FEVER: Absolutely not. For one thing, they drive me away with hunger. For another, they chase me far away from them with their hard labor.

HUTTEN: How would it be if I sent you to the homes of princes or wealthy people, or to the great merchants—even the Fuggers, say?

FEVER: Nothing doing. Whenever I have visited them they have been surrounded by a crowd of physicians. That's no place for me. Someplace else, if you please, in return for past favors.

HUTTEN: Favors? What favors? What kind of fairy tale are you trying to pass off on me now? Do you mean that you do people a favor by staying with them?

FEVER: Yes, and you more than anyone. Have you forgotten how diligent, patient, docile, and God-fearing I made you when I stayed with you for four days eight years ago—although the effect didn't last more than six months?

HUTTEN: The truth of the matter is that you tormented me so much and I was so sick of you that I devoted myself to my books, for I couldn't do anything else. But now I see through your maneuver, for, as I recall, you invoked one of your patrons, the one who taught you the speech you deliver to those you are not content to plague with sickness but also have to feed with those sentiments and similar ones, pretending to make a person diligent, virtuous, and capable. But if what your protector writes about your alleged good deeds is true, namely that a person recovering from the four-day fever is healthier, why didn't you leave me healthier after mine? In all the years since your departure I have been incessantly sick with one ailment or another.

FEVER: That's because I never intended to leave you for good. When I departed that time, I was firmly resolved to return to you soon. And if what you have just said means that you are not about to send me to proper lodgings, I'm determined not to leave you, no matter how angry you get, but to stay on with you for six or seven years, if it suits me.

HUTTEN: In that case I shall do what the cardinal does and have threepenny meals and live an ascetic life.

FEVER: But I can counteract that by giving you a sweet tooth and a craving for forbidden things.

HUTTEN: Then I shall immediately summon doctors—Dr. Heinrich Stromer, for example, a man in whom I have complete confidence.

FEVER: Oh, of course, doctors—oh yes, Dr. Stromer—as if I didn't know the way you are. You'd rather be sick a whole year than take a dose of two of rhubarb, or even a few grains of hellebore or other purgative. Rather give me that doctor who finds an oat grain in the urine bottle and concludes that the patient has swallowed a horse.

HUTTEN: I'll make an effort to avoid all that and send you to other hosts. Since you have a preference for people who live well, follow me to the monks' place. They have it easy in every respect. You can tell by looking at them. They are all sleek and plump and well fed. They enjoy life and revelry. They live in their cells and rarely exercise, something you hate; they also drink wine and eat fish ravenously. You see, that's the kind of lodging for you.

FEVER: No, you won't get rid of me with those words because those fellows hear confession from old women, and from them they learn plenty of magic spells to drive me away, even when they see me at a distance.

HUTTEN: How about going to the cathedral canons? They have all those things in abundance. They do occasionally ride out to hunt, for exercise and pleasure, but they ought to be quite to your liking, really, since you have a predilection for well-fed people. They eat well, sleep soundly, and do everything at a nice leisurely pace. No need to worry that they'll fortify themselves with medicines, for they live without cares and thumb their noses at the doctors you seem to fear so much in the case of the Fuggers. I can't see why, because those who have physicians are usually sicker than those who do without them, like the Saxons. Since you fear them, however, take note of what I have told you: these people detest doctors. They are also fond of bathing and stuff themselves at meals and are surrounded by wenches, often all night long, all of which results in their having bad stomachs and poor digestion.

FEVER: That sounds like the right kind of people to harbor a fever, and it might pay me to stay with them for a while. But I'm afraid a number of other sicknesses may reside with them already, considering the sort of life they live. Don't you imagine that one of them must already be ailing with gout or gallstones, or dropsy, sciatica, leprosy, jaundice or epilepsy, the French disease, or scabies with the worst kind of abscesses, or cancer, polyp, fistula, throat tumor, or, as a result of long-continued gluttony and drinking, tremors of the hands and feet, or a stitch in the side, or other ailment, so that there will be no room for a fever? Because all of the ailments named, as well as countless others, head for the kitchen and see to the cuisine and to gourmandizing, enjoying life with plump, gluttonous folk, as I do, and hastening in droves to wherever such gorging and feasting abound, as I do too.

HUTTEN: Take my word for it, they aren't all sick. There's that man Curtisan, for instance, who has recently come from Rome. After learning the art of sumptuous living from a cardinal, he has enthusiastically thrown himself into the midst of our local gluttony and is enjoying it enormously.

FEVER: Does he drink wine too?

HUTTEN: Yes, he guzzles it.

FEVER: Does he lace it with pepper, cinnamon, ginger, and cloves?

HUTTEN: Copiously.

FEVER: Does he have soft beds, fine carpets, cushions, down-stuffed pillows, and silken bedclothes?

HUTTEN: The most precious sorts.

FEVER: Then does he eat fish?

HUTTEN: Most assuredly. He fairly gobbles it, but only the best and most expensive kinds. He is also very fond of partridges and pheasants. When he eats a hare he thinks it makes him better-looking. And he finds winter too long because there is no asparagus to be had then.

FEVER: Does he bathe once in a while?

HUTTEN: He is very fond of bathing, and does so frequently.

FEVER: Isn't he stingy at times?

HUTTEN: No, as a matter of fact, he is generous to a fault.

FEVER: Does he have doctors attend him?

HUTTEN: He hates them and regards them as bitter enemies; he says they should be banished from German soil.

FEVER: Does he wear fur coats and other fine garments?

HUTTEN: Yes, like the man Martial writes of:

> He longs for frost, for rain, and snow,
> Has thirty score fur coats to show.

FEVER: If that's the way he is, I don't think he could stand me very long.

HUTTEN: You see to that. But why would you want to kill someone you can make use of for a long time?

FEVER: For the reason of getting too attached. But, tell me, does he have minstrels too?

HUTTEN: Yes, also court jesters.

FEVER: Does he have a mistress too, who will take care of the pair of us?

HUTTEN: Yes, he does, a pretty little thing, as a matter of fact.

FEVER: Does he have a big fat paunch?

HUTTEN: It's beginning to develop.

FEVER: Suppose he refuses to accept me; where else would you send me?

HUTTEN: I'll give you a runaround.

FEVER: Then I'll give you a sound beating.

HUTTEN: Then I'll despise you.

FEVER: Then I'll strangle you.

HUTTEN: Then I'll befoul you.

FEVER: You? Befoul me?

HUTTEN: Yes, with the help of hunger, moderate exercise, and a completely ascetic life.

FEVER: Then I'll give this Curtisan fellow a try; after that I shall consider what to do about you.

HUTTEN: As you will. I'm getting out of here.

Fever to Curtesan

Mr. Curtesan, I bid you good day.
  In your house abundance prevails;
That's why I'm coming to stay with you.
  Have food and drink served up; don't stint!
But first let's have a bath made warm
  And let ourselves enjoy its benefits
With rubbing and stroking, hot baths and cold.
  From that we'll go at once to dine.
A lavish banquet will be held,
  No cost too great, with splendor untold,
  To last until beyond midnight.
Let there be dishes there galore,
  Fish, poultry, game, plus beer and wine.
Spare not the condiments nor spice,
  No matter what the cost may be.
Whether it hails from India
  Or grows in far-off Araby.
Or is from the Neue Insel.
  Just serve it, the Fuggers can get more.
Create the mood with meat and drink;
  With stomach full one soundly sleeps.
For me to join in this act too
  Is quite all right, won't demand much.
  Each creature has his goal in life.

I've said my piece.

Translated by Robert A. Fowkes

CROTUS RUBIANUS

Crotus Rubianus (c.1480–1539) made literary history with
the satire from which the following samples are selected. As
the Hebraist and Humanist Johann Reuchlin became more
and more deeply involved in the controversy over Jewish
books, a feeling of indignation against the Dominicans in
Cologne began to sweep the nation. Every scholar of reputation eventually wrote to Reuchlin expressing sympathy and
solidarity with his cause and imploring him not to give up,
and Reuchlin published these letters of support under the title
Letters of Famous Men.

In an obvious play on this title, Crotus, together with von
Hutten, designed his brilliant satire *Letters of Obscure Men*
(1515), in which fictitious provincial clergymen from all over
Germany write in support of Ortwin Gratius, the spokesman
of the Dominicans. They reveal themselves as ignorant, vul-
gar, naïve, and bigoted simpletons whose enthusiastic support is an embarrassment to the Dominicans. Ulrich von Hutten wrote a sequel to this satire (1519) of which one letter is
included here (I, 1).

This parody worked extremely well. Genuinely funny, it
nonetheless unmasked the questionable, even despicable,
methods with which the Dominicans sought to suppress the
Jews. *Letters of Obscure Men* is a milestone in German cultural history, in that it transformed a potentially ugly anti-
Semitic incident into a nonviolent victory of intelligence over
stupidity—a peculiarly Humanist approach.

From Letters of
Obscure Men

I

1

THOMAS LANGSCHNEIDER, *duly qualified, albeit unworthy, Bachelor in Theology, sendeth greeting to the supereminent and high-scientifical Herr Ortwin Gratius of Deventer, Poet, Orator, and Philosopher—Theologian too, and whatsoever else he listeth.*

Since, as Aristotle hath it, "To inquire concerning all and singular is not unprofitable," and, as we read in the Preacher, "I purposed in my soul to seek and ensearch wisely of all things that are made under the sun," so I, therefore, am purposed to propound to your worship a question about which I have a doubt.

But first I call the Lord to witness that I seek not to craftily entangle your excellence or your reverence; I do but heartily and sincerely crave of you that you will instruct me on this perplexful matter. For it is written in the Gospel, "Thou shalt not tempt the Lord thy God," and Solomon saith, "All wisdom is of God."

Now, it was you who imparted to me all the learning that is mine—and all right learning is the beginning of wisdom—therefore, to speak as a poet, you stand to me, as it were, in the place of a god, because it was you who imparted to me this beginning of wisdom.

Now, the aforesaid question arose after this manner: The other

247

day a Feast of Aristotle was celebrated here—the doctors, the licentiates, and the magisters were in high feather, and I too was present. To begin with, by way of a whet, we drank three bumpers of malmsey, and for the first course we had fresh wastel bread and made sops; and then we had six dishes of meat, and chickens, and capons—and one of fish; and between the courses we ceased not to drink Kotzberger and Rhine wine, and beer of Eimbeck, and Torgau and Naumburg; and the magisters were full pleased, and vowed that the new-fledged graduates had acquitted themselves right well, and greatly to their credit.

Then began the doctors over their cups to argue canonically concerning profundities. And the question arose whether *magister nostrandus* or *noster magistrandus* is the fitter to denote a candidate eligible for the degree of doctor in divinity. (As is now, for example, the mellifluous Father Theodoric of Gouda, friar of the Order of Carmelites, most reverend legate of the benign University of Cologne, most sagacious artsman, philosopher, and syllogizer—and withal theologian preeminent.)

Forthwith made answer Magister Warmsemmel, my compatriot—a right subtle Scotist and a master of eighteen years' standing. (He was, in his time, twice rejected and thrice impedited for the master's degree, and yet he resided until, for the honor of the university, he was graduated.)

He knoweth his business right well, and hath many pupils, high and low, young and old; and, speaking with ripeness of knowledge, he held that we should say *nostermagistrandus*—in one word—because *magistrare* signifies to make master, and *baccalauriare* to make bachelor, and *doctorare* to make doctor (whence come the technical terms "magistrand," "baccalauriand," and "doctorand"). Now doctors in divinity are not styled "doctors," but on account of their humility and sanctity, and by way of distinction, are named and styled *Magistri Nostri,* because in the Catholic faith they stand in the room of Our Lord Jesus Christ, who is the fount of life, and the *Magister* of us all: wherefore are they styled *Magistri Nostri* because it is for them to instruct us in the way of truth—and God is truth.

Rightly, he argued, are they called "our masters," for it is the bounden duty of us all, as Christians, to hearken to their preachments, and no man may say them nay—wherefore are they the masters of us all.

But *nostro-tras-trare* is not in use, and is found neither in the vocabulary *ex quo,* nor in the *Catholicon,* nor in the *Breviloquus,* nor even in the *Gemma gemmarum,* notwithstanding that this containeth many terms of art.

Thereupon uprose Magister Andreas Delitzsch, a very subtle scholar—on the one hand a poet, and on the other an artsman, physician, and jurist—who lectureth in ordinary upon Ovid in his *Metamorphoses,* and explaineth all the fables allegorically and literally (I myself have attended his lectures, by reason that his exposition is mightily fundamental), and he lectureth privately on Quintilian and Juvencus—and he held, in opposition to Magister Warmsemmel, that we should say *magisternostrandus;* for as there is a difference between *magisternoster* and *noster magister,* so there is a like difference between *magisternostrandus* and *nostermagistrandus.* Because *magisternoster* signifieth a doctor of divinity, and is one word, but *noster magister* consisteth of two words, and is used for a master in any Liberal Science, whether it concern handicraft or braincraft. And it booteth not that *nostrotras-trare* is not in use, for we may devise new words—and on this point he quoted Horace.

Then the company marveled greatly at his subtlety, and a tankard of Naumburg beer was handed to him. Quoth he, "Now I wait awhile—but, with your leave!" and, laughing heartily, he touched his cap and pledged Master Warmsemmel, saying, "Marry, Herr Magister, think not that I am out with you!" He made but one draught of it, and bravely did Master Warmsemmel respond thereto, for the honor of the Silesian "nation."

Then all the magisters waxed merry, till at last the bell rang to vespers.

I beseech your excellence, therefore, to set forth your opinion, seeing that you are mightily profound, and, as I said at the time, "Magister Ortwin will easily unfold the truth of the matter, for he was my teacher at Deventer when I was in the third class."

Let me know, too, how standeth the strife between Doctor Johann Reuchlin and yourself. I have heard, indeed, that the scoundrel, albeit a doctor and a jurist, will not yet recant.

Send me also, I prithee, Mag. N. Arnold von Tongern's book of *Articles,* which he hath drawn up; for it is vengeance subtle, and treateth of many theological profundities.

Farewell—and take it not amiss that I write to you thus familiarly, for you told me once on a time that you loved me as a brother, and desired to advance me in all things, even if it should cost you a pretty penny.

Leipzig

37

Lupold Federfuchser, *Licentiate—in a little while—sendeth to Mag. Gratius greetings as many as are the blades of grass in a goose's supper.*

Herr Magister Ortwin, among the quodlibets at Erfurt a vengeance subtle question hath been mooted in the two Faculties of Theology and Natural Philosophy.

The one part hold that when a Jew becometh a Christian there ensueth a preputial regeneration, or retrieval of the virile deprivation inflicted in childhood under the Judaic law.

These disputants are of the Theological Faculty, and they allege for their part sundry weighty reasons, one whereof is that were it not so, Jews who had become Christians might be regarded as being yet Jews at the Last Judgment—their virile deficiency being made manifest—and hence an injury would be done to them; but the Lord doth injury to no man.—Q.E.D.

And they find another argument in the words of the Psalmist, who saith, "He covereth me in the day of evils, in the secret place he covereth me"; but "the day of evils" meaneth the Day of Doom in the Valley of Jehoshaphat, when account of all sins must be rendered. Other arguments I omit for brevity's sake, for we at Erfurt are moderns, and the moderns ever delight in brevity, as you know. Moreover, in that my memory is weak, I cannot learn by rote a multitude of citations, as do the jurists.

But there are others who contend that this argument holdeth not, and they quote Plautus on their side, who saith, "What is done cannot be undone." From this they prove that if a Jew in the days of his Judaism hath lost any portion of his corporality, he will by no means recover it in Christian baptism. They argue, too,

that their opponents' proof concludeth illogically, for from their
major premise it would follow that Christians who had, through
loose living, suffered some carnal deficiency—as happeneth many
a time to both secular and spiritual persons—would also be held
to be Jews at the Last Judgment.

But this is a heretical conclusion, and our masters, the Inquisi-
tors of Heretical Pravity, will by no means grant it, seeing that
they themselves are now and then a trifle lacking thereabouts—a
mishap which occurreth to them by no means from consorting
with wantons, but from lack of care at the baths. Most humbly
and devotedly I pray your worship, therefore, to determine the
truth of this matter once and for all by your decision, and to make
inquiries of Herr Pfefferkorn's wife, seeing that you stand in her
good graces, and she will not be backward in telling you whatsoever you ask in the name of the close friendship you have with her
husband. Moreover, I hear that you are her confessor, and therefore you may compel her to due obedience under pain of penance.

Say to her, "Madam, be not bashful! I know you for as honest
a lady as any in Cologne, and nothing dishonest do I ask from
you. I do but seek to learn the truth from you: Is your husband
of the circumcision or not? Speak boldly, without shame! 'Od's
life! Have you lost your tongue?" But I must not presume to instruct you, for you know much better than I how to deal with
women. I write in haste.

From Erfurt: At the sign of the Dragon

II

1

JOHANN LABIA, *by the grace of God Apostolic Prothonotary, to the
Reverend Herr Magister Ortwin Gratius of Deventer, as to a well-
beloved brother, of Salutations a hundred thousand Sesterces, as
the New Grammarians have it.*

I received the day before yesterday, honored sir, a book that
your worship will have sent me from Germany. This work was—

or is—entitled *Epistolae Obscurorum Virorum.* Sonty! How rejoiced was I in mine heart when my eyes fell on that book—for it hath goodly contents, in prose and eke in verse. And I had great joy with dulcet jubilation when I perceived that you have many allies—poets, and rhetoricians and theologians—who write to you and are your friends in opposition to Johann Reuchlin.

Yesterday there was a feast toward—and certain Curialists were present—scholars and men of affairs—and I laid that book before them on the board. And after that they had dipped into it here and there, I mooted a logomachy, saying, "Masters, how think ye? Wherefore hath Magister Ortwin named this book of his *Epistolae Obscurorum Virorum*—seeming thereby to call his friends and allies 'obscure men'?"

Then answered a priest from Münster, a learned jurist, and he declared that "obscure" was a word of many meanings, as, following *Lex Ita fidei sqq. de Jure Fisci,* the first Solution hath it. He said, too, that it might be some family name. For it is recorded that the parents of Diocletian and some other kings were "Obscuri."

Then I nudged him and said, "By your favor, sir, this is beside the point." And next I put the question to a famous theologian who drank with us. He is of the Carmelite Order and a native of Brabant. Full solemnly spake he his reasons: "Most eximious Herr Prothonotary, since, as Aristotle saith, it is profitable to make inquiry concerning each and all; therefore hath your Eximiousness proposed to me a question, to wit: For what cause did Magister Ortwin, in publishing a new collection of letters, entitle them *Epistolae Obscurorum Virorum.* By favor of these gentlemen, I pronounce my opinion that Magister Ortwin, who is a learned man and a philosopher, cognominated his friends 'obscure men' in a mystical sense: for I once read in an authority that truth lieth in obscurity. Wherefore also saith Job, 'He discovereth deep things out of darkness.' Also in the Seventh of Micah we read, 'When I sit in darkness, the Lord shall be a light unto me.' And again, Job xxviii.: 'Trahitur autem Sapientia de Occultis.' Whence also, as I have heard tell, Vergil hath it, 'Truth is wrapped in obscurity.' And it may be presumed that Magister Ortwin and his friends are men who seek out the secrets of the Scriptures, and truth and justice and wisdom—which things are not to be understood of all men, but by those who are illuminated of the Lord.

"As it is written in Kings cxxxviii: 'Yea, the darkness hideth not from thee, the night shineth as the day: the darkness and the light are both alike to thee.' "

And after the aforesaid theologian had made an end of speaking, all regarded me, to mark whether I was persuaded. But I pondered over these words.

There was present Bernhard Gelff, a magister of Paris, a youth indeed, but, as I hear, of good parts, and one who studieth much and maketh fair progress in the arts, and moreover hath good grounding in theology. And he, after his manner, shaking his head this way and that, spake thus with a grave countenance: "Learn, gentlemen, the weighty and reasonable cause wherefore Magister Ortwin calleth his friends 'obscure men.' He doeth it for humility's sake. For, you may know, and even if you know not it may be presumed that you do know, how that three years ago Johann Reuchlin, when he published a collection of letters from his friends, entitled it *Epistolae Clarorum Virorum*. And Magister Ortwin chewing upon this, and perpending much thereon, said within himself, 'Lo, Reuchlin believeth that none save he himself hath any friends. What will he do if I prove that I too have many friends—worthier far, and able to write better metrifications and compositions than his friends?' And so, to put him to shame, he sent to the press those letters and entitled them *Epistolae Obscurorum Virorum*. As saith the Psalmist, 'He sent darkness and made it dark.' But this he did in lowliness, belittling and humbling himself, that he might say with the Psalmist, 'Lord, my heart is not haughty, nor mine eyes lofty.' Wherefore the Lord, beholding his humility, will in due time give him grace to send abroad mighty works and name them with exalted titles. As saith Job, 'And again after darkness I hope for the day.' But it must not be supposed that that letter book of the friends of Magister Ortwin is not artistically composed—for Johann Reuchlin's friends never in their lives could compose anything better; no, not to save their necks— but, as I have declared, more excellent conceits will ensue; and, by God's help, I hope we may see great things.

"Magister Ortwin layeth no store by swelling titles. Wherefore he saith, 'The Lord is my light and my salvation, whom then shall I fear?' For he knoweth that in belittling himself he will hereafter be magnified. As saith the Scripture, 'Whoso exalteth himself will be brought low.' And, as we read in the twentieth of Ecclesiasticus, 'There is an abasement because of glory, and there is that lifteth up his head from a low estate.' These things the prophet Nahum prophesied when he said, 'And darkness shall pursue his enemies.' "

Then, desiring that the disputants should not be out with one another, and that neither of them should fall foul of me for saying "This or that is the subtler reasoning," I quoted that line of Horace in which he saith, "The case is still before the judge." "When next I write to Magister Ortwin," I added, "I will ask him to tell me his motive. Forgive me, therefore, if I have in any wise perplexed you."

So then they disputed no longer, though Magister Bernhard muttered that he would contend to the stake that he had rightly apprehended your motive. Therefore, Herr Ortwin, I adjure you in friendly wise that you reveal to me what you had in your mind when you entitled that fardel of letters *Epistolae Obscurorum Virorum*.

And now farewell, in all health and honor.

The Court, at Rome

Translated by Francis C. Stokes

THOMAS MÜNTZER

Thomas Müntzer (1489–1525) was born in Stolberg (Harz), the son of a well-to-do family. He began his studies early and started upon a long odyssey whose individual stations remain largely uncertain. He was a member of the generation that at first enthusiastically embraced Luther's teachings. Upon Luther's recommendation, he went to Zwickau, where he fell in with a sect of religious fanatics who believed in "inner enlightenment." He also became an ardent admirer of the Bohemian reformer John Hus (who was burned at the stake in 1415).

After working as a pastor (again on Luther's recommendation) with congregations in eastern Germany and Bohemia, Müntzer turned against Luther, began to organize the peasantry of Thuringia politically, and led them in their revolution against the nobility (1525). He was taken prisoner during the Battle of Frankenhausen in 1525 and executed.

Sermon to the Princes [1]

The text of the aforementioned [second] chapter of the prophecy of Daniel has been presented and interpreted in the clear words of the original, in translation, and the entire sermon is provided with references to the text of the Bible and set forth as follows.

It is easy to see that there is neither aid nor help for poor, suffering, and crumbling Christendom, unless diligent and indefatigable men of God use the Bible every day in song, reading, and preaching. But that might cause the delicate heads of the priests to suffer severe shocks, or even to abandon their function. Yet what else can be done while Christianity is being so deplorably devastated by ravenous wolves? Thus it is written in Isaiah 5 and Psalm 80,[2] with reference to God's vineyard. And St. Paul also teaches us to sing religious songs of praise (Eph. 5).[3] For just as in the times of the beloved prophets Isaiah, Jeremiah, Ezekiel, and the others the whole congregation of God's elect had so completely fallen into idolatry that even God could not help them but had to let them be carried off into captivity and to suffer agonies among the heathen until they once again acknowledged His holy name, as is written in Is. 29, Jer. 15, Ezek. 36, and Ps. 89, so too has poor Christendom in our time and that of our fathers become more and more impenitent, though under the unspeakable semblance of a godly name (Lk. 21, 2 Tim. 3) with which the Devil and his henchmen so smartly adorn themselves (2 Cor. 11), so smartly, indeed, that the real servants of God are seduced by it and, even when exerting the greatest care, fail to note their error, as Mt. 24 clearly shows. All this is the result of sham sanctity and hypocritical apologies for the godless foes of the Lord, when they say that the Christian Church cannot err; whereas it actually needs constant instruction by the word of God if it is to avoid error and is to be saved from it. It must, in fact, admit the sin of its own ignorance (Lev. 4, Hos. 4, Mal. 2, Is. 1). Yet this is true: Christ the Son of God and His Apostles, like the holy prophets before them, established a pure Christianity, sowing pure wheat in the field; that is, they planted the beloved word of God in the hearts of the elect, as is written in Mt. 12, Mk. 4, Lk. 8, as well as Ezek. 36; but the lazy and neglectful servants of that same Church have not been willing to tend and support it with watchful care, but have sought their own benefit and not that which was Jesus Christ's (Phil. 2). Consequently they allowed the mischief of the godless— that is, the weeds—to proliferate (Ps. 80), while the cornerstone referred to was still small. Isaiah 28 speaks of this too. Indeed, it has not yet filled the world, but will very soon do so and make it complete. This cornerstone, set up at the beginning of the new Christendom, was then soon rejected by the builders, that is, the rulers (Ps. 118, Lk. 20). Therefore I say the early Church became dilapidated everywhere down to the time of the divided world (Lk. 21, Dan. 2, Esdras 4). Hegesippus and Eusebius say (Bk. IV, Chap. 22 of the *History of the Christian Church*)[4] that the Christian community remained virginal only to the time of the death of the Apostles' disciples, and shortly thereafter became an adulteress, as had been predicted by the beloved Apostles (2 Pet. 2).

And, in the Acts of the Apostles, St. Paul has told the shepherds of God's sheep in plain words (Acts 20), "Take heed therefore unto yourselves, and to all the flock over which the Holy Spirit has made you overseers, to feed the Church of God which He has purchased with His own blood. For I know this, that after my departing shall grievous wolves enter in among you, not sparing the flock. Also of your own selves shall men arise, speaking perverse things, to draw away disciples after them. Therefore watch." The Epistle of St. Jude says the same thing, and Rev. 16 proclaims it also. Therefore Christ our Lord warns us to beware of false prophets (Mt. 7). Now it is, most lamentably, plain as day that nothing is so lightly and slightly regarded as the Spirit of Christ, and yet none can be saved unless that same Holy Spirit assures his salvation beforehand, as is written in Rom. 8, Lk. 12, Jn. 6 and

17. But how are we poor miserable worms to attain to that? For we hold the godless in such high esteem that, compared to the great titles and names of this world, Christ the precious Son of God is like a hempen scarecrow or a painted manikin. Yet He is the true rock that is cast into the sea (Ps. 46) by the lavish splendor of the world. He is the rock cut from the mountain without human hands, whose name is Jesus Christ (1 Cor. 10), who was born at the very time the chief villainy was on the ascent (Lk. 1 and 2), at the time of Octavianus, when all the world went to be taxed. Then a feeble-minded man, a wretch of a dungsack, wanted to take the whole world for himself, although he had no use for it save for the purposes of splendor and vanity. Why, he even let himself believe that he alone was great. Oh, how small the cornerstone was, Jesus Christ, in the eyes of men! He was consigned to a cattleshed, like the scum of the earth (Ps. 22). Afterward the scribes rejected Him (Ps. 118, Mt. 21, Mk. 12, Lk. 20), and continue to do so today. Yes, they have even made fun of His passion since the death of the beloved Apostles. They have made the Spirit of Christ a laughingstock and still do, cf. Ps. 69. They have quite obviously stolen it, like thieves and murderers (Jn. 10) and have robbed Christ's sheep of their true voice and have turned Christ crucified into some grotesque idol. How did that come about? The answer is that they have rejected the pure concept of God and in its place set up a fine golden god before which the poor peasants smack their lips and kowtow, as Hosea clearly says in chapter four and Jeremiah in the fourth chapter of the Book of Lamentations, stating that those who once ate well-spiced foods now accept dunghills instead. Alas, for the woeful abomination, of which Christ Himself speaks (Mt. 24), that He is so wretchedly scorned and mocked with the Devil's Mass, with idolatrous preaching, gesticulating, and conduct, and is, withal, nothing but a vain wooden god. Yea—an idolatrous, wooden priest and a coarse, foolish, and loutish people, without the slightest conception of the true God, is that not a sin and a shame and a disgrace? I maintain that the beasts of the belly (Phil. 3) and the swine that are described in Mt. 7 and 2 Pet. 2 have trampled the precious stone Jesus Christ with their feet as hard as they could, and He has become a foot cloth for the whole world, and it is no wonder that the Turks, heathens, and Jews mock us and take us to be fools. How else should one

regard people who are unwilling even to hear the spirit of their religion named? Thus Christ's suffering has become nothing more than a country fair for desperate knaves, such as no scoundrel has ever known, as Ps. 69 says.

Therefore, beloved brethren, if we are to rise above this filth and become God's true disciples, taught by God Himself (Jn. 6, Mt. 23), we shall need great might and power, bestowed on us from above, to chastise and reduce such unspeakable wickedness. That power is the brightest knowledge of God (Wisdom of Solomon 9), springing from the pure, unfeigned fear of God, which alone will arm us with a mighty hand for vengeance against the enemies of God and with the utmost zeal for God, as is written (Wisdom of Solomon 5, Jn. 2, Ps. 69). There can be no exoneration through human or rational schemes; the appearance of the godless is beautiful and deceptive beyond measure, like the lovely cornflower among the green spikes of wheat (Eccles. 8), and such will be identified only through the wisdom of God.

In the second place, we shall continue to detect clearly the abomination that loathes the cornerstone. But if we are to recognize its nature distinctly, we must rely on the revelation of God every day. Yet that has become exceedingly rare in this treacherous world. For the deceitful schemes of the acutely clever would assail us every moment and hamper us most severely in the true knowledge of God (Prov. 4, Ps. 37). This must be countered with the fear of God. If we were armed with that alone, wholly and purely, then holy Christendom could easily return to the knowledge and revelation of divine will. All this is contained in the Scriptures (Ps. 111, 145, Prov. 1). The fear of God must, however, be really pure and not adulterated by the fear of any humans or creatures (Ps. 19, Is. 66, Lk. 12). Ah, that fear is urgently needed by us. For just as no man can with impunity serve two masters, so nobody can fear both God and creatures. But God cannot have mercy on us (as the mother of Christ our Lord says) unless we fear Him, and Him alone, with all our hearts. God says, regarding this (Mal. 1), "If, then, I am your father, where is my honor? If I am your master, where, then, is the fear of me?" Thus, beloved princes, it is necessary for us in these highly perilous times to take extreme care, as all beloved fathers in the Bible have specified from the beginning of the world, to resist cunningly deceitful evil. For the time is now perilous and the days are bad (2 Tim. 4, Eph. 5). Why? Only because the noble power of God is so lamentably profaned and reviled that poor ordinary men are led astray by the infamous scribes with their great chattering, such as the prophet Micah speaks of (Chap. 3), which is now, with few exceptions, the manner of all scribes. They teach that God no longer reveals His divine mysteries to his Beloved friends by means of true visions or the words of His mouth (Eccl. 34, etc.) and make a joke of people who rely on God's revelation, as the godless ridiculed Jeremiah, saying (Jer. 20), "Tell us, has God spoken to you lately? Or have you recently asked God's advice and consulted with Him? Do you have the Spirit of Christ?" They do so with great scorn and derision, but was it not a momentous thing that occurred at the time of Jeremiah? Jeremiah warned the poor blind people of the coming agony of captivity in Babylon, just as pious Lot had warned his daughters' husbands (Gen. 19), but it seemed foolish to them and they told the prophets so. God should, indeed, warn men thus, like a loving father; but what happened to the sneering crowd in their Babylonian captivity? Nothing other than that they were abused by the heathen king Nebuchadnezzar—see the text. He acknowledged God's word, yet he was such a powerful tyrant and a scourge to the chosen people who had sinned against God. But out of the blindness and impenitence of God's people, the highest good was to be explained to the world, as St. Paul (Rom. 11) and Ezekiel (23) say. Therefore I say here for your instruction that not only did Almighty God show the heathen king the things that were to happen many years in the future, to the unspeakable shame of the obdurate ones among the people of God who would not believe any prophet, but also of those inexperienced people of our own times who are just the same, being unaware of the punishment of God even when they see it right in front of their eyes. What, then, should Almighty God do with us? He must because of that withdraw His loving kindness from us. Now follows the text.

King Nebuchadnezzar had a dream in which he, etc.[5]

What shall we say to that? It is an unmentionable, unusual, and odious thing to speak about people's dreams now, because the whole world has been deceived by dream interpreters from the beginnings to the present, as is written (Deut. 13, Ecclesiasticus

34). In the chapter of Daniel being discussed (Chap. 2), it is shown that the king was not inclined to believe the cunning soothsayers and sorcerers when he said, "Tell me my dream, then give your interpretation of it, otherwise you will tell me nothing but trickery and lies." What was that dream? They were unable to tell him and said, "Your Majesty, no one on earth can tell you the dream, only the gods, and they do not maintain communication with humans." To the extent of their understanding they spoke quite reasonably. But they had no belief in God, being godless hypocrites and sycophants, saying what their rulers wanted to hear, just like the pedantic divines in our times, who love tasty morsels at court. But they are refuted by what is written in Jeremiah 5, also in Chapter 8. Here the text says that there would be people who had communication with heaven. Oh, that's a bitter pill for the cunning ones to swallow! Yet St. Paul says it to be so too (Phil. 3). Such learned scribes still claimed to interpret the mysteries of God. Oh, the world now has a great number of such rogues who publicly arrogate that function to themselves. Of these Isaiah speaks (Chap. 58), saying, "They delight to know my ways, as a people that did righteousness." Such learned scribes are the soothsayers who publicly deny God's revelation, but interfere with the work of the Holy Spirit and yet would instruct the whole world. That which is beyond the feeble power of their poor intellect must come straight from the Devil. Yet they have no assurance of their own salvation, which should be of utmost concern (Rom. 8). They babble nicely about faith and brew a drunken faith for poor confused consciences. All this is caused by the uninformed judgment and terrible abomination they have from the hateful trickery of those accursed and venomous monks' dreams by means of which the Devil puts his pet schemes into operation and has, in fact, irreparably deceived many of the pious elect, because, lacking all discernment, they have straightway granted credulity to those visions and dreams. Thus their rules and frivolous hocus-pocus[6] are prescribed by the revelation of the Devil, against which the Colossians are so urgently warned by St. Paul (Col. 2). But the accursed monk dream-mongers have not known how to draw upon the power of God, and for that reason are now obdurately headed in the wrong direction and are a matter of sin and shame to everybody, as much as are indolent good-for-nothings. They are still

blind in their folly. Nothing else has led them astray, and is leading them still further astray in these times, but false belief. For
without any experience of the arrival of the Holy Spirit, the Master of the fear of God, they cannot distinguish good from evil,
since they spurn divine wisdom. God cries out against the likes of
them through Isaiah (Chap. 5), "Woe unto them that call evil good,
and good evil." Therefore it is not in the nature of decent people
to spurn good for evil. For St. Paul says to the Thessalonians (Chap.
5), "Despise not prophesyings; prove all things; hold fast that
which is good," etc.

In the third place, you shall grasp the significance of God's being
so completely gracious to His elect that whenever He was able to
warn them in the slightest (Deut. 1 and 32; Mt. 23), He did so to
the highest degree, if only they could have accepted the warning,
despite their great disbelief. Here the text of Daniel agrees with
that of St. Paul to the Corinthians (1 Cor. 2), taken from holy
Isaiah, Chap. 64, saying, "Eye has not seen, nor ear heard, neither
have entered into the heart of man the things which God has prepared for them that love Him." But God has revealed them to us
by His spirit, for the Spirit searches all things, even the deep things
of God, etc. In brief, the meaning of that is: We must know, and
not merely believe in some vague airy way, what is given us by
God and what comes from the Devil, or nature. For if our natural
understanding is to be made subservient to faith (2 Cor. 10), it
must reach the highest degree of all its judgment, as is indicated
in Rom. 1 and Baruch 3. But it can form no well-founded judgment of its own knowledge without God's revelation. Man will
find that he cannot dash through heaven with his mind; he must
first become inwardly a complete simpleton (Is. 29 and 33, Obad.
1, 1 Cor. 1). Ah, to the clever, carnal, sophisticated world of the
flesh that is a strange bit of nonsense. There follow pains like those
of a woman in labor (Ps. 48, Jn. 16). Daniel, and all decent men
with him—it is as impossible for him as for all ordinary mortals
in all circumstances to fathom the things of God. That is what the
wise man means (Ecclesiasticus 3) when he says, He who would
find out God's glory is overwhelmed by that glory. For the more
human nature tries to get at God, the farther is the action of the
Holy Spirit estranged from it, as is clearly shown in Ps. 138. Indeed,
if man knew the prescience of the natural light, he would doubtless

not have to resort to the aid of misappropriated Scripture, as the learned scribes do with one or two scraps (Is. 28, Jer. 8), but would soon feel the effect of God's word springing up in his own heart (Jn. 4). Yes, he would not have to take foul water to the well (Jer. 2), as our learned scribes do now, being unable to distinguish between nature and the grace of God. They prevent the Word from taking its true course (Ps. 119), which comes from the depths of the soul, as Moses says (Deut. 30): The Word is not far from you; it is in your heart, etc. Now you may perhaps ask how it gets into the heart. The answer: It comes down from God in a sublime wonderment, a topic which I shall reserve for discussion at some other time. But this wonderment, whether it is God's word or not, begins when a child is six or seven years old, as is reckoned in Num. 19. For that reason St. Paul quotes Moses and Isaiah to the Romans (Chap. 10) and speaks there of hearing the inner word of God in the depth of the soul through the revelation of God. And he who has never been aware of nor experienced this through the living testimony of God (Rom. 8), cannot say anything about God, even if he has swallowed a hundred thousand bibles.

From this anyone can judge how far the world still is from true Christian faith—but nobody wants to hear this, or read it. If, then, a man is to become aware of the word and be receptive to it, God must take away from his carnal desires. The incentive comes from God, moving his heart to wipe out all lasciviousness of the flesh, so that he may receive the effect of the word. For a man of the flesh cannot perceive what God speaks to the soul (1 Cor. 2) but must be taught by the Holy Spirit the serious contemplation of pure understanding of the law (Ps. 19). Otherwise he will be blind in his heart and picture to himself a wooden Christ, thus deceiving himself badly. Note, therefore, how painful a task it was for Daniel to interpret the king's dream for him, and how he prayed and besought God to help him. Thus, for the revelation of God, one must set aside all frivolous pleasure and approach the truth with a serious mind (2 Cor. 6) and must, by the exercise of such truth, distinguish real visions from false. To this Daniel speaks in the tenth chapter. A man must have understanding of visions, and not all of them are to be repudiated by any means.

In the fourth place, you shall know that an elect person who wants to be able to tell whether a vision is from God, or nature, or the Devil must with heart and soul and inborn understanding be cut off from all temporal ease and comfort of the flesh, and he must undergo what beloved Joseph did in Egypt (Gen. 39) and Daniel in the chapter discussed here. For a sensual man will receive only the thorns and the thistles—that is, the pleasures of the world—which, as the Lord says (Mk. 4), will stifle the entire effect of the word that God speaks to the soul. Thus, when God sublimely speaks His holy word to the soul, man cannot hear it, for he is inexperienced, for he does not search his soul nor look into the depths of heart (Ps. 49). Man is not willing to mortify his depraved and carnally lustful life, as St. Paul the Apostle teaches; therefore the field of God's word remains full of thistles and thorns and huge clumps of bushes, all of which must be eradicated if the work of the Lord is to be accomplished and if man is not to be judged remiss and negligent (Prov. 24). Accordingly, when one sees the fruitfulness of the field and eventually the rich growth, he will become aware for the first time that he is the dwelling of God and the Holy Spirit and will be as long as he lives (Ps. 93, 119)—in fact, that he is created only that he may search for the testimony of God in his life. He now realizes this, in part, through parables and figuratively, but also fully in the depths of his heart (1 Cor. 13). Secondly, he must realize that such parables in visions or dreams are attested to in Holy Writ, with all attendant precautions, so that the Devil may not interfere and ruinously deprive the ointment of the Holy Spirit of its sweetness, as the wise man says of the dead flies (Ecclesiasticus 10). Thirdly, the elect one must take care that the progress of the dream is not that of rapid gushing but rather a steady flow in accordance with God's unshakable will; he must also take care that not a bit of what he sees is lost, for it must all take complete effect. When, however, the Devil tries to perpetrate something, his shady tricks ultimately give him away, and his lies clearly show up, for he *is* a liar (Jn. 8). The same thing is plainly shown in Nebuchadnezzar in this chapter, and also in the following one. For he quickly forgot God's admonition. That was no doubt the result of his carnal desires and lust for creature comfort and pleasures. For that is inevitable when a person wants to pursue his own voluptuousness and, at the same time, be concerned with God's work without suffering. The power of God's word will in such a case shelter him (Lk. 8). God almighty shows His beloved only true dreams and visions, most especially when they are in times of greatest trouble, as He did to righteous Abraham (Gen. 15 and 17), appearing to him while he was undergoing great fear and terror. Furthermore, when beloved Jacob was fleeing from his brother Esau, a vision came to him in which he saw a ladder leading up to heaven, with the angels of God ascending and descending it (Gen. 28). Later, when he returned home, he was exceedingly afraid of his brother Esau; the Lord appeared to him in a vision and wrestled with him, crushing his hips (Gen. 32). Furthermore, the good Joseph was hated by his brothers and, in the midst of this trouble, he had two critical visions (Gen. 37). Afterward, while he was suffering sadness of heart in prison in Egypt, he received such enlightenment from God that he was able to interpret all visions and dreams (Gen. 39–41). The unenlightened, lascivious, clever swine are deprived of all such power. The other Joseph, St. Joseph (Mt. 1–2), had four dreams while sorely troubled. Similarly, the Wise Men were instructed by the angel, as they slept, not to return to Herod. Moreover, the beloved Apostles must have constantly relied on visions, as is clearly related in their accounts. Yes, the true apostolic, patriarchal, and prophetic spirit waits for visions in time of painful distress. Thus it is no wonder that Brother Hog and Brother Soft Life [Luther] rejects them. If, however, man has not received the clear word of God in his soul (Job 28), he must needs have visions. St. Peter, for instance, in the Acts of the Apostles, did not understand the law. He had doubts about sharing food with Gentiles and about taking them into his company (Acts 10). Then God sent him a vision in the fullness of his soul, and he saw a linen cloth with four corners let down from heaven to earth, filled with four-footed beasts, and he heard a voice say, "Slay and eat." Similarly, Cornelius, a just man, when he did not know what to do, had a vision (Acts 10). Also, when Paul was on the way to Troas, a vision appeared to him during the night: A man of Macedonia was standing there, saying, "Come down to Macedonia and help us!" And after he had had that vision, according to the text (Acts 16), "immediately we endeavored to go into Macedonia, assuredly gathering that the Lord had summoned us there."

Moreover, when Paul had fears about preaching in Corinth (Acts 18), the Lord spoke to him in the night through a vision, saying,

"Be not afraid," etc. "No one shall dare to harm you, for I have many people in this city." But what need is there to cite numerous other attestations of Scripture? It would never be possible, in such serious and far-reaching matters, for righteous preachers to have dukes and rulers to protect and support them on every hand and to act without reproach, unless they lived in the revelation of God, such as Aaron heard from Moses, and David from Nathan and Gad. The beloved Apostles, then, were quite accustomed to visions, as the text proves (Acts 12). When the angel came to Peter and led him out of Herod's prison, he thought he was having a vision, not knowing that the angel was really performing the act of delivering him. If, however, Peter had not been familiar with visions, why would he have taken this to be one? From that I now conclude that whoever is, because of the judgment of the flesh, so unwise as to oppose the idea of visions and to reject them all, or to accept them all without discrimination, with the result that false dream-mongers have done the world so much harm, because of ambitious or pleasure-seeking people, will not succeed but will come into conflict with the Holy Spirit; cf. Joel 2, where God plainly speaks, as in this [second] chapter of Daniel, of the transformations of the world. In the last days He shall bring it about that His name shall be praised; He will free it from all its disgrace; and He will pour out His Spirit on all flesh. And our sons and daughters shall prophesy, and shall dream dreams and see visions. For if Christendom is not to be apostolic (Acts 27), as is proclaimed in Joel, why should anyone preach? It is really true, and I know it to be so, that the Spirit of God is now revealing to many elect righteous people that a tremendous, invincible reformation is due and must be carried out, regardless of who resists it. Then the prophesy of Daniel will remain unassailed, whether anyone believes it or not, as Paul also says to the Romans (Chap. 3). This text of Daniel is as clear as day, and the work is now proceeding in full swing from the end of the fifth kingdom of the world. The first, symbolized by the golden knob, was the kingdom of Babylon. The second, represented by the breast and arms of silver, was the kingdom of the Medes and Persians. The third was the kingdom of the Greeks, clanging with cleverness and symbolized by resounding brass. The fourth was the Roman, which was won by the sword, a realm of coercion and force. But the fifth is the one we see before us now, also, like Rome, a kingdom of iron, and would feign compel with coercion, but it is spotted with dung, as we can see the impact of hypocrisy, which wriggles and swarms over the whole world. For anyone who cannot succeed at hood-winking today must be a fool indeed. It is neatly observed how the eels and snakes carry on unchastely in a heap. The priests and all the evil clerics are snakes, vipers, as John the Baptist says (Mt. 3), and the wordly leaders and rulers are eels, designated as fish in Leviticus (Chap. 11). At that time the kingdoms of the Devil were smeared with clay. Ah, beloved leaders, how finely the Lord will smash the old crocks with a rod of iron (Ps. 3).

Learn, then, all you beloved rulers, to take your decisions directly from the mouth of God, and do not let your hypocritical clergy mislead you and impede you with the false concern of sham goodness. For the stone that was torn from the mountain without hands has grown huge, and the poor laymen and peasants see it more sharply than you do. Yes, praise be to God, it has become so great that if other leaders, or neighbors, were to persecute you for the Gospel's sake, they would be banished by their own people. That I know for sure. Yes, the stone is great. Yet if, when it was still small, the foolish world long feared that the stone would fall on it, what shall we do now that it is so huge and mighty and has so irresistibly swept against the great column and shattered it to potsherds? Therefore, beloved rulers of Saxony, stand boldly upon the cornerstone, as St. Peter did (Mt. 16), and seek the true stability of the will of God. He will preserve you on that stone (Ps. 40). Your paths will be right; seek at once the justice of God, and valiantly seize the cause of the Gospel. For God is so close to you, you would hardly believe it. Why do you let yourselves be terrified by the specter of man (Ps. 118)? Pay close attention to the text of Daniel here: King Nebuchadnezzar wanted to slay the wise men because they could not interpret his dream. It would have been just punishment for them, for they intended to rule his whole kingdom through their cunning, although they did not succeed in that intent. Our clergy are like that today. I am telling you the truth. If only you would recognize what harm is being done to Christendom, and rightly thought it over, you would achieve as much zeal as King Jehu evinced (2 Kgs. 9–10); see also the whole book of Revelation. I know that you have had great difficulty refraining from using the power of the sword. For the lamentable damage inflicted on holy Christendom has reached such proportions that no tongue can begin to exhaust the topic. Therefore it is necessary for a new Daniel to arise and interpret your revelation for you and, as Moses teaches us (Deut. 20), he must go to the van of the army. He will reconcile the anger of the princes and of the enraged people. For once you really come to know the harm to Christendom and the treachery of the false clerics and desperate villains, you too will become enraged at them; nobody can imagine how much! It will doubtless cause you exceeding displeasure that you have been so kind after they have duped you with the fairest words into making the most shameful decisions (Wisdom of Solomon 6) against the sincere truth. For they have really made fools of you, each one swearing by the saints that princes are, by virtue of their office, heathens and should do no more than preserve civil unity. Alas! The great stone will soon roll and fall upon them and dash all that spurious reasoning to bits. As Matthew says (10), "I came not to send peace but a sword." But what is to be done with that sword? Nothing less than banishing and doing away with the evil ones who hinder the Gospel—if you do not want to be devils but the servants of God, as Paul calls you in his Epistle to the Romans, 13. You must have no doubt: God will smash to pieces all the adversaries that presume to persecute you. For His hand is not yet shortened, as Isaiah 59 says. Therefore He can still help you, and will do so, as He stood by the chosen king Josiah and others who defended the name of God. Thus, you are angels, if you are willing to do the right, as Peter says (2 Pet. 1). Christ has most earnestly commanded us (Lk. 19), "Take my enemies and strangle them before mine eyes." Why? Because they undermine Christ's authority and, at the same time, defend their villainy under the guise of the Christian religion and, using their deceitful cover of shame, ruin the whole world. Therefore Christ our Lord says (Mt. 18), "Whoever shall offend one of these little ones, it were better for him that a millstone were hanged about his neck, and that he were drowned in the depth of the sea." Let him who will play pedantically with the wording, these are the words of Christ. Now, if Christ can say, "Who shall offend one of these little ones," what can be said when a whole multitude is harmed in its faith? That is what the arch-scoundrels do who would ruin the whole world and make it turn from the true Christian faith, saying, "No one shall know the secrets of God." Everyone shall act according to their words, not their deeds. They say it is not necessary for faith to be tested with fire, like gold (1 Pet. 1, Ps. 140). But in that way the faith of Christians would be worse than the faith of a dog, for he hopes to get a piece of bread when the table is set. That is the kind of faith the false learned men hold out to the poor blind world. That is no wonder, for they preach only for the sake of the belly (Phil. 3). They cannot say anything else from the heart (Mt. 12). Now, if you are to be real rulers, you must seize the rule by the roots and, as Christ commanded, drive His enemies away from His chosen ones. For you are the ones to do that. Please do not hand us some polite distortion to the effect that the power of God should do this, without your taking up the sword, for then it may rust in the sheath. God grant this, no matter what any false scholar may tell you. Thus Christ speaks amply about it (Mt. 7, Jn. 15): "Every tree that does not bring forth good fruit shall be torn out and cast into the fire." If you do away with the bugbear of the world, you will at once identify it, with a righteous judgment (Jn. 7). Make a righteous judgment at God's command; you shall have ample help for it (Wisdom of Solomon 6), for Christ is your master (Mt. 23). Therefore do not let those evildoers live any longer who turn us from God (Deut. 13). For a godless man has no right to live when he impedes the righteous. In Ex. 22 God says, "You shall not allow evildoers to live." St. Paul also means this when he says that the sword of the rulers should be employed for vengeance against the evil and for the protection of the righteous (Rom. 13). God is your protection and will teach you how to do battle against His enemies (Ps. 18). He will make you skilled in battle, and He will preserve you. But, because of that, you will have to bear a heavy cross and suffer oppression, so that the fear of God may be made clear to you. This cannot be done without suffering, but it costs you nothing more than the danger risked for God's sake—also the idle chatter of the opponents. For although the righteous man David was driven from his palace by Absalom, he ultimately returned to it when Absalom was hanged and stabbed to death.

Therefore, beloved fathers of Saxony, you must dare this for the sake of the Gospel. But God will chasten you lightly, as His most beloved sons (Deut. 1). Since He is exceedingly slow to wrath, blessed are all who rely upon God. Speak freely in the spirit of Christ, saying, "I will not be afraid of a hundred thousand if they besiege me." I suppose that our learned men will point out the graciousness of Christ, which they distort in their hypocrisy. But they should, on the other hand, have regard for the wrath of Christ (Jn. 2, Ps. 69), when he destroyed the roots of idolatry, as Paul says in the first chapter of his Epistle to the Colossians that, for the same reason, the wrath of God cannot be taken away from the congregation. If He has now humbled those who are slight in our estimation, He would doubtless not have spared the idols and images, had they been there. He himself commanded through Moses (Deut. 2), saying, "You are a holy people, you shall have no mercy for the idolatrous, but shall destroy their altars and smash their images and burn them, so that I may not be angry with you."

Christ has not abrogated those words but will rather help us fulfill them (Mt. 5). Figures of speech have all been interpreted by the prophets, but there are plain, clear words which will always endure (Is. 40). God cannot say yes today and no tomorrow. He is unchangeable in His word (Mal. 3, 1 Kgs. 15, Num. 22). To the fact that the Apostles did not destroy the idols I respond thus: St. Peter was a timorous man who fawned hypocritically in the presence of the heathens (Jn. 21); he was, though, at the end, intensely afraid of death, and there is no reason to accept him as a norm in this. But St. Paul spoke out most severely against idolatry (Acts 17), and if he had been able to put his teaching into full effect among the Athenians, he would without doubt have entirely eliminated idolatry, as God had commanded through Moses, and was later done by the martyrs in well-attested accounts. Therefore, the failings or shortcomings of the saints do not give us any reason to allow the godless to persist in their ways. Since they have acknowledged God's name with us, they shall choose one of two things: either to renounce the Christian religion completely, or to put away their idols (Mt. 18). But for our learned hypocrites to come forward and say with Daniel, in their godless and warped way, that the Antichrist should be abolished without violence, is going too far. He is already discouraged, as were the elect when they were about to enter the Promised Land. Joshua writes, "He did not spare them the sword." See Ps. 44 and 1 Chron. 14; you'll find the solution there. They did not conquer the land with the sword but by the power of God, though the sword was the means of annihilating the godless (Rom. 13), as eating and drinking are the means of living. In order that the same thing may now happen in fit and proper manner, our beloved fathers, the princes who profess Christ with us, should act. If, however, they fail to do so, the sword will be taken away from them (Dan. 7), for they profess Him with their words but deny Him in their acts (Tim. 1). Therefore, if they make peace with the enemies, if they claim to be spiritual yet still do not take into account the power of God, they shall be done away with (1 Cor. 5). But what I ask for them, with righteous Daniel, is, if they are not against the revelation of God but act contrary to it, that they shall be strangled without mercy, the way Hezekiah, Josiah, Cyrus, Daniel, and Elijah destroyed the priests of Baal (1 Kgs. 18). Otherwise the Christian Church cannot return to its pure pristine state. The weeds must be eradicated from God's vineyard at the time of harvest. Then the fine red wheat will take permanent root and will rightly thrive (Mt. 13). The angels who sharpen their sickles for that purpose are the sincere servants of God who complete the zeal of divine wisdom (Mal. 3).

Nebuchadnezzar perceived the divine wisdom in Daniel and fell down before him after the powerful truth had overcome him, but he was moved like a reed by the wind, as Chapter 3 proves. Similarly, there are now great numbers of people who accept the Gospel with great joy as long as all goes smoothly (Lk. 8); but when God puts such people to the test of the crucible or the fire (1 Pet. 1), they, alas, take offense at the slightest word, as Christ proclaimed (Mk. 4). By the same token, many inexperienced people will no doubt be annoyed by this pamphlet, since I say, with Christ (Lk. 19, Mt. 18) and with Paul (1 Cor. 5), as well as with the instruction of the whole law of God, that godless leaders, especially priests and monks, who call the Gospel heresy, while simultaneously claiming to be the best of Christians, should be put to death. Hypocritically feigned piety becomes tremendously enraged and bitter and will defend the godless, saying that Christ never killed anyone, etc. It will shamefully toss the friends of God to the winds. In this, the prophesy of Paul (2 Tim. 3) is fulfilled: In the last days lovers of pleasure having a form of godliness will deny its power. Nothing on earth has a better semblance and guise than sham holiness; therefore all corners are full of vain hypocrites, among whom none is bold enough to tell the real truth. Thus, in order that truth may be brought to light, you rulers (God grant it, whether you do it willingly or not) must conduct yourselves according to the conclusion of this chapter of Daniel, namely: Nebuchadnezzar made the holy man Daniel a high official, so that he might render righteous verdicts, as the Holy Spirit says (Ps. 58); for the godless have no right to live except that which the elect may grant them, as is written in Ex. 23. Rejoice, you true friends of God, that the hearts of the enemies of the cross have been broken; they must do what is right, though they have not even dreamt of it. If we fear God, why should we be afraid of good-for-nothing, worthless men? (Num. 14, Josh. 11).

Just be brave. He to whom all power is given in heaven and on earth will wield the authority Himself (Mt. 28). May He preserve you beloved ones forever. Amen.

Translated by Robert A. Fowkes

Notes

1. This *Fürstenpredigt* ("Sermon for Princes," or better, "Sermon to the Princes") was delivered before Duke Johann of Saxony and his son, Duke Johann Friedrich, as well as various Saxon officials, in the palace at Allstedt on July 1, 1523.

2. Müntzer's numbers of the Psalms are in each case one lower than those in more recent German and English bibles. Therefore each of his references to the Psalms has been increased by one.

3. The following abbreviations of the names of the books of the Bible are used in this translation: Gen. (Genesis), Ex. (Exodus), Num. (Numbers), Deut. (Deuteronomy), Kgs. (Kings), Ps. (Psalms), Prov. (Proverbs), Is. (Isaiah), Jer. (Jeremiah), Ezek. (Ezekiel), Dan. (Daniel), Hos. (Hosea), Mal. (Malachi), Mt. (Matthew), Mk. (Mark), Lk. (Luke), Jn. (John), Rom. (Romans), Cor. (Corinthians), Eph. (Ephesians), Tim. (Timothy), Pet. (Peter), Rev. (Revelation).

4. The works of Hegesippus (second century) are preserved only in fragmentary form in Eusebius, but the latter makes clear that certain sections of his *History of the Christian Church* are taken from Hegesippus.

5. The "etc." is in Müntzer's sermon itself. He refrains from giving the whole text of the chapter of Daniel, presumably because people were expected to turn to their bibles.

6. "Hocus-pocus" is a conjecture here. The strange word *pockfintzerey* seems to cause trouble for everybody. The context seems to make hocus-pocus as likely a meaning as any.

Well-Warranted Speech
in My Own Defense

To the most Illustrious, First-born Prince and Almighty Lord Jesus Christ, gracious King of all Kings, valiant Duke of all faithful, my most merciful Lord and trusty Protector, and to His own distressed bride, poor Christendom.

All glory, honor, dignity, titles, and splendor be yours alone, eternal Son of God (Phil. 2). Your Holy Spirit has always had such a fate at the hands of those merciless lions, the pedantic scribes, that it would appear to be the worst of devils, whereas you have had it from the beginning without measure (Jn. 3), and all the elect have had it handed down to them from your fullness (Jn. 1), and thus it dwells in them (1 Cor. 3 and 6; 2 Cor. 1; Eph. 1; Ps. 6). You give it to all who hasten to you according to the measure of their faith (Eph. 4, Ps. 68). And he who does not have it to give infallible witness to his own spirit, does not belong to You, O Christ. You hold the invincible testimony (Ps. 93).

Therefore, it is no great wonder that the very worst of all the self-seeking pedantic scribes, Dr. Liar,[1] is becoming a bigger and haughtier fool all the time, putting on the covering of Your holy scripture, without mortifying his reputation or his comfortable ease, and making use of it in the most deceptive way. And he wants nothing less than to deal with You with the utmost effrontery (Is. 58), although he has received Your judgment through You, the portal of truth. He is so insolent as to scorn Thy true spirit in Thy presence, for he clearly and irrevocably announces that, out of ferocious envy and bitterest hatred, he is making me, Your limb purchased by You, a laughingstock to his scornfully mocking and violent associates, while he most scandalously depicts me to the simple-minded as a Satan or devil, reviling and taunting me with his perverted, calumnious verdict.

In You, however, I am joyous and blissful, quite satisfied by Your gentle consolation. For You have graciously proclaimed to Your sincere followers that the disciple is not above his master. Now, if they were blasphemous enough to call You Beelzebub, You leader without guilt and blessed bestower of salvation, how much more will they revile me, Your unremitting soldier, after I have expressed myself about the sycophantic scoundrel at Wittenberg, obeying Your voice (Jn. 10). It absolutely has to be that way, if the easy-living opinionated fellows with their spurious faith and their Pharisaic trickery are not to be allowed to go unchallenged or to be deprived of their reputation and their pomposity. You would be unable to surpass them in those matters Yourself, for they would be presumptuous enough to claim to be more learned than You and Your disciples. Indeed, the Pharisees, with the literal obstinacy of their pedantry, were probably more learned than Dr. Ludibrii[2] ever can be. They also had a great name and repute in the whole world, though it was not right for them to oppose You with their reason and to try to refute You with Holy Writ, just as they rebuked Nicodemus (Jn. 7), and attacked You for healing on the Sabbath (Jn. 5 and 9). They cited the whole Scripture against You, to the nth degree, to prove that You should be put to death for claiming to be the Son of God, born of the Eternal Father—even as we confess Your Spirit. Therefore they said, "We have a law according to which He must die." For they had distortedly applied the text of Deuteronomy 13 and 18 and would not look further in that text for a complete view. That crafty scribe now acts the same way to me, as he points to the Scripture but ridicules it most mockingly, calling the Spirit of God a devil.[3]

The entire scripture speaks (as all creatures also attest) of nothing but the crucified Son of God. Thus He began with Moses, proceeding through all the prophets, to reveal His mission, namely that He must suffer and enter into the glory of His Father. This is clearly stated in the last chapter of Luke. Paul also says that he can preach nothing other than Christ crucified (1 Cor. 1). After searching the law of God more thoroughly than all his associates, he could not find in it (Gal. 1) anything other than the suffering Son of God, who says (Mt. 5) that He came not to destroy the law or to break God's covenant, but rather to complete, explicate, and fulfill it.

The Hessian scribes were unable to realize all this, for they did not search the scripture with their whole hearts and minds as they ought to have (Ps. 119) and as Christ also commanded them to (Jn. 5). They were learned in the scripture, like apes attempting to imitate the cobbler making shoes but only succeeding in ruining the leather. Ah, why? They want to receive the consolation of the Holy Spirit, yet all their lives long, because of the gloom of their own hearts, never get to the root of it as they should. But the real light ought to shine in darkness and thereby give us the power to be children of God, as is clearly written (Ps. 55 and 63; Jn. 1).

If now Christ, as preached through the Old and New Testaments, were taken without enlightenment of the Spirit, a more confused monkey farce could result than among Jews and heathens, as everyone can now see with his own eyes, since present-day scripture-mongers do not act otherwise than did the Pharisees of old. They vaunt their knowledge of Holy Writ; they scribble and write whole books about it and babble more and more, saying, "Believe! believe!," yet they deny the coming of faith, mock the Spirit of God, and believe nothing at all, as You can see. None of them is willing to preach unless he gets forty or fifty florins. In fact, the top ones demand over a hundred, or even two hundred florins. They thereby exemplify the prophecy of Micah: The priests preach for the sake of reward and want a life of ease and leisure, along with the highest acclaim on earth. Yet they boast of understanding the origin of everything, while actually opposing that origin with all their might, branding the genuine Spirit as false, and as Satan, under the cover of holy scripture, as happened to Christ when, in His guiltlessness, He proclaimed the will of His Father. That was far too lofty for the scribes and consequently annoyed them no end (Jn. 5 and 6).

You will find it no different at the present time. When the ungodly have the law thrown up at them, they say, most frivolously, "It has been set aside." But when it is explained to them that the law is written in the heart and that one must have regard to what the heart teaches (2 Cor. 3), to observe the right paths to take to the origin (Ps. 37), the wicked attack the righteous and trot out St. Paul with such idiotic misunderstanding that it could serve as a puppet show for children (Ps. 64). He still claims to be the cleverest person in the world, boasting that he has no equal. On top of that he calls all poor folk sentimental fanatics and cannot bear to hear the word "spirit" spoken or read. He has to shake his clever head; the Devil doesn't care to hear the word (Prov. 18). If one speaks to him of the origins, he is cast out. Therefore he has recourse to deception (2 Cor. 11). He sings, from the words of St. Paul, in the highest register of music called disdiapason, to the effect that one should not worry about lofty things but should condescend to men of low degree. He likes the porridge, nothing else, and he shudders at the thought of soup in the morning, saying that one must simply believe, yet does not see what is requisite for that. Therefore Solomon speaks of such a person as a stupid fool. Cf. Proverbs: God's wisdom is too high for a fool.

Like Moses, Christ began with the origin and explained the law from the beginning to the end, saying, "I am the Light of the world." His preaching was therefore true, and so well set forth that it captivated human reason even in the ungodly, as the evangelist Matthew writes (Chap. 13) and as Luke explains (Chap. 2). But since the teaching was too high, and the person and life of Christ too lowly, they became annoyed at Him and His teaching and said openly that He was a Samaritan and was possessed of the Devil, for their judgment was of the flesh, as pleases the Devil, and it had to burst right out, for they do not displease the world of the flesh, which likes the role of Brother Soft-living (Job 28). All this they did to please the world (Mt. 6 and 23).

That is the way the godless Wittenberg flesh acts toward me when I, through applying the first chapter of the Bible, strive for the purity of God's law (Ps. 19), trying to explain through all statements the fulfillment of the spirit of the fear of God (Is. 11). And I will not allow him his perverted way of treating the new covenant of God without explication of God's commandments and the coming of faith, which is made known only after chastisement by the Holy Spirit (Jn. 16). For only after realization of the law does the Spirit chasten the unbeliever, whom no one recognizes unless he has acknowledged it previously, as plainly as the most unbelieving heathen. Therefore all the elect have from the beginning recognized their unbelief by observing the law (Rom. 2 and 6). I affirm Christ with all His adherents as fulfiller of the law (Ps. 19). For the will of God, and His work, must be fulfilled on earth by observing the law (Ps. 1, Rom. 12). Otherwise nobody would distinguish belief from unbelief, except in a deluded way, as the Jews, with their scripture and their sabbath, failed to become aware of their foundation.

I have not done anything to the treacherous raven which Noah, as a sign, let fly out of the ark, but flapped my wings like a simple dove, coating them with silver, brushed seven times, and letting them turn to gold on my back (Ps. 68). I flew over and detested the carrion on which he likes to sit, as I want to inform the whole world that he acts hypocritically and fawns on the ungodly, as you see in his booklet against me, actually going so far as to defend them. From this it is quite evident that Dr. Liar does not dwell in the house of the Lord (Ps. 15), for the ungodly are not rebuked by him, whereas the godly are chided as devils and rebellious spirits. The black raven well knows that this will turn to carrion for him. He pecks out the eyes of swine and blinds voluptuous flesh, being so considerate of the evildoers that he gets fed up with them as far as honors, property, and lofty titles go.

The Jews wanted Christ to be slandered and disgraced in every way, as Luther is now undertaking to do with me. He abuses me most violently and reprovingly reminds me of the graciousness of the Son and His beloved friends, after I have preached of the sternness of the law, saying that it should not be set aside when it comes to punishing impious transgressors, even if they are rulers, but that it should be strictly enforced, as Paul instructed his disciple Timothy (1 Tim. 1) and, through him, all ministers of souls, to preach to the people. He clearly says that the punishment must be imposed upon those who fight and struggle against sound doctrine, something nobody can deny. This judgment is plainly rendered in Deuteronomy, Chap. 13, and by Paul (1 Cor. 5) concerning immoral transgressions, as I have also published and have preached, before the princes of Saxony, without any deception, showing them the sword mentioned in Holy Writ for them to use, so that no rebellion might arise. In short, transgression must be punished; neither great nor small can escape (Num. 25).

Straightway Papa Pussyfoot steps forth, mild chap that he is, and says I am trying to stir up insurrection, as he reads my letter to the miners. He mentions one part of it but omits the most significant. As I clearly expounded to the princes, the entire congregation has the power of the sword, as well as the key to loosing it, stating on the basis of Dan. 7, Rev. 6, Rom. 13, and 1 Kgs. 8, that the princes are not masters of the sword, but servants. They are to act, not arbitrarily, but justly (Deut. 17). Therefore, in keeping with ancient and honorable custom, the people must be present when a man is tried, justly tried and justly sentenced, according to the law of God (Num. 15). Why? If the authority were to attempt to pervert the sentence (Is. 10), the Christians present would repudiate it and not stand for it, for God demands an accounting for innocent blood (Ps. 79). It is the greatest outrage on earth that no one will take up the cause of the needy. The great ones do as they want, as Job says (Chap. 41).

The wretched sycophant spuriously tries to cloak himself in Christ's mercy, contrary to the text of St. Paul (1 Tim. 1). He says in his book on commerce[4] that the princes shall walk confidently among thieves and robbers. But he fails to mention the source of all thievery. He is a crowd pleaser and wants to win approval by shedding people's blood, for the sake of temporal gains, which, however, God did not order him to do. Lo, the nourishment of the profit of thievery and robbery are our lords and princes. They take all living things to be their own property: the fish in the water, the birds of the air, the plants of the earth—everything must be theirs (Is. 5). On this subject, they let God's commandment be circulated among the poor, saying, "God has commanded; thou shalt not steal." But it avails them nothing, for they cause all men— the poor peasant, the artisan, and all that live—to scrimp and scrape (Mic. 4). If anyone steals the slightest thing, he must hang for it. And then Dr. Liar says, "Amen." The masters themselves are the cause that the poor man becomes their enemy, but they will not do away with the cause of insurrection. How can it, in the long run, ever be changed? If I say that, I shall probably be found guilty of stirring up rebellion. Very well, so be it.

He is absolutely incapable of being ashamed. When the Jews (Jn. 8) brought to Christ a woman caught in adultery, they tested Him to see whether He would transgress the strict law of the fathers and would deservedly have called Him an evildoer if He had released the woman without any statement, branding Him a defender of injustice. In the Gospel, Christ has illumined the strictness of the Father by His own mercy. The mercy of God is over all His works (Ps. 145). It is not diverted by the pain of the law, which the elect do not desire to escape. As Jeremiah says, also Ps. 7, he wants to be judged with righteousness and not punished in anger, which God has never had in all eternity, but which springs from the perverse fear of men for God, terrified as they are of the pain and not aware how God will lead them, after pain, in pleasant enticement into His eternal life.

All evildoers of original wrongdoing among the generality of Christendom must be subjected to the law, as Paul says, in order for the severity of the Father to do away with the ungodly Christians who resist the saving doctrine of Christ, so that the righteous may have the time and place to learn God's will. It would never be possible, under such tyranny, to pursue His contemplation, with the result that evil would be free to punish us with the law, and the innocent would let themselves be tortured, so that the wicked tyrant acts against the truly religious, saying, "I must martyr you; Christ suffered too, you must not resist me" (Mt. 5). That would be an utter distortion. There must be made a very careful distinction, now that the persecutors claim to be the best Christians.

The Devil has the most crafty treachery to employ against Christ and His followers (2 Cor. 6 and 11), at times with insinuating graciousness, as when Luther defends the ungodly with the words of Christ; at times with grim severity, showing destructive self-righteousness for the sake of worldly goods. One to whom Christ's finger, the Holy Spirit, does not point out the friendly sternness of the law nor hold up the crucified Son of God for the revelation of God's will, with the comparison of both, will scorn the law of the Father and hypocritically pretend to embrace the most precious treasure of the mercy of Christ, thereby making a disgrace of the Father by means of the forbearance of the Son (Jn. 15 and 16), and scorning the distinction of the Holy Spirit, thus ruining each with the other. He has been doing this for so long that there is almost no true judgment left on earth.

Christ was called a devil when he reminded the Jews of Abraham's deeds and provided them with the best possible distinction between punishing and forgiving: to punish on the basis of righteous justice. He did not, then, set the law aside, but said, in the seventh chapter of John, before proceeding to His remarks in the eighth, "You shall pass a just sentence, not one based on appearances." There are for them no verdicts other than the ones written and set forth in the law: to judge according to the spirit of the law, thus to forgive with the Gospel, calling on the Spirit of Christ, and with no impediment of the Gospel (2 Cor. 3 and 13), the way Dr. Liar does in trying to make me a devil, saying with his scriptural pedants, "Have I not rightly taught with my writing and publication? But you have no other result to show but disruptiveness. You are a Satan, and a poor one at that, etc. See, you are a Samaritan and possessed of the Devil."

Ah, Christ, I count myself unworthy of bearing with You such precious suffering in the same cause, although the adversary's judgment has many improper judges on its side. I say, with You, to the haughty, conceited, and malicious dragon, "Do you hear? I am not possessed of the Devil; I seek to proclaim the name of God through my calling, comfort to the troubled, obstinacy and illness to the healthy" (Is. 6, Mt. 9 and 13, Lk. 8 and 4). And if I were to say that I want to drop this subject because of the evil lyingly attributed to me, I'd be on the same level as you, Dr. Liar, with your perverse slander and abuse. You are able to nothing but quarrel with the ungodly. But now that things have turned out for you the way they have, you have put yourself in the place of the evil ones you have disgracefully whitewashed. Now that you perceive that it may get to be too much for you, you want to pass on your name, when it is at its worst, to another, to whom the world is already hostile, and to escape cleverly, as the Devil is wont to do, so that no one will observe your evilness. Therefore the prophet calls you a basilisk, a dragon, a viper, and a lion, because with your venom you first flatter and then rant and rave, as suits your nature.

The faultless Son of God has with justification compared the most ambitious scriptural pedants with the Devil and, through the Gospel, has left us the power of judging them, with the formulation of His unblemished law (Ps. 19). Their greedy cravings were bent on sheer murder, for they said (Jn. 11), "If we let Him go, all men will believe in Him, the people will cling to Him; look in what great numbers they flock to Him already. If we let Him continue the way He's going, we are done for and will be poor men." Thus Caiaphas—Dr. Liar—came and gave his princes a good piece of advice. He was concerned about his countrymen around Allstedt. It is no different, in truth, as the whole land can attest: The poor folk are so thirsty for the truth that all the streets were full of people coming from all directions to hear the service that was arranged for singing and preaching the Bible there. If he was also to speak, he could not do so at Wittenberg; one can see from his German mass how holy he was. This so irked Luther that he at first prevailed upon his princes to prevent the printing of my service. When that Pope of Wittenberg's order was not heeded, he thought, "Just wait, I'll find a way to smash this pilgrimage to bits." The godless man has a shrewd head to be able to think up such things (Ps. 36). For his plans were such as you can see: to promote his teaching through the hatred of the laity for the clergy. If he had a real desire to punish a person, he would not have put himself in the place of the pope, and he would not have hypocritically posed to the princes, as you can clearly see written (Ps. 9). He has the same psalm neatly translated by himself and made to apply not only to the pope, but to him, aiming to turn Sts. Peter and Paul into mere bailiffs, thereby defending his own henchmen.

Dr. Liar is, though, a simple man, in that he writes that I should not be prevented from preaching. But you should see to it that the spirit of Allstedt keeps its fists still. Let's see, dear brothers in Christ, if he is not less simple than he pretends. Of course that is so; he's clever. The world will not find out for two or three years what murderous, treacherous damage he has done. The reason he writes the way he does is that he wants to wash his hands most innocently, so that nobody will notice that he is a persecutor of the truth. For he defiantly boasts that what he preaches must be the true word of God, because it evokes so much persecution. I am amazed, too, that the disgraced monk can endure being so horribly persecuted. He cannot act differently from the scribes (Jn. 10): "We do not do anything to you for your good works, but for blasphemy we shall stone you to death." That's how they spoke to Christ, as this man does to me: "You shall not be banished because of your preaching, but because of inciting to riot."

My most beloved brethren, it is really not a bad thing that is going on at the present time. You are not actually in a position to judge. You think that if you stop giving the priests anything, everything is settled. You do not know that you're a hundred thousand times worse off than before. From now on they will befoul you with a new logic based on deceptive use of the word of

God. But, in opposition to that, you have Christ's command (Mt. 7). If you contemplate it with all your heart, no one will deceive you, no matter what he may say or write, but you will take care, as Paul warned his Corinthians (2 Cor. 11), "Let not your minds be corrupted by the simplicity of Christ." The scribes have applied that simplicity to all the treasures of godly wisdom and knowledge (Col. 2), contrary to Gen. 3, where God warned Adam, with a single commandment of danger to come, not to be led astray by the pleasures of living creatures but to have delight in God alone; as it is written, "Your delight shall be in the Lord."

Dr. Liar would like to bring a great case against me, showing how simple his teaching is, while allegedly resulting from the application of his penetrating thought. Yet it seems that, after all, it is not preaching that bothers him, since there must be sects, and he asks the princes not to forbid my preaching. I expected nothing different from him but that he would discuss with me and allow me a hearing before the world, while maintaining that he relied on the word alone. But then he turns things around and would hold the princes to it, as if it were a prearranged game, so that nobody says, "Well, as long as they follow the Gospel themselves, they may as well let me preach and not deny me that." But I am to keep my hand idle and not even have my words printed. Yes, that's a nice subtle point, as if saying, with the Jews, we are not doing anything to you for your good works, only because of your blasphemy. The truly pious folk said that even if a man swore an oath, but not by the sacrifice on the altar, it was not binding. They made abundant use of that trick (Mt. 23, Lk. 11). They were still pious people, not hurting anybody. If you believe that, you must spare the weak.

Blasphemy did not bother the Jews very much, as you can see from the Gospel. And good works concerned them hardly at all, just as they do not matter much to Luther. Therefore God called their attention to the works of Abraham (Jn. 8). But there was in them a fierce hatred that had to burn brightly before men, as is true of Virgin Martin now. Ah, the chaste Babylonian virgin (Rev. 18)! He would act entirely for the sake of the word, yet he will not seize the word to try my case and to find for or against it— he will only make a bad case of it, to the big leaders, that nobody should follow my teaching because it is inflammatory, and whoever would have a clear verdict here must not love violence. He must also not be opposed to righteous indignation; he must hold to a very rational mean, otherwise he will either hate my teaching too much or will love it excessively, according to his nature, something I will never want.

It would be more beneficial for me to instruct the people with good teaching than to get involved with the blasphemous monk, now that he would be a second Christ who has gained much good for Christendom with his blood. Yet what shall I reply to the subtle argument that it is all right for priests to take wives? I will probably find no answer, for you have completely covered yourself—as you let youself think. See how nicely you have sacrificed the poor priests in the declaration of the First Imperial Mandate, when you say, "There would go over them . . . etc.," so that the doctrine stated by you is at first not justified. For you hypocritically would pretend to allow them to be taken. Thus you would have kept on making new martyrs, and once you had sung a little song or two about them, you'd have become a certified sanctifier. To be sure, you'd then sing in your own fashion, "Nunc dimittis . . . ," etc., so that they would all sing after you, "Will you dance, Monk?" Then everybody would kowtow to you.

But if you are a saint-maker, you must be a strange sort of one. Christ gives the credit to His Father (Jn. 8), saying, "If I honor myself, my honor is nothing." But you want to get a lofty title from the people at Orlamünde. In the manner of the carrion crow, you take and steal the name of God's Son and would earn thanks from your princes. Have you not read, learned chap that you are, how God spoke through Isaiah (Chap. 42), saying, "My glory I will not give to another." Can you not name the good people, as Paul names Festus (Acts 25)? Why have you called them serene, illustrious princes? The title is not theirs, but Christ's (Heb. 1, Jn. 1 and 8). Why do you call them high-born? I thought you were a Christian, yet you are an arch-heathen. You make Jupiters and muses of them, as if they were not born of woman (Wisdom of Solomon 7) but from the brow of Zeus.

Shame on you, you arch-rogue. You insinuate yourself into the good graces of the erring world (Lk. 9) and you wanted to justify all men. But you know perfectly well whom to accuse—the poor monks and priests and merchants who cannot defend themselves; that's why you can abuse them with impunity. But nobody is supposed to condemn the ungodly rulers, even when they trample Christ with their feet. But, to appease the peasants, you say that the princes will founder on the word of God, and say in your interpretation of the latest imperial mandate, "The princes shall be deposed from their thrones." You also regard them as merchants. You ought to twist their noses too; they've deserved it perhaps more than the rest. What do they ever reduce? Their interest rates? Their oppression? Yet you can atone for this reprimand of the princes, you new pope, very easily by giving them monasteries and churches. Then they will be content with you. I advise you thus, for otherwise the peasants may make trouble for you. Since, however, you insist on speaking about faith all the time, and write that I am battling under your protection and safeguard, one can see my sincerity and your folly: I've been under that protection and safeguard like a sheep among wolves (Mt. 10). Did you not in that very protection have more power over me than otherwise? Had you not anticipated that? I was in your principality, so that you could have no excuse. It is you who speak under our protection and safeguard. Oho, how you give yourself away! I suppose you are a prince along with the rest of them. Why should you boast about your protection and safeguard anyway? I have never wanted his protection in any of my letters. I wanted him not to make his own people antagonistic to him because of the goat stable and the statue of Mary at Malderbach. Thus he would fall upon villages or towns and not see that the poor people were in peril day and night for the Gospel's sake. Do you think the whole country doesn't know this? How to protect them? God have mercy on Christendom if it does not have as its protector the One who created it (Ps. 110).

You say I was expelled and had to wander around for three years. You mention that I complained of great suffering. Look at what the facts of the case are: With your pen you lied about me and calumniated me to many an upright man—I can supply the details. With your slanderous big mouth you publicly branded me a devil. Yes, that's the way you treat all who oppose you. What else can you do—the raven screams its own name. You with your half-baked Laurentius of Nordhausen well know what has been offered malefactors to kill me. You are not a murderous, inflammatory spirit, but you chase and incite like a hound of hell. You make no fuss about Prince George's invasion of the country of

Prince Friedrich and the general disturbance of the peace. You are the ground snake that creeps across the rocks (Prov. 30). Christ says (Mt. 10 and 23), "If they persecute you in one city, flee into another." But this apostle of the Devil—his arch-chancellor, in fact—says that if I am banished, I am a devil, and he tries to prove it (Mt. 12), attaining an understanding contrary to the Holy Spirit, which he ridicules as he "beats his chops."

He makes a lot of useless drivel and nonsense out of God's word, saying I call it a heavenly voice and that I say the angels speak to me, etc. The answer to that is that what Almighty God does with me or speaks to me I cannot boast very much about, only about what I proclaim to people out of the holy scripture through the testimony of God, and I will—God willing—not preach my own presumption. If, however, I do, then I will gladly let myself be punished by God and His beloved followers and will be willing to take the consequences. But I don't owe the scorner anything (Prov. 9), for I must not eat the cuckoo (Lev. 11) nor take into me the filthy food of the ungodly mocker. I wonder what the model may be. Since you hail from the Hartz, should you not call the mystery of God's word a heavenly bagpipe, perhaps? Then the Devil, your angel, would play your little ditty on it. Monk, if you will dance, all the ungodly will serve you.

I speak of God's word and all its manifold treasures (Col. 2) which Moses offers to teach us (Deut. 30). And Paul tells the Romans (Chap. 10) of the eighty-fifth psalm, that it should be heard by those who are converted with all their hearts, and in the doctrine of the Spirit, rendering equally all judgments of the mercy and justice of God. But you deny the true word and present to the world only the outward show. Therefore, without any understanding, you grossly turn yourself into an arch-fiend and distort the text of Isaiah to mean that God is the source of evil. Is that not God's most horrible punishment of you? You are still blinded, yet you would be the world's leader of the blind, and want to blame God that you are a miserable sinner and a poisonous bit of vermin, with your lousy, stinking humility. That's what you have produced with your weird reasoning, based on your Augustine, truly a blasphemous affair of free will, brazenly to despise mankind.

You say I have favored proceeding at once to violence and that I will not allow anyone time to consider. I say, with Christ, he who is of God hears His word; are you of God? Then why don't you hear it? Why do you mock it? Why do you damn it, when you have not grasped it? Do you first want to think about what you should teach others? You ought more logically to be called a crook than a judge, so that poor Christendom may come to realize how your carnal mind has actually worked against the incorruptible Spirit of God. Let Paul pronounce sentence on this (2 Cor. 11). You have always managed everything with simplicity (symbolized by an onion with its nine skins), just like a fox. See, you have become a brent fox that barks hoarsely before dawn. Now that real truth will rise, you are going to rebuke the small and not the great. You will act, as we Germans say, like the fox who got into a bucket to climb down into the well and ate the fish, afterward luring the unsuspecting wolf into the other bucket. Then the fox rises to the top and the wolf stays at the bottom. Those princes who follow you will also experience the same thing, and the noble footpads and highwaymen that you have set upon the merchants. Ezekiel gives the verdict on the fox (Chap. 13 and 34) and on the beasts, the wild animals that Christ calls wolves (Jn. 10). Then the same thing will happen to all as happened to the trapped foxes (Ps. 73). When people wait for the light, the little dogs will run into the holes with the foxes (Mt. 15). Then they will be able to bite but a little in their mouths, but the insolent dog will shake the fox's fur, so that he has to leave the hole, having eaten enough chickens. See, Martin, haven't you smelled the roasted fox that is passed off as a hare to the inexperienced game wardens? You, Esau, really deserved to be pushed aside by Jacob; why did you sell your birthright for a mess of pottage?

Ezekiel tells you (Chap. 13), likewise Micah (Chap. 3), you have confounded Christendom with a false belief and cannot put it right now that distress is on the increase. Therefore you hypocritically flatter the princes and think matters have gone well, since you have acquired a big name. And you go to endless extremes, as you did in Leipzig, when you stood before the most solemn conclave; why will you blind people? You were in such high spirits in Leipzig, going out the gate with a bunch of carnations and drinking good wine at Melchior Lother's. But the fact that you went to Augsburg could not result in your achieving any solemnity other than having Stupicuanus Oraculum stand right beside you. He wanted to help you but has now turned from you and has become an abbot. I am really worried that you may follow him. The Devil cannot stand on the side of truth, he cannot leave off his little pranks. But, in his booklet, he's afraid of insurrection, of the prophecy of his abomination. Therefore he also speaks about new prophets the way the scribes did of Christ (Jn. 8). Thus I have used almost the whole chapter for the present judgment. Paul says of the prophets (1 Cor. 14) a true preacher ought to be a prophet. No matter how ridiculous it seems to the world, the whole world ought to be prophetic. How will you judge people if you utter your divine service in the "Monk's Calf" [title of one of Luther's writings]? When you say you hit me in the mouth, you're lying. Yes, you're lying in your teeth, for I haven't been near you for six or seven years. But if you have turned the good brothers who were with you into fools, that must surely come to light; otherwise it would make no sense. You shall not despise the little ones (Mt. 17).

One could fall asleep listening to you boast; you're such a fool. You can thank the German nobility that you stood before the Reich at Worms. You have smeared their mouths with honey, for they thought nothing less than that you would give Bohemian [Hussite] gifts of monasteries and convents, such as you are now promising the princes. If you had faltered at Worms, you would very likely have been slain by the nobility, instead of being released, as any fool knows. You really should not write that you would risk your noble blood, as you boast. You and your followers use wild treachery and cunning. You had yourself arrested at your own request and acted most insufferably. Anyone not familiar with your knavery would swear by the saints that you were a pious Martin. Sleep peacefully, dear flesh. I'd prefer to smell you stewed in the juice of your own defiance by God's wrath in a vessel by the fire (Jer. 1). For, stewed in your own juice, the Devil should eat you (Ezek. 23). You are asinine flesh, you would take a long time to cook and would be a tough dish for your mealy-mouthed friends.

Oh, most beloved brothers in Christ, I tired at the start of this quarrel because of the inevitable offense of the poor masses. But if Dr. Liar had let me preach, or had defeated me before the people or his princes when I was before them in Weimar, and they questioned me through the proposal of the same monk, I would have preferred to go into this matter at a leisurely pace.

It was finally decided. The prince wanted the severe Judge to prolong the case until the Day of Doom; he did not wish to refuse the tyrants who wanted to come under his care for the Gospel's sake. It would be fine if it were turned over to the court, too; then the peasants would see it. It would be a splendid thing if it could be postponed to the Last Judgment; then the peasants would have a good case for doing right. They say, "I am keeping it for the judge." But the rod of the ungodly is meanwhile the medium of judging.

When I got home from the hearing at Weimar, I intended to preach the solemn word of God; then my councilman came to hand me over to the worst enemies of the Gospel. When I heard that, I could delay no more. I wiped the dust off my shoes. Then I saw with my own eyes that they esteemed their oaths and obligations much more highly than the word of God. They undertook to serve two masters, playing them off one against the other. For God had clearly stood by them and had saved them from the power of the bear and the lion and had also rescued them from the hand of Goliath (1 Kgs. 17). And Goliath relied on his armor and his sword, yet David taught him a lesson. Saul also started something good, but it remained for David to complete it, after a long period of roving about. What a symbol of Thee, O Christ, in Your beloved friends, whom You will diligently preserve forever. A.D. 1524.

Vulpis, Fecisti, etc., which is, translated, O Doctor Liar, you Treacherous Fox: You have with your dirty lies saddened the hearts of the righteous, whom God has *not* saddened. Thereby you have strengthened the power of the ungodly so that they still persist in their old evil ways. You will therefore be treated like a trapped fox. The people will be liberated and God alone will be master over them.

Translated by Robert A. Fowkes

Notes

This bitter diatribe against Martin Luther, Müntzer's one-time mentor, stems from frustration at what seemed betrayal of the Reformation. Luther's earlier pronouncements had called for sweeping social, political, and religious changes. But Luther soon adopted a point of view that made a sharp distinction between the realms of politics and religion and told his followers to submit to civil authority, even at the price of suffering.

Müntzer, ever a ferocious activist in word and deed, had led the first Anabaptist revolt in Zwickau, Saxony in 1521, where he was a rough but eloquent preacher. Expelled from Zwickau, he went to Prague, there acquiring a few adherents, then to Allstedt, Thuringia, where, as preacher of the Church of St. John, he delivered intensive attacks on Luther; his offensive utterances resulted in his being asked to leave town. Transferring his activity to Mühlhausen, Saxony, he was expelled once more, together with his colleague Heinrich Pfeiffer, after causing an uprising. Following a trip through southern Germany, during which he continued to preach against Luther and also to advocate communal ownership of property, he returned to Mülhausen, where he and his followers overthrew the municipal government and proclaimed a communistic theocracy.

In the Peasant's War Müntzer made himself leader of an armed band and set up camp at Frankhausen. Luther had by now expressed horror at violent revolts, while admitting the legitimacy of some of the grievances of the rebels, and went so far as to urge the authorities to crush insurrection, ruthlessly, if necessary. He regarded the peasants as having no scriptural justification for their acts and as thus being motivated by satanic evil.

This speech, ostensibly addressed to Christ, also speaks at times directly to Luther and simultaneously, of course, to hearers or readers. The vitriolic assault equates Luther with the scribes and Pharisees of old, also with Satan. In his colossal—but possibly sincere—egotism, Müntzer compares himself to Christ by virtue of having been accused of the same offenses as Jesus.

Not satisfied with those reformers who relied on scriptural authority alone for justification of their actions, Müntzer, while also invoking that justification and displaying a thorough knowledge of the scriptures in doing so, claimed that, more importantly for him as a "spiritualist" (or fanatical mystic, some would say), the Holy Spirit communicated directly with him and all true believers and prompted their deeds. Despite such exalted sponsorship, the peasants were utterly routed at Frankhausen on May 15, 1525. Müntzer managed to escape from the battlefield but was soon captured and put to torture. On May 25 he was decapitated, together with some 25 other leaders of the peasants.

1. Müntzer's sardonically bestowed aliases for Luther are, in German, closer to the real form of the name than is usually possible in English translation (*Lügner, Leisetritt*, etc.).

2. "Idle Play."

3. Müntzer's followers, like those in other radical groups of the Reformation, derived some of their ideas from various heterodox trends of thought going back at least to the thirteenth century. One cardinal principle was that which accepted belief in direct revelation stemming from the Holy Spirit, which gave simple folk the true meaning of scripture. Such a view was anathema to Luther, who, paradoxically, owed some of his own ideas to the same sources. The numerous references in this speech—more than a dozen—to the "spirit" are all references to this belief and to Luther's rejection of it.

4. *Von Kaufshandlung und Wucher*, 1524 ("On Commerce and Interest"—or "Usury").

Manifesto to the Miners

May the pure fear of the Lord be with you, dear brothers—how long will you sleep? How long have you been unaware of the will of God, so that He has, in your view, abandoned you? Ah, how often have I told you how it has to be, that God can no longer reveal Himself to you unless you take a stand? If you don't, your sacrifice of broken and contrite hearts is for nothing, and you must consequently fall into suffering again. I tell you this: If you will not suffer for the sake of the Lord, you will have to be the Devil's martyrs. Therefore, take care not to be despondent or remiss. Stop kowtowing to the wrong-headed madmen, the godless villains. Take up and fight the battle of the Lord. It is high time. Urge your brothers not to scorn God's witness, otherwise they will all go to ruination. All Germany, France, and Italy are aroused. The master is about to make a move. The villains are done for.

Four collegiate churches were destroyed at Fulda during Easter Week. The peasants in the Klettgau, the Hegau, and the Schwarzwald are up three hundred thousand strong, and their number is increasing all the time. Yet I am worried that the foolish people may enter into some false agreement, since they do not recognize the potential harm. If there are only three of you who, relying on God alone, seek His honor and His name, you will not fear a hundred thousand.

Up, then, arise, arise! It is time. The scoundrels are disheartened, let them be hunted down like dogs! Persuade the brethren to come to an agreement and to gather their testimony. It is exceedingly urgent: Arise! arise! arise! Let yourselves not be moved to pity if, like Esau, they give you good words for bad (Gen. 33); pay no heed to the moaning of the godless. They may beg, beseech, and implore you as piteously as children, but do not be moved by them. Remember how God commanded Moses (Deut. 7) to show them no mercy. And He has made the same revelation to us. Stir up things in the towns and villages, especially among the miners and other good fellows who will be useful to the cause. We must sleep no more. Even as I was writing this, word came from Saltza that the people were about to seize Duke Jörgen's officer and drag him from the palace, since he had planned to kill these men in secret. The peasants of Eichsfeld are happy as far as their Junkers are concerned; in short, they won't accept any mercy from them. All sorts of things are happening that can serve as examples to you. You must get a move on! Balthasar and Barthel Krump, Valtin and Bischoff, lead the procession! Have this letter circulated to the miners. In a few days my printer will come. I've got the message. I cannot act any differently in my instruction to the brothers; I must say that their hearts shall be sturdier than all the castles and armor of the ungodly villains on earth. To the fray! Strike while the iron's hot! Let not your blood-covered sword grow cool. Forge it, cling-clang, on the anvil of Nimrod. Dash their tower to the ground. As long as they live, it is impossible for you to get rid of human fear. One cannot speak to you about God as long as they rule over you. Get moving! While there is daylight! God is leading you; follow! The story is written; Matthew 22 says, "Therefore let yourselves not be dismayed. God is with you, as is written (2 Paralipomena 2). Thus saith the Lord, Ye shall not be afraid, you shall not dread this great multitude. It is not your battle, but the Lord's. It is not you who fight. Act valiantly and you will see the Lord's help above you. When Jehosophat heard these words, he fell down. Therefore, act through God; may He strengthen you in the true belief without fear of men.

Mülhausen, the 25th year.
Thomas Müntzer, a servant of God against the ungodly

Translated by Robert A. Fowkes

SEBASTIAN LOTZER

Sebastian Lotzer's *Twelve Articles of Peasantry* is a political and social document of unusual significance. Very few facts are known about Lotzer, except that he was a journeyman in the Furriers' Guild who knew his Bible extremely well and became very involved in the social upheavals of the Peasant Wars of 1525. His is a rare voice, indeed, at this early point. It announces in haunting simplicity and modesty the basic demands for social justice and human dignity among the working classes. This voice, though forced into submission (with Luther's collusion) this time, would never again be entirely silenced.

The Twelve Articles
of Peasantry

*To the Christian reader, the grace and peace of God
through Jesus Christ.*

There are many Anti-Christians who, because the peasants are
assembled, are now disparaging the Gospel, saying, "So these
are the results of the new gospel! To be obedient to no one, to
rise up and rebel everywhere, to gather together in violence and
band together in hordes, to reform, eradicate, and perhaps even
kill religious and secular authorities." The following articles will
answer all those friendly godless critics, first, to remove the dis-
paragement of God's word, and second, to exculpate the rebellious uprising of the peasants on Christian grounds.

First of all, the Gospel is not a cause of rebellions or disturbances, as long as the talk is of Christ the promised Messiah, whose
words and life teach nothing but love, peace, forbearance, and
unity, so that all who truly believe in that Christ will be loving,
peaceful, forbearing, and united. If, then (as will be clearly seen),
the fundamental basis of all the peasants' articles is directed toward listening to the Gospel and living by it, how can the Anti-
Christians call it a cause of rebellion and disobedience? If, though,
certain Anti-Christians and enemies of the Gospel oppose it and
rise up against such desired aims, it is not the Gospel itself that is
to blame, but the Devil, that most pernicious foe of the Gospel,
who instigates such acts in his followers through unbelief, so that
the words of God (love, peace, unity) are suppressed and deleted.

Secondly, it clearly follows that since the peasants in their articles desire that sort of gospel as a basis for their doctrine and life, they cannot rightly be called disobedient or seditious. If, however, God deigns to hear the peasants (who are desperately crying for a chance to live according to His word), who is to blame the will of God? Who will dare to interfere with His judgment? Yes, who would presume to oppose His majesty? When the children of Israel cried out to Him, He heard their cry and delivered them from the hand of Pharaoh. Can He not rescue His people today? Indeed, He will rescue them. And very soon! Therefore, Christian reader, read the following articles with care, then judge them. The articles follow.

Article One

In the first place, we humbly desire and request, and we all intend henceforth to have, the power and might for a whole congregation itself to choose and elect its priest, as well as the power to remove him if he acts improperly. That same elected priest shall preach the Gospel to us, clearly and purely, with no human admixture, doctrine, or commandment, but always proclaiming to us the true faith, prompting us to pray to God for His grace to implant and confirm that same true faith within us. For if His grace is not implanted in us, we shall always remain mere flesh and blood, which avails nothing, as is clearly stated in the Scripture, which says that we can come to God only through true faith alone and will be saved only by His mercy. Therefore, such a pastor and leader is needed by us and is thus based on the Scripture.

Article Two

Second, since a just tithe has been established in the Old Testament and completed in the New, we shall gladly pay the grain tithe. But we shall do so in the proper way: accordingly, one shall pay it to God, and it will be passed on to His people, it being fit and proper for a priest who proclaims the word of God to do so. Henceforth we are willing for our church priors, elected by a congregation, to collect and receive this tithe. Out of it they shall give a pastor, duly elected by the congregation, enough for an adequate living for himself and his family, according to the findings of the whole congregation. Whatever is left over shall be given to the poor and needy in the village, in keeping with the circumstances and the findings of the congregation. Whatever is left after that shall be held in reserve in case there is need of traveling for the sake of the land. In order that no land tax shall be imposed on the poor, it shall be derived from that surplus. Also, in the event that one or more villages may have, out of necessity, sold their tithe rights, with proof, the whole village shall not have to make restitution, but we shall come to an arrangement with them in a reasonable manner, according to the circumstances of the case, and redeem them at a reasonable time. But if anyone has not bought such tithes from a village, but has them from his forefathers who appropriated them for themselves, nothing shall, will, or ought to be given to him, except as our elected priest shall see fit to arrange—reappropriating the tithes or passing them on to the needy, as the Scriptures demand, be they clergy or laity. We shall not pay the "small tithe," for the Lord God made cattle for man and we deem this an improper tithe, devised by people. We shall, therefore, no longer pay it.

Article Three

Third, it has hitherto been the custom for us to be regarded as bondsmen, which is to be deplored, since Christ redeemed all of us with His precious blood, the shepherd as well as the man of highest station, without exception. Thus it is provided by the Scriptures that we are and shall be free. Not that God teaches us to be absolutely free and recognizing no authority at all. We shall live by the commandments, not in the capricious freedom of the flesh, for we shall love God, acknowledging Him as our Lord and as being in our neighbor, and willingly doing all that He commanded us to do at the Last Supper. Since we live according to that commandment, does it tell us not to obey authority? We not only obey authority but also shall humble ourselves before everybody, and we shall obey our elected and appointed authorities (as appointed for us by God) in all proper and Christian matters, if they will release us from bondage as true and proper Christians in accordance with the Scripture.

Article Four

Fourth, it has hitherto been the custom that no poor man is granted the right to hunt game or fowl or to catch fish in flowing streams. This seems to us completely improper and unbrotherly, being self-serving and not in keeping with the word of God. Also, in some localities the authorities defiantly withold game from us to our great detriment, for God has let the animals grow for the benefit of mankind, and we have been forced to look on and bear it in silence when they wantonly and willfully destroy dumb beasts. This is contrary to the law of God and to the responsibility to one's neighbor. For when God created man He gave him power over all the animals, the birds of the air, and the fish in the water. If a person has a body of water and can prove with proper documents that it was knowingly sold to him, it is not our wish to take it away from him by force; one must have Christian insight in this matter and brotherly love. If, however, anyone cannot satisfactorily prove his ownership, it is only right for him to give such property to the community.

Article Five

Fifth, we also have grievances concerning woods and forests, for our masters have appropriated them all, and when a poor man needs wood he has to pay double price for it, as we see it. We believe that whatever woods are held by clerics or laymen without having been bought by the holder must revert to the community, which shall be free to permit anyone to carry home the wood he needs for firewood without charge, also whatever he needs for building, but this must be with the knowledge of those elected by the community. If, however, no woods remain but those which have been legitimately bought, one shall come to an agreement with the owners in a brotherly and Christian manner. But if the property was originally appropriated but subsequently sold, an agreement shall be reached as the facts in the case warrant and with due regard to brotherly love and Holy Writ.

Article Six

Sixth, we have a serious grievance concerning the number of people in servitude, which is increasing day by day. We want to be granted understanding in this matter and not to be so seriously aggrieved but shown gracious consideration, inasmuch as our parents served only according to the provisions of the law of God.

Article Seven

Seventh, we shall henceforth not let any masters plague us but shall insist that they act in decent fashion and according to the agreement between masters and peasants. The master shall no longer compel him to render service without compensation. The peasant is entitled to his leisure. If, however, the master has need of services, the peasants shall be willing to provide them, but at a time that shall not be inconvenient for the peasant, and for suitable compensation.

Article Eight

Eighth, we demand that in those numerous instances in which the landowners cannot bear the expense of the land, thus causing the peasants to lose their own holdings, that the owners summon trustworthy people to inspect and assess the properties and arrive at a reasonable payment, for every workman is worthy of his hire (Mt. 10).

Article Nine

Ninth, we protest against the extreme arbitrariness with which new regulations are constantly made, so that we are penalized, not according to the nature of the case, but at times with animosity, at times with favoritism. We believe we should be penalized according to well-established written law, and that the case shall be treated accordingly, not on the basis of caprice or favor.

Article Ten

Tenth, we are aggrieved that some have appropriated to themselves fields properly belonging to the community. We shall repossess these for our common ownership unless they have been legitimately purchased. If, however, they have been improperly acquired, an equitable and friendly settlement shall be reached, in keeping with the nature of the case.

Article Eleven

Eleventh, we insist that the practice known as *todt fall* [death duties?] be entirely abolished, and we shall never tolerate or condone robbing widows and orphans, as so shamefully happens in many places (and in many ways) contrary to God's will and honor, and that at the hands of the very ones who are supposed to protect and defend them but who have bruised and abused them. If they had a little sense of what is right, they would realize that God will no longer tolerate this and that the practice must cease entirely. Henceforth nobody shall be required to pay these duties, whether great or small.

Conclusion

Twelfth, our final statement and summation is this: If one or more of the articles herein set forth shall prove to be out of keeping with the word of God, we shall retract them, provided we are shown scriptural reasons for so doing. If certain articles should later be found unjust, they would from that moment on be null and void, likewise any articles found to be in opposition to God and oppressive to our fellow man. We reserve the right, and are determined to change them, acting according to all Christian doctrine and praying God to grant us this, as He alone can, and nobody else. The Peace of Christ be with us all.

Translated by Robert A. Fowkes